The House That Hitler Built

by

STEPHEN H. ROBERTS

M.A., D.Sc. (Econ.), Litt. D.

Challis Professor of Modern History,
University of Sydney

Harper & Brothers Publishers

New York and London

1938

PREFACE

This book is written primarily for the man-in-the-street who wishes to have some idea of the German experiment. It may best be explained by a personal note. Most of my work for the last twenty years has been concerned with contemporary history, and I spent most of the study-leave which the University of Sydney granted me (November 1935 to March 1937) in Germany and neighbouring countries. My main aim was to sum up the New Germany without any prejudice (except that my general approach was that of a democratic individualist), and to contrast the state of affairs to-day with that which I knew in Germany at the end of the inflationary period, then at the height of the Weimar Republic's temporary success, and lastly immediately prior to Hitler's accession to power. I may have gained—or suffered—from the detachment of view which is natural to one living in a distant Dominion.

Owing to a fortunate conjunction of circumstances, I was afforded unusual facilities in Germany. The Nazi authorities did everything possible to aid my investigations, although they knew from the outset that my attitude was one of objective criticism. Indeed, they had even filed copies of all my articles and summaries of my wireless and other talks on Germany over a period of years. Despite this, no request of mine was too much for them, and the only refusal I encountered in the whole of Germany was in being denied access to their collection of banned literature.

I wish, then, to acknowledge my indebtedness to them, even in cases where they knew that they could never convert me. I should also like to point out that, in every case, the judgements are my own. None of the scores of officials who helped me must in any way be blamed for the conclusions I have drawn. To a man, they did their duty as officials of the Party and the State. I wish to be quite clear on this point.

Under the conditions I cannot mention individuals, but should like to thank the many officers of the Foreign Office, the Ribbentrop Bureau, the Labour Front, the Labour Service Headquarters, the Reichsbank, the *Reichskreditgesellschaft*, the Ministry of Finance, the department of Public Works, the Ministry of the Interior, the Ministry of Propaganda, the Finance Ministry, the Ministry of Labour, and many other departments. I am particularly indebted to scores of Party officials, especially to those who arranged that I should meet such persons as Hitler, Hess, and Schacht, and those who invited me to the Nuremberg Party Rally in September 1936. A special mention must be given to the officials who made available to me the resources of Party Headquarters in Munich. I also owe much to private industrialists and business leaders for their frank discussions, although naturally I can be no more specific than this under existing circumstances.

I must also pay tribute to the ordinary people of Germany who made my investigations such a great pleasure. Although we motored many thousands of miles through every German province but one, and although we showed what must often have been a disconcerting persistence in trying to find out what tinker and worker, professor and farmer thought, we met not the slightest discourtesy and found everywhere a striking eagerness for friendship with Great Britain.

Explanatory mention must be made of the use of S.A. and S.S. throughout this book. The term S.A. is used for *Sturmabteilung*, and is synonymous with Storm Troopers or Brownshirts or the Brown Army (the original private militia of Hitler) ; S.S., on the other hand, is an abbreviation of *Schutzstaffel*, the smaller body of praetorian guards, often referred to as Black Guards.

In writing this book, I have tried to give an account of Hitler's first four years of power and to throw light on this by mentioning my own experiences in Germany. Wherever necessary, I have gone back to the origins of certain movements, but in general have made no attempt to cover the period between 1921 and 1933, because many adequate surveys of this formative period exist. The presentation has often been interpretative rather than factual, although in places (as when dealing with Party organization) I have gone into great detail because the facts are not easily accessible to the kind of people for whom this book is written. I claim no finality or completeness. I have merely tried to put on record one observer's idea of Hitlerite Germany as it existed after four years of power. The faults of omission in attempting to sum up most aspects of so vast a subject in a hundred thousand words are everywhere obvious ; and I can but apologize for them in advance. It will be obvious, too, that many sections (especially those on economics and foreign policy) are not written for the expert, but, as I explained earlier, this book is directed towards a wider public. I put it forward hesitatingly as a general survey and interpretation.

A few dates are necessary. My last personal contact with Germany was in the early days of January 1937, and I have not seen this book since the manuscript left my hands on June 1st, 1937.

Lastly, I must express an especial obligation to the Senate and Vice-Chancellor of the University of Sydney for granting me facilities to undertake this work.

S. H. ROBERTS

Sydney University,

CONTENTS

PART I. ORIGINS

PART II. FOUR YEARS OF POWER

PART III. THE ECONOMICS OF HITLERISM

PART IV. THE BALANCE SHEET OF HITLERISM

SECTION I. WHAT THE ONLOOKER SEES

SECTION II. WHAT THE ONLOOKER DOES NOT SEE

PART I

ORIGINS

Chapter One

THE RIDDLE OF HITLER

I.—*Hitler's Origins*

With a blaze of emphasis on every other part of his life, Hitler is extremely reticent about his family. While we may dispose of the stories of Jewish ancestors, we must still admit that there are very weak spots in the official family tree evolved at the Munich headquarters and the Rehse Museum. Even granting the dubious marriages, *der Führer* can trace the peasant Hiedlers only as far back as 1725. The name frequently appears as Huttler or Hittler, but is usually Hiedler. The curious point is how narrowly Hitler escaped being called Schicklgrüber. Hitler's father was illegitimate for forty years and was known for most of his life by his mother's name, Alois Schicklgrüber— a name which not even Hitler could have carried off in his rise to dictatorship. *Heil Schicklgrüber* would have been impossible.

His father was an amorous peasant cobbler who became a minor Government official in Austria through his wife's generosity. It was a strange family. Hitler was born of Alois's third wife, a maidservant who was a distant connexion of his. It is an interesting point to know how much of Hitler's mental narrowness is due to the habit of his Waldwiertel ancestors of inbreeding for centuries.

Certainly his upbringing was not normal. He was the neurotic child of a neurotic, repressed mother. She warped him by impressing upon him how different he was from other children[1] ; and it is to Klara Poelzl that we must attribute that supreme conception of his difference from other men. She greatly reinforced his resentment complex. Indeed, it

[1] In her own words he was *mondsüchtig*—moonstruck.

might almost be said that, through her son Adolf, Klara Poelzl is making the world pay for her fancied wrongs. This domestic atmosphere may also explain why Hitler has done nothing for his Austrian kinsmen.

He also ignores his former schoolfriends, because he was just as much an unhappy rebel at his *Realschule* as he was at home. He says in his autobiography that he took only the subjects he liked and refused to be disciplined with the others. He excelled in geography and world history. Last year I met a schoolfriend of his who told me that Hitler frequently incurred his father's wrath by burning lamp-oil until the early hours of the morning. Laughed at by his comrades for poring over an atlas, he fixed them with a glassy stare and replied with crushing dignity : 'I am wiping out the German boundaries and making them larger—making them larger !' Here already we have the essential Hitler—lonely, dreaming, ignoring facts, living in a world of fancy, and happy in his artificial isolation.

He has never been disciplined. He was spoiled by his mother, who made much of his physical weakness. He was so weakly that his schooling was interrupted for a year and he was rejected for military service. From his thirteenth to his eighteenth year he just loafed and was told that he was too good to work at sums like his fellows. Then came four more years of frustration. Trained for nothing, he made no effort at training, having all the failure's contempt for preparation for any job.

Irrational and unbalanced, he gave way to delusional manias about everybody with whom he came into contact— Jews or capitalists or labourers. It is one of the ironies of history that world affairs to-day depend on the accidental contacts of a spoilt down-and-out in the Vienna of thirty years ago—on the resentment complexes of an adolescent who had failed solely because he refused to submit to authority and had not the stamina to achieve normality.

He went to Vienna as a labourer ; and it is significant that he despised physical labour and his workman associates. 'I was nice in my speech and reserved in my disposition.' He left Vienna hating Jews and workmen, and, as Konrad

Heiden shrewdly points out, these attributes were signs of gentility in pre-war Vienna. He was already the perfect mirror of the lower middle classes—a gramophone of respectability. He even left Vienna in 1912 because it was not respectable. In his own words, it was ' the embodiment of incest ', a typically meaningless Hitlerian phrase. Vienna had given him nothing more than a men's doss-house, and, until he returned to it as a conqueror, he would go to Munich.

His next two years were more normal. The jolly life of Bavaria did much to wean him back to mental averageness, although material success still passed him by—this strange young man who painted posters or houses or birthday cards.

Without hope and definitely ousted in the battle of life, he was saved by the war—' a redemption ', he calls it. ' I sank down on my knees and thanked Heaven from an overflowing heart.' Incredible as they are, these words are still the German dictator's account of his reaction to the bloodbath of 1914. He thanked Heaven and joined the regiment of Colonel List, the Sixteenth Bavarian Reserves, entraining for the front in time for the first battle of Ypres.

In the next four years he fought in forty-eight battles. It is ridiculous to belittle his war services, for he served throughout the war on the Western Front and bears to-day the physical signs of that service. At the same time it must be pointed out that for much of the time, from October 1915, when he was promoted lance-corporal (with the privilege of exemption from mounting guard), he was at the regimental base as a *Meldegänger* or orderly. The museum at Party Headquarters in Munich has not been able to discover many souvenirs of his war experiences. They have a few rough snapshots since circulated (and copyrighted) by his assiduous photographer Hoffmann, and a plentiful supply of such trifles as menus for officers' dinners. Obviously Lance-Corporal Hitler's drawing ability stood him in good stead.

Nevertheless, he took his fair share of the fighting. He obtained an Iron Cross (second class) in the first December, and lived reasonably quietly until a foray at Le Barque on October 5th, 1916, when a grenade splinter took him away from the front for five months. On September 17th, 1917, he was awarded the Military Service Cross (third class) with palms, and followed this up by a regimental mention for his part in the attack on Fontaines on May 9th, 1918. The great push of 1918 saw him in the front lines again. Already decorated with the black wound-badge, he now received the Iron Cross (first class) for bravery at the bridge of Montdidier on August 4th, and a fortnight later the *Dienstauszeichnung*. Altogether this is a considerable array of decorations for an infantry non-commissioned officer. Hitler has undoubtedly seen service. He has known hand-to-hand affrays and has taken part in bayonet raids. He can recollect the hell of no-man's-land, the enervation of trench warfare, and his body has suffered the ravages of shells and gas.

He does not appear to have been popular at the war. He was a 'patriot', and the ordinary grousing infantry-men found him a prig. The job of Hans and Karl and Johann was to live ; that of Hitler—this Austrian volunteer who should have been with his own countrymen—was to express a patriotism that kept him on another plane. They lived on their bellies, he on his nerves, and neither his fellows nor his officers liked him. An emotional idealist has no place in the lousy, scrounging life of the trenches, and, after all, good-fellowship is of far more importance there than heroics. Perhaps this explains why a man who is supposed to be so loyal to his old comrades has not elevated any of his wartime friends, with the exception of his sergeant-major, Max Amann.

Servile to his officers, he came out of the war with the third element of his mental equipment. He already despised Jews and workers ; he now felt himself ineffably superior to the rest of mankind, this patriot who remained a lance-corporal after four years of war in which promotion came to most men.

On October 14th, 1918, the battered remnants of the List Regiment, now a regiment only in name, were trying to hold up the Allied advance near Montagne. Suddenly the gas alarms clanged metallically, and Hitler put on his helmet— a poor contraption of cracked cloth and artificial rubber which was of no more use than a handkerchief in keeping out the biting phosgene. Days of jolting pain followed, until he regained consciousness on the morning of October 21st in

Pasewalk hospital, a reserve institution far away from the Front in the heart of Bavaria. How he got there, he did not know, and cared still less. A week passed, two weeks ; and then he became conscious of his surroundings. To his disgust, he found that the hospital was just as much a receptacle for mutinous broadsheets as the trenches had been in the last few months of his service. His room-mates even spoke of Socialist revolution, whereupon he turned to the wall and scarcely cared if he were doomed to blindness or not. If Germany fell, there was nothing to live for.

It is significant, however, that he summoned enough courage to receive delegates from the mutineers before he finally made up his mind. But his contempt for the workers and his peculiarly sublimated form of patriotism turned him away from the People's Revolution, and he gladly escaped to the delightfully situated camp of Traunstein to recuperate in the mountains. As he has repeatedly said : ' On November 9th, 1918, I resolved to become a politician.'

II.—*The Man Hitler*

It is almost impossible to give any idea of Hitler's personality, because every interpretation of necessity reflects the viewpoint of the interpreter. There can be no finality. All that one can do is to set down the attributes that one has noticed in listening and speaking to Hitler oneself.

Hitler undoubtedly has a very complex personality. People like Stalin and Mussolini are much simpler—easier to analyse and understand ; but there is something elusive about Hitler, and one feels that the simplest solutions fall short of the whole truth. The two most popular views picture him either as a mere ranting stump-orator, or as a victim of demoniacal possession, driven hither and thither by some occult force that makes him a power of evil. But these are as unsatisfactory as the view of his believers that he is a demigod, revealing the path Germany is to follow by some divine power of intuitively knowing what to do.

I think that he is primarily a dreamer, a visionary. His

mind, nurtured by the other-worldness of the Alpine scenery
round his mountain retreat of Berchtesgaden, runs to visions ;
and I have heard his intimates say that, even in cabinet meetings
when vital questions of policy are being discussed, he is
dreaming—thinking of the light that never was on sea or land,
the consecration and the poet's dream.

South Germany has always produced dreamers and roman-
tics, like the Swan-king Ludwig of Bavaria. The romantic
side of medievalism is always with them. They live in an
impracticable world of unbelievable mountains ; their fields
and houses are like stage settings ; they dream of treasure-
trove and speak of masses of emeralds on the peaks illuminated
by the moon at her full ; they accept the fairy-tale castles of
Neuschwanstein and Hohenschwengau as part of normal
existence ; they live, as it were, in a typical Wagnerian
opera.

Hitler is one of them—a peasant's son with little more than a
peasant's education, but now holding a position that outrivals
the most magical transformation in their wildest fairy tale.
Indeed, he always has the air of being faintly surprised. An
eminent neurologist who accompanied me to the Nuremberg
Partei-Tag pointed out again and again that Hitler obviously
' pulled himself up ' at the great public functions and stopped
dreaming. It is almost a case of dual personality. He cannot
allow his normal, average peasant-being to come into ascen-
dancy, but has constantly to remind himself that he must act as
the *Führer*, the demigod, of a great people. The neurologist
told me that another symptom of this is the way in which he
quickly removes the self-satisfied smirk that so often creeps
over his face at public demonstrations.

Of course it is his dreaminess that hard-bitten advisers like
Goebbels and Göring have capitalized. He is so transparently
honest when he is weaving visions of his own creation that
nobody can doubt him. He is ready, like a medieval saint,
to go through fire and water for his beliefs. I am not certain
that he would not actually like being tortured ; he would love
playing the martyr, if only for his own mental delectation.
He sees himself as a crusader ; he thinks the whole time of
saving mankind. That is why he reaches such a stage of

mystical exaltation when he talks about saving the world from
Bolshevism. It is the old Siegfried complex once again.
Just as the young German knight of old went out into the
dim, dark forests to kill dragons, so he goes out to exterminate
Bolshevism. He is simply living again the romantic frescoes
which mad King Ludwig painted round his castles to express
the Wagnerian operas, and Hitler's spectacles are nothing
more than an enlargement of this Wagnerian drop-scene, with
the improvements offered by modern science.

That accounts for his popular appeal, and it also makes
him dangerous. I heard him make the famous speech when
he spoke of absorbing the Ukraine and Siberia. Under the
cold analysis of foreign newspaper reporters, this speech read
like a declaration of Germany's Eastern Imperialism. Actually
it was nothing of the kind. Hitler merely forgot his audience
and wandered off into a dream-world of his own. He spoke
of the wonders he would do if he controlled the fields of
the Ukraine and the hidden treasures of Siberia, just as one
of us might meander on about the riches of Cathay or the
mother-lode from which all gold was thought to have come.

The same remarks apply to his other speech in that same
week, when he held out his arms, rolled his eyes to heaven, and
said that he must thank God for giving him Germany and
that they must thank God for giving them Hitler. In retrospective analysis this seems either silly or blasphemous, but it
did not appear so to his listeners. It did not seem incongruous
even to foreigners like ourselves—at least, not in that place
and time. Imagine an English premier speaking in the same
way ! Nothing shows more clearly the enormous gulf
between Hitlerian psychology and our own.

I am convinced, further, that all the brutal sides of his
movement pass him by. The killings, the repressions, the
imprisonments, do not belong to the world of his imagination.
He is too remote for them. People have scoffed at the story
of him weeping over music on the night of June 30th, 1934,
when so many of his oldest associates were being brutally
murdered, and foreign cartoonists took delight in depicting
his hypocritical tears. That is not fair. The plain truth is
that the music reached home to him and was part of his feeling,

whereas the killings would be very remote. Göring could look after those while his leader was dreaming.

It is the combination of men like Göring with a dreamer like Hitler that has made Nazidom possible. They could not supply the mysticism and the dreams without being laughed at, and he could not do the necessary dirty work. Hitler without his Party organization behind him would be inconceivable, so too would the Party without his pixy-ridden other-worldness.

He is a romantic through and through, and he lacks the education or the reading to temper his romanticism by the balance of philosophy. Everything that he does is Wagnerian —this is the *leitmotif* of the whole Hitler piece. He has the trappings of mysticism everywhere. He blesses banners ; he makes a workaday shovel a symbol for mysterious ritual ; he believes in macabre rites about the resurrection of the Nazi dead ; he fosters midnight ceremonies on the sacred Brocken mountain ; he talks of Valhalla and knight-errantry ; he wants to be Siegfried and Frederick the Great rolled into one. The mystical trappings of Hitlerism are always strongly in evidence ; and the normal mind reacts against it knows not what. Experts have shown that, consciously or unconsciously, Hitler uses the very phrases that have been the formulae of occult observations ever since the Middle Ages.

Hence comes the uncertainty. A Mussolini has everyday ambitions, and thinks in terms of men and guns and machines. His foreign policy is in terms of iron and steel and frontier posts, but with a Hitler one never knows. He may be carried away by some obsession of reconstituting Vienna as the capital of a new Germanic Empire, or he may see himself as a crusader in Eastern Europe, like the Teutonic Knights of the olden days.[1]

Realism in foreign policy is bad enough, but romanticism leaves us at the mercy of a dreamer's will-o'-the-wisp ideas, especially when a new army is at its beck and call. That is

[1] In Munich in the early autumn of 1936 I saw coloured pictures of Hitler in the actual silver garments of the Knight of the Grail ; but these were soon withdrawn. They gave the show away ; they were too near the truth of Hitler's mentality.

why many foreign experts hope that either the Nazi Party machine or the army will retain power, for there at least are men who, brutal realists as they may be, are in touch with ordinary affairs. Then the aloof dreamer of Berchtesgaden can keep on looking through his telescope at the eternal snows and keep on dreaming his visions and making speeches to himself.

Nobody would claim that Hitler is of outstanding mental stature. If he really expresses the Romantic Ideal carried to the point of absurdity, and if romanticism is the liberation of the less conscious levels of the mind (as one recent writer has described it), extreme mental clarity would not be expected from him. His life, as I see it, can be expressed as an attempt at escaping from reality and a more or less constant intoxication of his imagination by a free indulgence in fantasy. He has none of that ' great measuring virtue ' without which Ruskin asserts true greatness is impossible. The psycho-analysts have a marvellous subject for discussion in Herr Hitler. Some of them say that he shows the salient features of schizophrenia (split personality) because of his overwhelming ambition and conceit, his favourite role of himself as the saviour of mankind and his habit of speaking as if he received personal revelations from the Deity. Others hold that he is a manic-depressive ; others again a paranoiac. The paranoid tendency is shown in his ambivalent persecutory fantasies. He seems to suffer from what the Germans call *Gewissensbisse*, which means roughly a confusion of ideas and fears associated with good and bad objects. The typical paranoid is terrified of imaginary persecutors, and defends himself against this fear by the annihilation in fantasy of his persecutors. Sometimes, as in the case of Hitler, the annihilation can to some extent be translated from fantasy into fact. Hitler's persecution of the Jews and Communists, for instance, can be explained from this point of view. This is all a matter for the experts, of course, but some of the facts certainly appear as evidence for the psycho-analyst's stress on Hitler's persecution mania, his ways of escape from reality, his great anxieties, his over-keen but distorted observation of realities, his alternating moods of melancholy and elation, his recurring doubts of himself—and contrasting sense of omnipotence.

The feeling of persecution appears to be in the ascendant. Every outside object is to him a potential enemy of that with which he has identified his own personality, namely, Germany. To an increasing degree he seems to be indulging in this identification of himself and his country. From the real or fancied persecutors of Germany he is always seeking means of escape, which latterly he tries to find in the sublimation of part of himself (but part of himself only) into the role of universal saviour.

How could such a mind be coldly analytical? Abstract intelligence and logic are not necessary in his scheme of things. He seems to have a single-track mind. Always a simplist, he cannot understand the complexities of most problems. He cannot, for instance, recognize the importance of diplomatic forms or the element of safety provided by the tortuous methods of conventional diplomacy. He simplifies every problem, even the most vital questions of domestic and foreign policy. He applies a general principle of an intuitive solution to a question complicated by centuries of history and arrives at some delusively simple outcome. *Mein Kampf* gives him away in this. After its publication he could never again claim subtlety of analysis or breadth of vision. His own autobiography reveals his mental processes to all mankind.

But he is transparently honest. He believes what he is saying, and throws every ounce of nervous energy into all that he says or does, even when he is answering the most casual question (this stands out as my keenest impression when I spoke to him in the *Deutscher Hof*). Nobody can doubt his utter sincerity. He cannot help himself; he cannot restrain himself. He is completely absorbed in the statement or policy of the moment. That explains why he carries the crowds with him—because he believes so utterly, so appallingly, in what he is saying.

Nevertheless, he can say different things in successive moments and believe in each with the same degree of fervour. It is not his honesty that is in question ; it is his terrific power of self-delusion that introduces such an element of uncertainty into everything he does. His advisers never know what he is going to say next. It is said that he could start talking about any subject under the sun and, before he got very far, he would be expounding it with all the zeal of a prophet of a new religion. ' Start Adolf on two sentences about religion, and he will make a heathen gathering like a revivalist meeting,' one of his lieutenants said years ago, and this is quite true. His emotion drags him along behind his surging words, and he can neither stop nor restrain his impetuous belief in what he is saying. Thus, unless he reads every line of his speech, an element of uncertainty is always present. What made the demagogue might ruin the Chancellor—were it not for Goebbels's astute control of the Press. Even Hitler has found himself censored on many occasions, when his tongue ran away with him, and Goebbels's blue pencil came into play.

It is often maintained that he is a man of strong decisions. But may he not occasionally and jerkily take positive steps to convince himself that he is energetic—to cut the tangle of his own mental procrastinations ? There are many opinions about this ; but there is certainly a spasmodic appearance about his so-called rapid decisions that would appear to belie the interpretation that he is a man of action, thinking clearly and acting energetically.

Indeed, he himself provides much evidence on the matter. According to his own statements, he loathes making decisions. He will not make up his mind unless forced along tumultuously by events. He could not come to any decision about Communism in 1919 until he had hesitated and heard both sides. He procrastinated in every way at the time of the first November *putsch*. When the Berlin Storm Troops were mutinying and their leader telegraphed to Hitler for a decision, he could not answer. Explaining the killing of Röhm, he said : ' During those months I delayed again and again making a final decision.' He apparently doubted and hesitated on the occasion of June 30th, even after he had issued instructions to take drastic action. He cannot make up his mind what to say in his public speeches, and it is common knowledge in Germany that the man who sees him last before he mounts the rostrum has a good opportunity of determining the nature of his speech. His strength, then, is the unduly assertive characteristic of a man not certain of himself and shunning a real analysis of the problems confronting him. It is a mixture of brazenness and empiricism, and above all, a form of escape from his own introspectiveness. He is harassed, tormented, tortured by imaginings and confused thoughts ; and the only way out of the tangle is to take some act that is seemingly decisive, or, more often, to find refuge in the endless reiteration of stock arguments, such as those against Semitism or Bolshevism.

Associated with this is his fear about breaking the law. The spitting machine-guns used by the police against him in 1923 converted him for ever to a fervent belief in legal methods. Indeed, he hesitated for long about attempting a *putsch*, and only embarked on it when reassured that, owing to the preparations of Frick and others, there would be no fighting. Legality then became an obsession with him, and he made the Legal Division one of the strongest departments of his Party organization. Some of the more turbulent Brownshirt leaders coined a scoffing word combining *Legality* and *Adolf*, and even Goebbels said that he had a 'legality complex'. His most drastic revolutionary acts had to be brought into harmony with the law. If the existing law did not cover them, then the law had to be changed. The interesting conjecture thus arises—would Hitler have achieved power if the Weimar constitution had not contained clauses that permitted a revolution by abusing the spirit of the law while adhering to its outward forms ? If it had been a matter of barricades and a bloody *putsch*, would Hitler have met the test ? Or would he have stood by, as he always stood, limp and helpless, on the platform, in the fighting days of his movement, watching the mêlée below him ?

The next obvious aspect of Hitler's make-up is that he is distinctly an associationalist. He can do nothing without some awakening hint. The association may come from music ; it may be suggested by war stories, or by the tramp of marching feet ; it may arise from something said by others or even by himself. He always needs a stimulus. That is why he can never keep his thread in a speech ; everything suggests something else to him. His speeches are curiously monotonous. He never loses his self-consciousness in the early stages of a speech. He stiffly proceeds from phrase to phrase, and only gathers momentum as he goes along. Finally the stage comes when his last words bring no association to his mind. That is why he so often ends in an anticlimax. He sometimes breaks off in the middle of an argument, and, nine times out of ten, his ending is abrupt and unexpected. He will stop suddenly and either raise his hand in the peculiar horizontal form of salute he has evolved or else cry in a broken voice : ' *Heil Deutschland !* ' or ' *Sieg ! Sieg !* ' and gaze vacantly and fixedly before him.

He is pathetic when he loses the thread of an argument. As long as he is rushing along like a torrent, all is well with him, but ugly pauses occur in most of his public speeches. He looks round stonily. Usually his henchmen tide him over by frenzied shrieks of ' *Heil ! Heil !* ' or that gasping ' *Ah-h-h !* ' which is the token of German erotic indulgence at the moment. In the old days he frequently stopped talking in the middle of a speech and sat down. He is very temperamental in his speaking. Anything in the atmosphere around him may upset him—maybe some revulsion to his surroundings, maybe the presence of some antagonism which he feels. This temperamentalism may have been an asset in the days when he was an agitator, for no other agitator arrogated to himself the moods of a prima donna, and it was part and parcel of his dramatic entries and exits and his studied eccentricities ; but it is a distinct weakness in a *Reichskanzler*.

Hitler, either by design or because of his lack of creativeness, hit upon an elementary electioneering truth and has adhered to it ever since. He knows that an uneducated political public wants endless repetition of a few trite phrases ; and he has kept on parroting certain fixed phrases for over fifteen years. A brainier man would have wearied of this rôle of human gramophone, but, even to-day, every speech of Hitler's is mainly composed of the same old generalizations, the same old denunciations, the same old form of patriotism. It is always a case of ' the dose as before ', with a dash of flavouring to meet the particular situation in question. The speeches I heard him give at Nuremberg could have been taken from any of his writings of the last decade, yet hundreds of thousands of people cheered themselves hoarse, as if they were the latest revelations of some political oracle. So far has he dulled the spirit of analysis and criticism in a great people.

His collected speeches do not make good reading; and it becomes clear from perusing them that their appeal comes entirely from the way in which they are delivered and the circumstances under which they are given. His first broadcast speech to the nation after becoming Chancellor, for instance, was nothing more than a prolonged ranting against 'Jewish Marxism'; so, too, with his last great speech surveying his four years of power.

It might have been supposed that the man's outlook would have expanded by the responsibilities of office. But it is difficult to see how the years of power have added to his mentality. I am firmly of opinion that the real clues to his character and to the whole of his later policy lie in the very early days of the movement. Therein are shown the tendencies that have been working themselves out ever since: the fanatical belief in himself; the conviction that he alone could save Germany (and later the world) from its ills; the attitude that it is sufficient for him to state a policy without justifying it in any way, as if he received it as a result of communing with the Almighty; and especially the self-delusion that leads him to justify any act, however starkly opportunist it may be, by cloaking it with a cover of high principles, a process which seems to be unconscious rather than deliberate with him.

Nevertheless, he certainly succeeds in winning his audiences. After all, he is appealing to their feelings, not their intellect, and he captures them in an ecstasy of emotion, whipping them hither and thither by the castigations of his rather harsh, and frequently breaking, voice. He always uses the same methods, the same tricks of oratory, the same half-dozen gestures (especially the outpointed finger and the curious corkscrew movement of his hand), the same appeal to the crudest emotions, the same exploitation of common hatreds, even the same words. Goebbels is an infinitely finer and more polished orator from our point of view, but it is always Hitler who grips the meetings.

No display of emotionalism is too crude for him. He frequently weeps. He wept at the Court which tried him in 1924. He wept to his Brownshirt leaders in Berlin when they were mutinying in 1930. He wept before Gregor Strasser at the time of the Party split in 1932, and roamed up and down the corridors of his hotel, threatening to commit suicide. He has often threatened his own life or offered his body to the executioner's axe. ' Crucify me if I fail you ! '— that is his ultimate (and often pathetic) adjuration, used to journalists and party gatherings alike. ' We can always get Adolf to weep,' Göring is supposed to have said when confronted with a difficult situation. Here again the contrast with, say, a Stalin is obvious.

III.—Hitler's Mode of Living

The man himself leads a simple life, preferring his chalet at Berchtesgaden to the pleasures of Berlin palaces. As often as possible, he shuts himself up as in a monastery. Probably Hess and Bruckner and the talkative, irrepressible Hanfstaengl know most about his private life ; Goebbels and Frau Goebbels, also, are frequent visitors, and he feels in his element when Göring goes up to Berchtesgaden, and dresses in the leather pants and figured braces of the countryside, and they reduce some complicated world problem to a simple discussion, ignoring all its complexities and dealing with it as if they were two peasants talking about the next meeting of the village band. It is the haphazardly *a priori* methods with which great problems are handled in the New Germany that leaves one so appalled ; there are, it is true, the departmental officials, but nobody would believe for a moment that they exercise the restraining influence they do in other countries. An empire is run from a simple mountain chalet in Bavaria, far from chancellories and files and advisers. The idea is pure comic opera, but is none the less true (unless, as many Germans say, the empire is run from Party Headquarters in Munich, and Adolf can amuse himself as he likes, so long as he says and does the appropriate things on the proper occasions!).

He is a restless being. He likes opera, but is intolerant of the drama. When he is free, he walks in the Bavarian hills (inside his own estate), or dashes around the countryside in his car at a great speed. It is typical of the man that he made such a personal friend of his chauffeur, Schrenk, who even attained high rank in the S.S., and whose death was made a day of mourning throughout Germany. Hitler constituted a special Schrenk formation in the S.S., and almost wept when its gilded banner passed him at Nuremberg this year for the first time.

He loves movement. A few years ago he invented the technique of aeroplane electioneering (everybody will remember his dash over the Polish Corridor), but carried it to extremes. Even in the earliest days, when the Party funds were counted in pfennigs rather than marks, Hitler would hire aeroplanes. The nebulous dash to Berlin at the beginning of 1923, with the unwilling Eckart as his companion, was by air; and in the next few years it became almost a joke at Headquarters to ask where Hitler was and to get the reply: 'Oh, Adolf is up in the air again!' At times when he was sky-ranging and could not be found, it was an advantage, because the cruder pieces of work could then be disposed of without long discussion and without hurting his delicate feelings. He gets the same feeling out of speeding in the fastest of his destroyers. A pathologist would tell you that it is an extreme manifestation of his escape-tendencies.

For the rest, he has no physical diversions. He cannot ride, he will not hunt or shoot, he has no athletic prowess or inclinations. Not for him the rapier and the swimming and the shooting of a Mussolini. He has no interest in games as such. During the Olympic Games in Berlin, it was almost tragic to watch his absolutely uncontrolled expression during the contests. In his eyes, the events were not just sporting fixtures; each was a war in which the Fatherland had to win. I could see from my seat just below his stand that he would grip the edges of his box, rise from his seat, and hold himself stiff and taut during the events. If a German won, he relaxed and smiled all over his face; if a German lost, he scowled. He was not too tired, as the official story runs, to receive the negro victors (in the same way that he had received all the others) ; he was merely being petulant. The idea of sportsmanship is beyond him ; a sporting contest is something in which a Nordic German must win. He is concerned with the result alone.

Of Hitler's relations with women there is no need to write. As was inevitable, the most scurrilous stories have spread in this connexion, and even the most serious biographies include accounts which have not the slightest evidence to support them. The mere raking up of libellous scandal in no way helps to solve the complicated riddle of Hitler's personality, and it is merely cheap to connect Hitler with the name of a charming young actress who films Nazi spectacles, or to say that one of his young henchmen (whose family life is obviously a happy one) married only to serve Hitler's convenience, or to spread the filthy libel that his niece committed suicide a few years ago as a result of Hitler's illicit attentions. There is not a tittle of evidence in any of these cases, nor is it reasonable that a man who is in every way a slave to his career should risk everything in scandals of this kind which even he could not weather.

Hitler is obviously uneasy in the presence of women (just as he is awkward at any social function), but that is no reason why whisperers should accuse him of a romance every time he acts uneasily before a woman. Why cannot the obvious fact be adopted—that Hitler eschews meat, wine, and women, and has always done so? He is immersed in his own dream ; that dream has afforded the clue to his whole career, and in the last fifteen years he has been living that dream in reality. This is enough to fill his every thought and action, especially now that it is connected with a myth about his monastic way of life. The myth in this case happens to be true ; the neurologists have informed me that such attributes are quite in keeping with ‘ cases ’ of Hitler's type. To picture him as a creature of sexual excesses—some romantic, some coarsely fleeting— is thus not only libellous : it is needless and obscuring to any real interpretation of the man. Even in his army days, one of the reasons of Hitler's unpopularity with his comrades— or rather, their negative attitude towards him—was his refusal to ' womanize '. He is too immersed in himself to be anything but aloof to women—he will not be distracted from moving inexorably towards his destiny by women or any other disturbing force. His sexlessness is the measure of his own colossal egotism, and he positively enjoys strengthening the myth of his difference from other men by his disregard for women. Probably no other factor has attracted women so much to his cause, for it piques and intrigues them—a demigod in this way must be almost as a deity in other directions, so they argue ; and Hitler's shrewd advisers know full well what value as propaganda this attitude has. Is it likely, then, that he would destroy all this for such petty passions, such low liaisons, as his enemies drag up ? His own psychology is all against it.

Apparently he never reads very much beyond official papers. Even in his agitating days he would never open a book. His personal room at the Brown House had no books, and none of the pictures taken at his chalet show any. It is doubtful if he has ever made a serious study of historical or philosophical works. He makes much of Houston Stewart Chamberlain, but it is said that even that is second-hand. He met Chamberlain only once (four years before he died). Characteristically enough, he brought Chamberlain in touch with Siegfried Wagner, and still more characteristically, this meeting took place in the troubled weeks just before the Munich revolt, when any other man would have lacked time for such gestures. His present views are distillations from Gobineau, taken from the tap-room gossip of old Dietrich Eckart and from the venomous attacks of Alfred Rosenberg on everybody and everything ; his knowledge of events was always gained—again verbally—from Goebbels. The written word has never had any appeal for him. Even in jail he would not read. He takes care, even to-day, to keep away from first-rate minds. He mistrusts intellect, even intelligence. Learning, as such, means nothing to him ; he will do nothing to aid it, unless it be in the form of propaganda that may be of use to him. The abstract pursuit of knowledge for its own sake, the company of brilliant talkers—he will have none of them. Instead, he narrows his world to his old friends—the propagandists and the fighters—and feels that he is cultured because he wallows in blatant Wagnerian music. Even there his interest is emotional and not intellectual— Wagner is to him what a luscious sugared cake is to a school-child.

His workroom in the Brown House is typical of the man. It is severely modern in its decoration, with buff walls relieved by green lamps and red carpets and tables. A small room, it is commanded by the *Führer's* writing-desk. There are four pictures of Frederick the Great, one of them on the desk itself. There is even a reproduction of Frederick's death mask. The only outside note is provided by a bust of Mussolini, presented to Hitler some years ago, and now obviously relegated to a corner. From where Hitler sits, he looks straight on to a vividly coloured painting of Bavarian infantry crossing a stream under fire in Flanders. It is said that it represented a battle in which Hitler himself fought. A very obvious piece of furniture is the elaborate bell-switch at Hitler's left hand, with no fewer than seventy-two buttons to press.

A strange man, this Adolf Hitler. He is infinitely polite and courteous in his interviews, pausing perceptibly after every statement in case there is something his questioner wishes to add. He is punctilious to the point of quixotism in acknowl-edging the salutes of his men and in himself saluting the standards. The odd feature is that he never seems at ease in formal gatherings or when being spoken to. He seems a hunted being and is always ready to find refuge in making a miniature speech, even when one asks him a question that could be answered by a single word. In making a speech he is at least on firm ground. There he does not have to think, there he can let himself go—for he has said it all thousands of times and will keep on saying it until he dies.

One fundamental fact is that Hitler never has any real personal contacts. The charming pictures one sees, in which he is taking bouquets from tiny tots or grasping the horny hands of picturesque old peasants, are all arranged. They are triumphs of the photographic skill of his old friend Hoffmann : Hoffmann blots out the surrounding guards and we see the result. The *Führer* is never alone. The giant Bruckner is always with him, and his ' suicide-brigade ' of special guards surround him everywhere. He goes out in his enormous Mercédès car (specially constructed so that he can stand up in front and receive support so that he is not wearied), and it is always preceded and followed by motor-cyclists and a whole fleet of cars with S.S. men. I was once present when he was talking to an English trade unionist at Nuremberg, and after leaving him the Englishman said : ' What he wants is to get away from his guards for a while and talk with a few ordinary human beings.' Most of his trouble, indeed, seems to be due to his enforced seclusion from mankind. When he is not walking in the grounds of his heavily guarded Berchtesgaden chalet, he is making public appearances inside his wall of S.S. men. He lives in an unnatural detachment that makes his disease of being a godhead batten on itself : the most balanced of human beings could not stand this kind of life without losing a sense of realities, and nobody would call Hitler emotionally balanced at the best of times. Most commentators make a great fuss about his diet or his celibacy : what seems to me far more important is his lack of ordinary human contacts. Abnormal himself, the constant adulation makes him pathological. He receives only the thrice-distilled views of the fanatics, intriguers and genuine patriots around him. Nobody can tell him anything or speak frankly, still less criticize his policy or himself. He lives in a mental world of his own, more aloof than any Sun-King, and he has only the narrow mental equipment and experience of an agitator to guide him. Unless one accepts the prevalent German view that he gets his inspiration direct from God (one of the most powerful Nazis once said he had a private line to heaven!), one must conclude that the future of Germany and the peace of the world rest on the tangled working of the mind of one man whom not even his friends would call normal. It is the most extraordinary comment on human evolution that, in this age of science and progress, the fate of mankind rests on the whimsy of an abnormal mind, infinitely more so than in the days of the old despots whom we criticize so much.

But the final enigma remains. Granting that Hitler is a dreamer, a creature of emotion, a man of ordinary mental calibre, a gripping orator, a simple-living *Führer* with an almost divine sense of his mission—how did such a man rise to power and consolidate the nation in his first four years of rule ? Many reasons seem to offer partial explanations of this. He was the greatest popular orator during a time of political chaos and national depression ; his general philosophy about *Deutschland erwache !* fitted in with the psychology of the nation, so that his movement became a national narcotic ; he had marvellous subordinates and, with them, built up the best Party organization ; his simplest mentality enabled him to carry through a complex revolution before which a mind more clearly analytical of the consequences would have quailed ; and finally he became the *Mythus* of the German people. The man was merged in the myth, and it became his task to think and act in terms of that myth, so much so that any power in the land which might supplant his Party would probably have to keep him as nominal *Führer*. The Hitler myth is the dominating fact in German life to-day. Indeed, he sees himself no longer as a person but as the Crusader who has captured the Holy City—the embodiment of a nation— the living and inspired voice of Germania—*Der Führer* in the most mystical sense of that word—and must one ultimately add : *Der Führer-Gott* ?

Chapter Two

HITLER'S LIEUTENANTS

I.—*Göring and Goebbels*

Captain-General Hermann Göring, the man of the decorations and uniforms, is usually dismissed too abruptly. Such stories as those about his 'Wardrobe' (the Air Ministry) and his weakness for medals are overdone. They are on a level with the publicity about his pet lion-cubs, and miss the essential qualities of the man. Göring is the second most powerful man in Germany, the second most popular (although his Berlin house has wire entanglements around its walls !) ; and no man could have achieved his position without capacity.

He was born in Bavaria in 1893, the son of a former colonial governor. Trained for the army, he became an infantry lieutenant in 1912. He fought throughout the war, first with the infantry and later, after a chance encounter with an aviator in hospital, with the air force. His war record was exceptionally fine, and he obtained the Iron Cross and the *Pour le Mérite*, the highest award of all. He became a squadron leader and, in the last months of the war, commander of the Richthofen squadron. A fighter of the reckless cavalier type, he refused to accept defeat at the Armistice, and would not hand over his aeroplanes to his own superior officers until forced to do so. Wiping the soil of Socialist Germany from his feet, he escaped to Sweden and became a civilian pilot. Returning to Munich as a student of history, he heard Hitler speak and immediately enlisted under his banner, being charged with the organization of the fighting Storm Troopers. He stood next to Hitler in the Munich *putsch* and, although dangerously wounded, managed to flee to the Tyrol and later to Italy. He was unable to return to Germany until the amnesty of 1927, when he became one of the first group of Nazis to enter the Reichstag. Displaying an ability for a rather summary kind of leadership, he displaced the more moderate parliamentarians and was elected President of the Reichstag in August 1932. After the Nazi revolution, he became Minister-president of Prussia, Minister of Air, Chief Forester and Hunting Master of the Reich, and, last year, co-ordinator of all departments dealing with raw materials and foreign exchange; and, last of all, dictator of the Four Year Plan in September 1936—an amazing record for a man who is now just forty-four years of age.

Göring is the embodiment of direct force, and if need be, insensate brutality. He has never concealed his belief in the efficacy of direct action and prefers to solve his difficulties by smashing through them. The best instance of this was his method of 'assimilating' Prussia to National Socialist ideas. There is nothing subtle or remote about him—none of the mental storms of a Hitler or the calculating precision of a Goebbels. He has no firmly fixed opinions, but is an opportunist who will do anything to make Germany strong. Eighteen stone of geniality or brutality, as the occasion may warrant, but never any light or shade—that is 'Iron Hermann'. He is so essentially human, a man of the crowds. He loves parade, eating, enjoyment, and fighting. Indeed, it is because he has all of a man's weaknesses that he understands others, and thus his greatest service to Germany is not so much in his air force as in his campaigns to keep up the country's morale.

When the people grumble about food restrictions, Göring roars at them with his sergeant-major's voice, gibes them in dialect, and, patting his huge stomach, cries : 'Look at me ! I have lost two stone in the service of the country ; why therefore do you complain at cutting down your meals a little ?' Elementary as his humour is, he at least makes the people laugh, and he is shrewd enough to realize the value of such tactics. It is probably not without truth that he has been described as the author of many of the stories against himself. He realizes that Hitler's symbolism and Goebbels's ceaseless nagging are not enough. The people must be kept in good humour, and it is his job to do it.

Even more important are his services in mediating between various factions within the Party. He has done this again and again, and it is said that, if the squabblers listen to him and become reconciled, he gives them a banquet, whereas if they remain obstinate, he will organize a different kind of party, as he did at Lichterfelde on June 30th. Again and again he has been called in. Last year he smoothed over the difficulties with Schacht and later won over the Party and the people to the Four Year Plan. He might indeed add another title to his long collection : ' Mediator-in-Chief.'

As a fighter, he tends to despise what he cannot understand, especially the mental qualities of Goebbels, although there seems no justification for the frequent stories of hostility between the two men. Their interests are too identical for them to quarrel, particularly because Goebbels knows that he is too unpopular ever to hope to succeed Hitler and knows, too, that a battering-ram like Göring must always have a subtle brain behind it to direct its energy. Yet, despite all his magnificence and popularity, it is doubtful if Göring would ever succeed in becoming *Führer*. The clash of rival interests behind the scenes would rather favour the emergence of one of the lesser-known men—such a man, for instance, who had command of a private army, and who controlled all the militarized police, and who could co-operate with the army (whose leaders would not feel towards him as they do towards politically-promoted Captain Göring)—such a man, in short, as Heinrich Himmler. On occasions like this, the stark directness and lack of subtlety of a Göring are positive hindrances, so that there would seem to be limits fixed to his future career. Yet he would indeed be foolish who ventured to cross swords with Captain-General Göring to-day, and, after all, Göring always has one card up his sleeve. Perhaps his belief in a sudden shattering blow against his enemies—his belief in an aggressive aerial war that would be a matter of days, perhaps hours—may yet be justified, and in that case the local manœuvres of rival politicians would not harm him.

With Dr. Joseph Goebbels, a forty-year-old Rhinelander of Westphalian peasant stock, the case is far different. If Göring is the battering-ram for Hitler, Goebbels is the brain. His record is a strange one. Educated in a Catholic school in his birthplace of Rheydt and later at seven universities, he became a journalist. Like so many others, he heard Hitler speak in 1922 and immediately joined the Party as a propagandist. He founded National Socialism in the Rhineland and the Ruhr, and was so successful there that Hitler at the end of 1926 made him Party leader for Greater Berlin and sent him to win over that nest of Communists for the Nazis.

Not the least of the mysterious features of Hitlerism has been the success of his ten years of fighting in Berlin, especially the way in which he perfected the methods of propaganda in his newspaper, *Der Angriff*. He also obtained a reputation for calculated brutality and a cold precision that took no heed of human values. Becoming a member of the first Nazi group in the Reichstag, his biting tongue made him the most feared of them all in debate. He was the only man, it is said, who could stand up to the Communist Torgler in the Reichstag. When Hitler became Chancellor, Goebbels was appointed Minister for Propaganda and Public Enlightenment. As such he became lord of the written and spoken word in Germany, and latterly he has even secured a dictatorship of the films. His huge department on the Kaiserhofplatz is the most efficient in Germany. It has grown enormously and already overflows into the Mauerstrasse. Contrary to general opinion, its main work is in Germany, not abroad. There is not a hamlet in the whole length and breadth of the country that is overlooked by it, and it must be remembered that the word *Propaganda* in a totalitarian State like Germany covers far more fields of activity than it does with us.

The outstanding feature about Goebbels is his searing contempt for humanity. One feels that he despises the human race and looks on the people as so many ants to be managed or stamped on. His attitude may easily be explained by a mixture of tortured nerves and acute resentment-psychosis, due to his physical defects.

His main contribution has been to the cause of propaganda.

That is why his book on the struggle for Berlin—*Das Erwa-chende Berlin*, apart from its intrinsic interest, marks an epoch in political methods. Tendentious, of course, and libellously insulting to his opponents, it is none the less a masterpiece, and the arrangement of its text, and especially the many hundreds of illustrations, have only to be contrasted with the cumbrous war efforts of Northcliffe to show the Nazi's contributions to propagandist methods. The most convincing test is that it temporarily converts the reader who knows its specious false-ness and its unfair methods. That is Goebbels's great inspira-tion—that propaganda seemingly fully documented by word and picture, may triumph over reason. Every investigator in Germany feels this—whatever his beliefs may be, the constant repetition of propaganda, in the Press, on the air, and through personal media, wears down his resistance, until he has to exert a conscious effort not to acquiesce in a campaign he would instantly question if considering it aloofly in his study in his own country. Goebbels has arrived at a mathe-matical relationship between the stream of propaganda and any individual's power of resistance, and if his margin is sufficient to wear down doubting foreigners, how much more effective is it for his own nationals, predisposed as they are to be converted to the achievements of the new régime ?

It appearance he is not impressive. He has a dwarfish deformed body, and is lame. He is never still for a second. Nobody is permitted to mention his extremely non-Aryan weakness of body. Not long ago a society for the aid of cripples mentioned him in one of their booklets as the supreme case in which mental powers triumphed over physical draw-backs. Berlin still talks of the fate of the unfortunate sponsors of that book!

It is impossible not to associate Goebbels with malignity. He appears to have an absolutely first-class mind, but one warped and embittered, and now, from his position of power, concerned with hate and revenge, especially against the Jews and the Communists. The way in which his diatribes against Russia dropped from his lips at Nuremberg made one shudder with their concentrated venom. He uses every device of oratory and effect to embellish his speeches ; he speaks a slow and limpidly perfect German (very different from Hitler's hoarse tumult of words or Göring's crude shouting) ; and he is far and away the best speaker among the Nazis. Nobody denies his claim to be the Party's brain, but he has always been an apostle of bitterness, and it is doubtful if anything constructive can ever come out of undiluted hate. Even his many books are concerned with tearing down rather than building up ; he has none of the dreams of a Hitler or even the wide theories of a Rosenberg.

He dislikes England, and thinks it ridiculous that our plodding trial-and-error methods should still leave us our position in the world. In foreign policy, he wants an understanding with Italy and activity in Central Europe. At the last rally in Nuremberg, when he was besieged by autograph-seekers, he replied over and over again : ' Only Austrians. I will sign only for Austrians.' Austria is obviously his next goal, although there is some discrepancy between this and his reliance on Mussolini's bayonets in the wider fight against Bolshevism.

I should call Goebbels the most dangerous man in Europe, precisely because he is so diabolically clever and so frankly Machiavellian in his views of mankind and the methods he would employ. Throughout the length and breadth of Germany, I heard nobody speak of him with affection. They all feared him, even where they admitted that the Party could not get on without him. Such is the man who, despising humanity, is engaged in the gigantic task of moulding the minds of 66,000,000 human beings into uniformity—to think and act as he dictates from his all-powerful Ministry of Propaganda. At close quarters he seems ageless, and that is in keeping—the forces he represents have always been with mankind.

Hitler is loyal to both Göring and Goebbels, whatever their faults. Whenever I mentioned in Germany that their removal would pave the way for easier understanding with other countries, most Germans told me that Hitler would keep them, even if he could afford to dispense with their services, because they are the oldest of his followers. The moral of Ernst Röhm seems to have passed over Germany !

Up to the present, however, Hitler has always shown a lively appreciation of the services of his two main henchmen, for, loyalty apart, he knows that they contribute qualities which he himself lacks. Each adds something absent in the others, and the group becomes stronger than the individuals.

II.—*The Patient Followers—Hess and Frick*

Rudolf Hess, Deputy of the Leader, was born in Egypt in 1894. He is a young man with dark skin, curly black hair, and enormous shaggy eyebrows ; his colouring is difficult to fit in to the Nordic descriptions. Well educated, he fought as an infantry and flying officer throughout the war, and, later, as a member of the Epp Freecorps which freed Munich from the Socialists. He joined the Party in June 1920, and was thus one of the earliest members. His particular tasks were to organize the university students and to build up the early Storm Troops whose function it was to keep order at public meetings. Participating in the Feldherrnhalle revolt, he was sentenced to imprisonment and served seven and a half months in Landsberg. Here he acted as Hitler's secretary in writing *Mein Kampf*.

Henceforth he was Hitler's secretary, and rose with the Party. In 1932 he became Chairman of the Central Political Committee and the next year Deputy for Hitler. He had charge of the departments in the Brown House and was really responsible for Party administration, while others waged the war in the Reichstag. After the seizure of power, he became Minister without portfolio and was given the difficult task of co-ordinating Party and State activities.

Hess is not very impressive personally. He would not stand out in a crowd. For the most part, he repeats Hitler's statements and makes speeches which it would be difficult for Hitler to utter in his capacity as Chancellor. Hess says what Hitler thinks but is restrained from saying. He appears washed-out and lifeless. That is why nobody in Germany believes that he will ever succeed Hitler, although everybody respects his simple mode of living. He has not the dynamic personality a dictator needs. He has much of the reticence and unassuming nature of the upper middle classes from which he sprang, and does not appear comfortable in the brusque hurly-burly of a Nazi meeting. On the other hand, fifteen years of power in the inner circles must have accustomed him to the cruder side of political agitation, although he takes none of the obvious steps to make himself a popular hero or even to assure himself a place in the event of anything happening to Hitler. He is, I repeat, curiously negative, almost anæmic, and has high moral character, apparently without any personal ambitions. That is why even Germans have no clear idea about his personality. He is the least known of all the major Nazi leaders. Content to give out the reflected brilliance of his *Führer*, he has drawn all light from himself and has really become a substitute—a *Stellvertreter*—for his Leader.

He is loyally supported by Dr. Wilhelm Frick, Reich Minister of the Interior (and since 1934 Prussian Minister of the Interior as well), one of the most powerful men in Germany. A thin sharp-faced man of sixty years of age, Frick looks like a medieval ascetic. He is admittedly one of the clean-living members of the Nazi inner circle and is respected for his personal integrity. All the scurrilous biographies of Nazi leaders have not been able to find out anything derogatory about him ; indeed, the main criticism we may levy against him is that he is an unreasoning zealot for his cause. A university man with good law degrees, he was a Government official and a chief magistrate in Bavaria until he became a convert to Hitlerism. He co-operated with his Leader in the November *putsch* and was sentenced to fifteen months' imprisonment, which, however, he did not serve. Then he became a leader of the Party in the Reichstag and had the distinction of being the first National Socialist to serve as a Minister, when he became Minister of the Interior in Thuringia in 1930.

Frick has the mind of a legal Civil Servant and a strictly Nonconformist morality. Critics have said that he applies ' the rule of thumb ' to every complex problem and thinks primarily whether he will be able to docket it in his administrative files ; and this seems not unfounded. He is a born administrator, with all the efficiency and limitations of that type of mind. As his Thuringian experiences showed, nothing could diminish his zeal in applying Nazi principles in practice, and he has pursued the same policy since then in the whole Reich. If he were corrupt or humorous, we would know how to deal with him, said a rival Party manager seven years ago, but, as it is, he is a walking application-of-a-moral-law. That is why he took such a stand against the immorality of Röhm and ' the third sex ', for the very idea shocked him. Nazidom becomes a dozen times more powerful when it is moralized by a Dr. Frick. For very different motives, he is as ruthless as Göring and Goebbels. Believing in a kind of puritanical predestination, he will continue in his ap-pointed path whatever the obstacles. Wanting to improve the race, for instance, he would sterilize half a million unsuitable parents. He sees his goal, estimates the difficulties statisti-cally, beautifully files them away, and then goes ahead. Frick represents something that is admirable and terrifying at the same time. His tight-lipped calculating inhumanity almost makes one prefer the hearty, though destructive, directness of a Göring ; a Frick makes one feel that human beings are so many insects to be driven along directed paths. And yet one admires him, as one does a slab of granite or some natural force that cannot be made to deviate from its set course. To him Hitlerism is Germany, the Germany of all ages, the Germany whose primitive pagan gods Frick is extolling to all schoolchildren.

Chapter Three

THE NATURE OF THE MOVEMENT

I.—The Party in Embryo

The prologue of this story commenced one cold day in the middle of the first September after the war, when an unemployed ex-orderly-corporal was admitted as No. 7 of the seven committee members of the German Workers' Party, one of the tremendous growth of political parties formed in the broken Germany of that time. The corporal's name was put down as *Adolf Hittler*, but one ' t ' was crossed out at his request. The chairman of the Munich group was one Anton Drexler, a small locksmith, and the Party, despite its paucity of numbers, boasted a national leader in the person of the journalist Karl Harrer.

The nucleus of this party was a vague group known as the D.A.P. (*Deutsche Arbeiterpartei*) which claimed to carry on the ideas of ' the Free Workers' Committee for a Good Peace', founded in 1915.

To this body—if body such a vague collection of individuals can be termed—came in the summer of 1919 the peculiar figure of Dietrich Eckart, destined to be the Delphic Oracle of the early days of Hitlerism. A heavy-jowled, fat little man of just over fifty-one, Eckart frequented the Munich beer-halls and inveigled against the Jews and ' the traitors of Berlin '. At the time he was planning a German Citizens' Union and pestered the students in the now dismantled artists' region of Schwabing. He naturally came into touch with several other discontented idealists of the time—with such persons as the over-earnest Balt, Alfred Rosenberg, who was obsessed with the importance of racial purity, or the engineer Gottfried Feder, who loathed capitalists and claimed that interest was the root of all evil. The last element came from a roystering, murdering soldier of fortune, Captain Röhm, a member of Colonel von Epp's staff and Hitler's actual paymaster. Röhm's creed was simple : ' Be a patriot or be a corpse ', and the streets of Munich in those days provided many object-lessons of both kinds.

All these diverse elements combined in the obscure German Workers' Party. Eckart, Rosenberg, and Feder already belonged to the queer group, when Hitler, the neurotic young fellow who was drawing a dole from military headquarters,[1] arrived at a meeting early in September. He had heard Feder speak three months before, he had known Eckart for some weeks, but now he began to attend group meetings and, after September 16th, to take part in the heated but sparsely attended discussions.

Affairs within the little Party were very confused. Hitler, the new-comer, was not popular, despite the name he obtained for being a good speaker after his spirited debate against Professor Baumann. Harrer, a genuine Socialist, mistrusted him because of his association with the military, and thought that he was abusing Anton Drexler's trusting faith in humanity for his own personal advantage. Most of the committee, however, were impressed by his zeal and by the number of new members he enrolled, and they acceded to Eckart's request that he should be made Party Propagandist (October 16th).

He gave the Party a programme and brought it out into the open. He leased a room in the *Sterneckerbräu* as its office, and persuaded the unemployed Rudolf Schüssler to become full-time but unpaid organizer. This was too much for Harrer. He resigned on January 5th, and lived in seclusion with his books until his death five and a half years later. Hitler was now in supreme control, for he could twist the nominal leader, the simple-minded Drexler, round his finger.

The great day of the new organization was February 24th, 1920, when the management of the Hofbrauhaus were per-

---

[1] He belonged to ' the Commission of Inquiry of the Second Infantry Regiment,' and was ' Organization Officer ' of the Bavarian Defence Regiment until April 1920. His work was practically peace-time espionage against the Communists.

suaded to allow a meeting in their gaudily decorated Festsaal upstairs. There, amidst noisy enthusiasm, the Twenty-five Points of the German Workers' Party were adopted on the voices, and, because of Marxist interruptions, it was decided to allow Emil Maurice, a burly fighter who is now a standard-leader in the Black Guards, to organize some of his young friends into a group of vigilants to keep order at Party meetings. At a single stroke Hitler had chanced upon his two key-weapons—the Party programme and the private army. On August 7th, the fuller title of *Nationalsozialistische Deutsche Arbeiterpartei* (N.S.D.A.P.) was adopted, and in the autumn Eckart bought a strange little anti-Semitic sheet, the *Völkischer Beobachter*, as the Party's newspaper. It was placed under a wild twenty-year-old named Hermann Esser, No. 2 on the Party's roll.

By the beginning of 1921, then, the N.S.D.A.P. was a party of 3,000 members, with a newspaper of its own, a central secretariat, and branches in a few other towns in South Germany. There was no mention yet of Goebbels or Göring ; these were essentially the days of Eckart, a drunken, but puckish figure who had a strange belief that, while he could never lead a great movement himself, he could inspire a lesser mind but a greater leader to bring about the regeneration of Germany.

II.—*The Background of the Movement*

The rise of Hitlerism was primarily the measure of Germany's disillusionment. The German people had been broken in body and mind by the sufferings they had undergone—four years of war ; starvation and the blockade ; the collapse of their ideals before what they called ' a stab in the back ' ; enemy occupation of their land ; 2,000,000 dead and the sur-vivors coming home to face street fighting ; humiliation on humiliation ; reparations ; the loss of their colonies and ' 10,000,000 Germans torn from the living body of the Reich ' ; inflation and collapse ; and the consequent wandering of the people along a path without hope and without faith. All they had in exchange was a cumbrously working Republic which seemed incapable of giving the people the unity and the inspired leadership they wanted. It is no wonder that private armies arose or that whole provinces, like Bavaria, were plunged into chaos for years. The wonder is that the German people did not sink so deeply into the mud that their nationality could never assert itself again, even under the stimulus of Hitlerism.

The Weimar Republic was bound to fail. It was doomed before Hitler's rise—doomed because of its own impotence and because its strongest supporters, in order to survive, had to use weapons that could only destroy it in the long run, once they had passed to other hands.[1] Chancellor Brüning was really Hitler's chief armourer. Hitler had only to use the constitutional tricks Brüning invented in order to become Chancellor himself. Brüning overlooked the importance of advertising his achievements and failed to provide a popular appeal to the masses. Hitler did so and then, grasping Brüning's weapons, became dictator by purely legal methods.

The trouble was that the Republic lacked what Wolff called ' the sacred fire '. Forgetting the power of inspiration it sank in the quicksands of dullness. Even its undoubted successes thus failed to receive recognition, and its virtues were submerged with its faults. No new constitution can sustain repeated errors in political tactics ; yet men like Stresemann and Brüning, much as we admire them, not only heaped error on error in the political realm but, what was more vital, failed to gauge the peculiar psychological stress under which Germany was labouring. A lesser man came and won, because the psychology of the crowds was no more subtle or more complicated than his own. He won, not because his point of view was superior to that of the average man but because it *was* that of the average man.

Brüning was separated from the crowds by the glacier of conscious leadership, whereas Hitler was one of them. His instincts were theirs, and the surety with which he could gauge those instincts (or, in other words, merely express his own feelings) swept him into power. A Brüning was too isolated, a Seldte too cautious, a Schacht too abstract to be a mass-

[1] See Part II, Chapter I, *infra.*

leader, but Hitler wagered all on the strength of his emotions. So he succeeded where a more capable mind, a more profound thinker, would have failed. His triumph was that of emotion and instinct over reason; it represented a great upsurge of the subconscious in the German people. He restored hope to the downcast, he gave visions of ultimate expression to the repressed. ' Arise, come with me, and ye shall feel '—that was the burden of his vehement message. Platitudinous it may have been, but it gave hope and virility to a people who do not take kindly to a depression.

The revolution of 1918, if indeed revolution it may be termed, was in no sense a great upwelling of a people. Rather did it represent the listless despair of sufferers who could only strike out and destroy. The subsequent Republic was linked from the first with defeatism and ' the dictate of Versailles '. No German could be proud of it. It was the symbol of a great enslavement, a cross which the mass of Germans had to bear. In their minds it was for ever associated with ' the stab in the back ' that ended the war, and they felt no pride in the new leaders, just as they felt no regret when the assassin's bullets reached Rosa Luxembourg, Karl Liebknecht, Kurt Eisner, and Rathenau. Theirs was the numbness of prostration, the enduring pain of a people whose past had been wrecked and whose future held no promise. They had lived only for *Volk und Heimat*—for people and Fatherland; but now the one was humbled and the other split into fragments, some of them lost for ever. They were drifting in a sea of false values with no steersmen and no instruments of navigation they could trust.

Indeed, they revelled in their own misery. As far as national virility was concerned, they were the living dead crowded into a tomb where the burial-urns of their ancestors had been broken and defiled. The false liberty of Weimar, excellent though it still seems to us, gave them no hope. They craved for sacrifices for a new Valhalla; instead they got only the verbiage of Weimar. Given that particular people and that particular time, and the psychology of defeat, the wonder is that the reaction was not immeasurably more violent.

Years before Hitler rose to eminence the people, especially the lower middle classes[1] (Hans Fallada's ' little men '), were craving for hope and leadership. The November revolution had seen the triumph of the ordinary man, the private soldier and sailor. But this was not what the people wanted. Equality meant little to them, for they were pining to be followers in the rise of some superman. Who it was they knew not—perchance Ludendorff (except that his political utterances were so ludicrous as to be incredible), perhaps somebody from the new parties.

III.—Why Hitler Succeeded

Then came the man given by Heaven to the German nation—the man heralded by every device of modern propaganda—the man whose virtues were dinned so repeatedly into the people's ears that most accepted his claims and the rest surrendered in the hope that the noise might give way to peace.

The people wanted some hope that would redeem the future, some romance that would take away the drabness of their recent suffering. They cried, in Boileau's words :

' Invent resorts that can take hold of me
  So that in all your speeches passion's dart
  May penetrate, and warm, and move the heart.'

Hitler saw that their feeling of suffering was the keynote of their whole existence. His early speeches raked and excoriated their wounds, and then, at the right moment, he turned the pleasure they were feeling in their suffering into the wider pleasure of future realization. The message was a simple one. ' You have suffered thus and thus, but, as you have suffered, so shall you rejoice. And the height of your rejoicing shall be as the depth of your suffering.' He merely preached to them. By diverting the feeling into political channels, he roused them as a revivalist pastor would have done—by threats of hell-fire if they drifted on in their old life, and by promises of heaven if they followed him.

[1] The *Kleinbürgertum.*

Ideas were burdensome under such conditions. All that was wanted was endless repetition of a few general phrases, an art in which Hitler has had seventeen years of constant practice. The thought behind them was always the same. ' Germany reborn ', ' Germany between night and day ', *Deutschland erwache* ! To an outsider they are simply trite admonitions monotonously repeated ; to the Germans they were for ever inspiring, and almost divinely revealed. ' Red Banners up ! ' the Horst-Wessel-*lied* aroused them as the Marseillaise did the France of '93, and Germany awakened to the tramp of marching feet.

But that is far from being the whole explanation of the rise of Hitlerism. Hitler was not looked upon as the prophet from the first. He was merely one of many political leaders, and it is often forgotten how frequently his movement was near the rocks, even in the months immediately preceding his appointment to the Chancellorship. No account of Hitlerism is at all complete without emphasizing his amazing luck. His ultimate success depended on a combination of time, place and events that could never be repeated, even if Hitler himself were starting out afresh. There was nothing inevitable about his rise. He had the message and the methods the people wanted, it is true, but a combination of quite extraordinary circumstances was also necessary. He is thus quite as much the creature of his times as the superman forcing his way inexorably to the front. I see him as the pawn of events in a time when even little men (and Hitler is far from being a little man) were rushed forward on the wave of circumstance. Ten years earlier or ten years later, Hitler would probably have remained in obscurity. As it was, fortune was always with him, and never more than when his enemies raised him to the Chancellorship at a moment when his Party was sinking into partial eclipse. He owed his supreme power more to the miscalculations of his adversaries than to his own handling of the political situation, although he made an unexpectedly full use of the opportunities presented by the Chancellorship once they were placed in his hands.

But, even if one emphasizes the element of luck in Hitlerism, the basic fact remains. On January 1st, 1920, Hitler was

No. 7 in a party of sixty members, yet by the time Brüning fell he had a million names on his Party roll, and a few months later he had achieved a position far more powerful than that of any German emperor. As his private room in the Brown House shows so clearly, his model has always been Frederick the Great, but no Prussian king could ever boast the omnipotence of this self-made man of the people, this for-eigner. If Hitler were to fall to-morrow, the abiding mystery of his rise to power would remain. His opponents have said that Nazi atrocities cannot be believed because they are un-believable ; exactly the same comment applies to Hitler's own career.

At first National Socialism was not very different from many other parties of the time. It started by being op-positionist and remained for some time merely an expression of discontent. Later the people were aroused to a growing resentment of their shackles, and Hitlerism developed into a popular movement. It survived because it had no fixed programme and could thus take advantage of every mood of national dejection and hatred. The ' dictate of Versailles ' was always a powerful weapon, but there were many others—the Ruhr, inflation, unemployment, 'the tyranny of the Young Plan', and, of course, the old stand-by of anti-Semitism which was dragged out when there was nothing more topical.

But other parties had these same grievances to exploit, and Hitler only ousted his opponents because of the efficiency of his Party machine and because of a succession of lucky acci-dents. Fate favoured him again and again. Even the Court which tried him in 1924 and which could have made him as insignificant as they had done the murderer Count Arcos shortly before, allowed him to babble about his vague philoso-phies for days on end.

After the reconstitution of the Party, it associated itself with national regeneration, and this motive, combined with an astute harassing of the successive republican governments, carried it to power. The Socialist aspect of National Socialism was of varying intensity in these years. At first much stress was placed on fighting Marxism (but more for political than doctrinal reasons, and one feels that if the governments of the day had been conservative Hitler would have been strongly Socialist). But Socialism waned as Nationalism grew, and the hopes of those who really wanted a 'second revolution' to supplement Nationalism by Socialism were rudely shattered on the night of June 30th, 1934. In power Hitler has stood for discreet and temporizing State Socialism rather than for his early ideas as set forth in the 'permanent and immutable' programme of 1920.

The movement ended by becoming a national dictatorship—a college of dictators with no immediate connexion with popular feeling. In a word, Hitler bred the myth of 'the German people'—the masses—while keeping effective power from them.

He survives his years of power partly because of his tremendous popularity and because of the feeling almost everywhere that he is genuinely concerned with the interests of his people. But these attributes are only part and parcel of a wider myth that has grown up around his personality. It is the story of the Hindenburg myth over again, this time with no Ludendorff to dim it. So keenly is it implanted that Hitler's constant problem is to live up to it, or, if that is impossible, to take no positive actions which will tell against the efficacy of the myth. It is just as futile to point to faults in Hitler as it was to faults in Hindenburg ; in both cases it was entirely a question of the myth.

It is this which makes his strength, this which various sections within the Party have had to consider in their quarrels, and this which will probably lead to the retention of Hitler as a nominal figurehead even if the political structure of Hitlerism collapses.

The Germans are a politically retarded race. They are still in the 'myth' stage of development. They need some national cult to weld the people into unity and, where this is lacking, as in the immediate post-war years, they split up into innumerable squabbling factions. A myth is what Bagehot would have called 'the cement of their society'. Brüning fell because he failed to provide a myth, and Hitler survives because he has deliberately built up the most showy, the most perfect myth of modern times.

He provided the myth from the first day in August 1921 when he ordered Lieutenant Klintzsch to work out a uniform for his adherents (the *Sportabteilung*, later to become the *Sturmabteilung*, the Brownshirts). Eight months before, when he called the first mass assembly—the *Generalmitgliederversammlung*—in Munich, he was already groping for the idea. By the end of the year it had fully grown, and the years since then have seen progressively bigger and brighter demonstrations, all of them contrasting the massed thousands of people with the one Leader. Those years may be described as a period of inculcating a myth by an appeal to instincts against reason and through the medium of mob-emotion aroused by public ceremonies. Hitler largely owes his success to the stage-hands who have produced the glamorous (and on occasion bloody and morbid) succession of spectacles. He realized at an early date that morbidity has almost as great an appeal to mass mentality as has more joyful entertainment, and his movement has always exploited the exhilarating results of the macabre.

He also offered the people power, and here he was on firm ground. The Germans have never wanted democracy; they crave for authority, and respect the strong arm. They do not want individual freedom. Accustomed to the restrictions of a police State, they quietly accept regulations that would provoke a rising in a British community, provided they feel that the State is benefiting thereby. The framers of the Weimar constitution thought that the Germans could be educated politically if they had the opportunity, but they erred in assuming that the political keenness possessed by a class-conscious minority could be extended to the whole nation. The average German would much rather salute a uniform than have a vote. He derives his feeling of strength and well-being from belonging to a strong community, and without that feeling of strength and respect, he is lost. The German is designed by history and nature to provide mass material for dictatorship, whether in time of peace or war, and Hitler realized this, even in the days when he was an unemployed house painter. Weimar gave them 'Freedom'; he raised the opposite slogan of 'Power' and won all along the line. A post-graduate student of Berlin said to me : ' I care nothing about being Johann Schmidt, but I want people to feel respect and awe when they see me pass and say : " *There goes a German* " ! ' Objectionable though this idea is to one who sees the greatness of the community existing only through the expression of the individual, it is quite typical of Germany to-day, and is the only bond uniting the disillusioned older sections of Germans with the young Nazi zealots. They all share this power complex, they all spurn the idea of individual expressionism if it weakens the community. Individualism, to them, is an anachronism taken over from last century and acting as a poisoning virus in the healthy body politic. It is not only negative, but treacherous.

Moreover, this idea is as strong amongst the working and middle classes as amongst the former ruling castes. Hitler always felt this to be the case. The revolution of 1919 attempted to organize the working classes, but Hitler realized that the *bourgeoisie* and the disappointed returned soldiers provided raw material just as malleable as the workers. It may be that he felt this only because of his innate instinct for social climbing to the middle-class Elysium painted for him by his mother ; but he was certainly convinced of it. His instincts made him loathe the horny-handed workers (the coarse fellows of the Vienna doss-house), and his military years turned him to the army. He therefore resolved (not consciously, but because he felt the need within him) to raise up the *bourgeoisie*. He made his success possible by the happy fluke or unconscious inspiration (who can say which ?) of organizing them, not on a class basis against the workers and the aristocrats, but on a broadly national basis which could be indefinitely enlarged to include all elements within the community. Here is the secret of the rise of Hitlerism ; and into this vaguely felt general background Hitler fitted in the accidental facts of the troubled post-war years. Everything was grist to his mill. Every suffering at home, every humiliation imposed by other nations, every domestic or foreign crisis contributed something for him. He held the master-key. The receptive Nationalism and the vague economic reforms he preached offered the Germans all that they wanted—hope, sacrifice, sympathy, striving, punishment or their foes, understanding of their past, a rally for their present, and a new world for the future.

Hitler had failed to reach the middle class himself; now, when the middle class fell with the mark, and were later exasperated by the world crisis, he offered himself as their saviour. Depressed, they wanted dreams; he offered them dreams for the moment and security for the future. He made them fight, and they made him a god—the god of the *Kleinbürgertum*—precisely because he thought and spoke what was inarticulate in their minds. His commonplace mentality, his unquenchable idealism, and his ready tongue combined to place a country at his feet. He saw that the *petite bourgeoisie*—the salaried classes, the small shopkeepers, the farmers and peasants—were crying for organization just as much as the factory proletariat were. He offered them *Folkic* as opposed to trade union organization, and later enwidened his organization to take in all sections—whether proletarian or even aristocratic—who were ready to place patriotic over class interests. This benevolent inclusiveness—like the amorphous pantheism of some Asiatic religion—gained him more and more adherents, so that at last his rally of the *Kleinbürgertum* could be reinterpreted as the rise of a nation. By starting with the plastic element of the lower *bourgeoisie*—a class more hardly hit in post-war Germany than in any other country—he was ultimately able to include the whole people. He solved the neurosis of a single class by invoking the idea of renascent Nationalism and discovered that the panacea he had hit upon could be indefinitely expanded. From being lord of the *Kleinbürgertum* he became the *Führer* of the nation as a whole.[1]

[1] For full details of the rise of the Party until 1933, see works of Heiden, Wickham Steed, Schumann, and Powys Greenwood in English ; or Bade, Czech-Jochberg, Ganzer, Goebbels, and Ruhle in German. Two excellent collections of documents (in German) are by Forsthoff and Krockow.

Chapter Four

THE PHILOSOPHY OF NATIONAL SOCIALISM

I.—The First Stages of Weltanschauung

At first National Socialism got on very well without a definite programme. Many of the leaders thought that Hitler had made a mistake in declaring the Twenty-five Points permanent. Goebbels, for instance, said later that if he were starting afresh he would have no programme at all. Gradually, however, Rosenberg and Darré evolved a policy which was officially sponsored by Hitler at the Party Congress of 1935. This was the famous *Weltanschauung*—the world-philosophy which is the present basis of Hitlerism.

Hitler says that all Germany must be educated up to this new way of thinking. National Socialism will be finally established when Germans not only act in accordance with his *Weltanschauung*, but think their every thought along its lines. He said specifically : ' National Socialism is a *Weltanschauung*.'

What is this *Weltanschauung* ? It is difficult to define. Nazi orators and writers make the task no easier when they say it is untranslatable, ineluctable, inexpressible, infallible, indivisible—which tells us nothing.

The truth is that it can be understood only as a kind of retrospective philosophical justification of Nazidom. It is well known that, with such a dynamic movement, the theory may follow rather than precede the events. Even to-day there is no clearly analysable doctrine behind the Third Reich. Hitlerism is still based on an aggressively patriotic emotion rather than a political philosophy.

Hitler has always proceeded through antagonisms. He started with anti-Semitism and tacked on to it opposition to

' the dictate of Versailles '.   His first mentor, Dietrich Eckart, went no further than this.   Hitler himself transformed these two plaints into a plea for a reawakened Germany.   *Deutschland erwache !*   Gottfried Feder, as I have mentioned earlier, contributed vaguely Socialistic economic ideas protesting against the tyranny of interest and the monopoly of the land. But this was always an uncertain element in Nazi ideology. Useful enough in the formative stages to gather in all manner of recruits, it receded into the background as the Party grew.

Hitler took stock of his ideas in *Mein Kampf* and declared the programme outlined in that book permanent and unalterable.   But this creed soon lost any relationship to practice. Indeed, it can only occasion mirth if compared with the actualities of National Socialism in the last four years.   *Mein Kampf* is still the gospel of Hitlerism.   Two and a half million copies of it have been sold (the local official paper at last year's Nuremberg Rally raised this to 25,000,000, regardless of the fact that such sales would have yielded the revenue of a millionaire !).   But the book is viewed only as a kind of inspirational guide and not a practical lexicon of conduct.   Its many discrepancies with Hitler's speeches to-day are very obvious ; and one can only conclude that the patriotic German has his nightly reading of *Mein Kampf*, approves its doctrines, then turns to the *Führer's* latest utterance, and approves that too—a desirable lack of that critical faculty which Dr. Goebbels has announced that he will stamp out in Germany.

We must look elsewhere than to Hitler for the philosophy of the New Germany.   The immediate source of the present *Weltanschauung* will probably be found in the writings of Arthur Moeller van den Bruck.   He published a book called *The Third Reich* in 1922, in which he pleaded emotionally for the rise of a new Germany out of the ashes of defeat.   Other writers did that about this time, but van den Bruck added the new idea of a Socialism that would be broadly national and in no sense based on class interests.   He advocated a peculiarly German form of patriotic Socialism.   In itself this idea dated back to the writings of Naumann and Lagarde forty years before, but it was now applied to Germany's post-war plight and changed from an idea held by a small minority of political thinkers into a great regenerative principle. It only needed some strong leader to arise and invoke the principle of leadership—*das Führerprinzip*—for Germany to be saved.

The basic contradiction in van den Bruck was that he emphasized the fundamental equality of man while talking in terms of Socialism. This juxtaposition makes his thesis clearer. He simply raised national Socialism in opposition to the international Socialism of the Marxians, and was seeking, not what we know as Socialism, but *Preussentum*—the revival of the old German authoritarian State, the State of Frederick the Great. This being so, it followed naturally that there had to be rule by a minority, by the supermen who were brought to light in the upward struggle. Van den Bruck said plainly that the progress of society depended upon the functional differences of mankind ; Marxism destroyed these differences and made societal advance impossible, but in ' the third Reich ' society would be balanced and progress would be made possible by the creative activities of the supermen—the *Übermenschen*. The community would be based on the ' folk ' as a whole—that is why it would be socialistic, but it would depend upon the emergence of a national aristocracy of talent who would govern in the interests of the whole.

This means that van den Bruck ended by advocating a nationalistic authoritarian State, based on the concept of the ' folk ' and ruled by a progressive minority—the very idea of a Folkic State ruled by a Nazi Party which applies to-day. Van den Bruck also contributed the emotionalism and the mysticism that made possible a flight from reality, and looked at the past history of Germany through rose-coloured spectacles in his attempts to reawaken the Germany of his time.

With all his paradoxes and lack of clear reasoning, van den Bruck gave Hitlerism its inspiration, and scores of political writers elaborated and extended his basic ideas about the Folkic State in which Socialism found its best expression in dictatorship, and in which progress meant nationalism. Van den Bruck died in the early days of the movement and his pioneering work was rather submerged by the later theorists.[1]　His book has run into only three editions, while those endorsed by the Party continue to pour from the printing presses every month, especially those of Alfred Rosenberg, the prophet of National Socialism.

II.—*Alfred Rosenberg*

It must be conceded that Hitlerism owes much to the out-pourings of Rosenberg.　He has been the real interpreter of Nazi ideology.　At first he followed events ; latterly he has become more ambitious and has tried to mould events so that they will conform with the philosophical theory he has now perfected, after fifteen years of frenzied writing.

His story is an amazing one, even in Nazi Germany.　Born at Reval in 1893 of an old family of Baltic handworkers, he was an architectural student at Riga and Moscow during the war.　His account in the Nazi *Who's Who* makes no mention of any war record, but it is stated that he turned his back on Russia after the revolution and went back with the German armies.　Drifting to Munich he came in touch with Dietrich Eckart, and later, Hitler, and was given a job on the *Beobachter* as soon as the Party acquired that paper.　He stood side by side with Hitler in the Munich *putsch*, but escaped punishment and did much to keep the records inviolate during the period when the Party was suppressed.　His main work for the Party was journalistic, although he took upon himself its cultural leadership for a time and later became head of the Foreign Affairs department within the Party, a role for which his experience in the Baltic lands was supposed to have fitted him.

---

[1] Oswald Spengler stands in a dubious position.　His preaching of the heroic idea in *The Decline of the Occident* and in *Preussentum und Socialismus* (1919), and his insistence on the replacement of democracy by Caesarism, should have made him the high prophet of Nazidom.　But the Nazis are doubtful about many of his writings, especially his *Hour of Decision* (1934) in which he rejected their racial theory and laughed at some of their wilder ideas.　Despite his increasing orthodoxy recently, they are not disposed to attribute to him much influence in the development of their philosophy.

Rosenberg is a young man with pasty features and a perpetual scowl. His face is curiously indeterminate, yet he rejoices in having a large photograph of himself on the covers of each of his books, a different portrait every time. He is not popular in Germany, and perhaps this accounts for his failure to obtain one of the really important posts despite his association with the Party from the pre-Hitler days. His cultural organization has declined in importance, his Foreign Affairs department has been shorn of most of its duties, and he only retains the functions of a *Reichsleiter*. He is a prophet at loggerheads with the practical men of the Party, and it is said that only Hitler's loyalty keeps him where he is.

Embittered by his unhappy private life, he has a curious incapacity for co-operation and, although nominally the cultural leader of 66,000,000 people, a misunderstanding of psychology. This was very obvious during his diplomatic visit to London four years ago.

I heard Rosenberg deliver his tirade against the Jews at the Party Congress last year. It was not impressive. For many minutes on end, in a rasping unpleasant voice, he read the names of hundreds of Jews who held office in Russia (remarkably enough, these were all condemned by their names alone, apparently on the principle that every other Rosenberg in the world except Alfred himself was a Jew !). He was a perfect foil to Goebbels who followed him and traversed much the same ground. His garrulity and harshness emphasized the silvery voice, the studied gestures and superb artistry of ' the little doctor ' ; and one felt that Goebbels had won another round in the long duel between the two men.

Mentally, Rosenberg owes his theories to Houston Stewart Chamberlain. He came to Germany with two ideas—a hatred of Jews and a loathing of race-mixture, rather ironical though this latter was for a man coming from the Russian Baltic States. These ideas he has kept ever since. He has written more prolifically than any other man in Hitler's Germany. Books have poured from him in endless spate, all of them bitter, all of them with the same philosophic content. He has written books attacking Marxism, the Jews, the Stock Exchange, international capitalism, the Freemasons, the democrats, the

November republicans (his *Thirty November Heads* attracted much attention in 1927, so much so that he followed it up by a still more outspoken attack called *The Swamp*, attacking the mentality of the Weimar leaders).   He has written biographies of Eckart and Chamberlain whom he calls ' the Prophet and Founder of a German Future ', and still more recently a eulogy of the first Jew-baiter in Germany.

His most important work, running to almost half a million words, was published in 1930.   It was called *The Myth of the Twentieth Century* and was sub-titled ' An estimate of the conflict of spiritual economic values of our time '—incidentally a fair specimen of his involved verbiage.   From whichever angle we approach it, it is an important work, for here we have the mature philosophy of National Socialism.

It is true that theoretically there is no marked advance from van den Bruck, or even Naumann, but the philosophy is now made more general and popular.   Rosenberg describes a *Weltanschauung* as the basis of the German State.   This combines the twin ideas of *Blood and Soil*.   Every German, whatever his religion or political nationality, is for ever a member of the German race—the People, *das Volk*.   The necessities of the *Volk* (as interpreted by the National Socialist Party) determine the acts and thoughts of every person in Germany.   Outside loyalties are therefore not only needless complications but absolutely incompatible with *Weltanschauung*.   A citizen enjoying full rights and responsibilities—a *Staatsbürger* —cannot logically owe allegiance to the Catholic or Lutheran Church.[1]   The unity of the People—the spirit behind mere political unity—forbids such clashing loyalties.   It is not enough for Party interests to be supreme ; they alone must count in a person's life.   No others can exist.   In other words, *Weltanschauung* claims the most exclusive form of possession the world has ever seen.

This point is important, because from its approach we can the most surely gauge the nature of Nazi philosophy.   It is idle, in Rosenberg's eyes, to say that a man can be a good Hitlerite and a good Catholic at the same time.   If he is really

[1] That is why the Papacy placed this book on the Index as soon as it was published.

a disciple of *Weltanschauung* he must surrender his every act and thought to it. He cannot divide his allegiances into watertight compartments and say that they are not incompatible because they never come into actual conflict. They must conflict, if the individual understands them properly. An international Church is as much an enemy of Hitlerian *Weltanschauung* as is international political faith of the type of Bolshevism. Both of them cut right across the idea of the all-embracing People. If the policy of the nation is founded on *Blood and Soil*, on the racial *Volk*, how can any allegiance be paid to a body with a worldwide organization? *Weltanschauung* ends at the German racial border; outside is a world of darkness whose inhabitants are doomed by nature never to share in this particular *Weltanschauung*. The border is impassable, for no man can change his race.

III.—The Racial Basis

Weltanschauung is thus determined by racial considerations, both for its extent and its nature. Race is at the bottom of National Socialist philosophy. 'The racial core of a nation is its characteristic, original, unalterable destiny', said Dr. Frank, the jurist who sought to make law conform to the facts of racial psychology. Race is a natural fact which cannot be changed. A man is born Nordic or Jew or of some other race, and he can no more change his racial characteristics than he can alter his skin from black to white. No society can exist except on the basis of racial purity. No Jew or coloured man can ever be assimilated into a Nordic society; social adaptability follows the facts of racial biology, and inescapable natural facts rule out any possibility of transformation.

The Nazi assumes that a society is an organism of people of the same race; he assumes that mentality follows race; he assumes that an accident of birth is the sole determinant of a man's fitness to be a member of a community. He does not attempt to justify these assumptions. He simply states them as facts that cannot be questioned, still less refuted.

This theory certainly reduces political science to a few

simple essentials. Indeed, the conception of the Volkic State dispenses with any need for political science. The simple fact of race covers everything. Politics, society, law—these have no existence otherwise than in conjunction with the racial norm. They all express race.

But that is not all. All races are not on an equality. Biologically, Hitlerism divides mankind into one superior race— the Aryans—and the other degraded slave-races. Among the inferior types two stand out (the Jewish-Slavs and the Jewish-Negro-French), and unfortunately accidents of history placed both of these in a temporary advantage over the pure Teutonic Aryans. Granting the Nazi racial theory, then, it follows that the only outcome must be a fight for that ultimate stage in which the Pan-Germans (including all people who have been lost to Germany by political shufflings) will rule the rest of the inferior races of the world. The more extreme theorists amongst the Nazis do not hesitate to draw this deduction.

This racial theory is not new, of course. It is merely a revival of the Aryanism of Gobineau and Chamberlain ; and Professor Hans Günther, in his many books about it, is only extending and giving pseudo-scientific form to a popular belief long held in Germany. People like Rosenberg and Günther honestly believe that most, if not all, creative works in the past came from the Nordics, and they carry this process of retrospective justification back even to the Stone Ages.

It is rather unfortunate that the Nazi leaders themselves are not typical Nordics. Indeed, the members of any other Cabinet in northern Europe would be a better advertisement for the Nordic ideal. Scarcely a man among the Nazi rulers could survive the first eliminating round in a Nordic contest. The dark Hitler, with his general physical flabbiness, is a fair Alpine example (although, in mentioning his state of health, one should remember his childhood diseases and the shrapnel and the gassing). Göring would be the last person to claim blond Nordic lithesomeness ; and Goebbels, a tiny bent cripple with dark colouring, may be dismissed even more abruptly. Günther's school, however, has come to his aid by saying that occasionally one finds ' dwarfish dark Germans ', throwbacks who were older racially than the blondes. And so it is with the others. Rudolf Hess, ' the Egyptian ' (he is sometimes called this because he was born of German parents in Egypt), certainly has the swarthiness which his friends ascribe to a tropical sun. The rotund little Dr. Ley and the big-nosed Julius Streicher have many points of physical resemblance to the Jews whose life they have made a misery. In fact, the only Nordic types within the inner circles were the Schleswiger Dr. Schacht (who is only tolerated because Hitler cannot do without him) ; Karl Ernst who was butchered on the night of June 30th for his ' immorality ' ; and Bruckner, the hefty blond giant who is Hitler's bodyguard and who is not supposed to be one of the Party's intellectuals.

But this is treason in Nazi eyes. Their racial theory leads inevitably to an emphasis on the governing class within the *Volk*. Indeed, Rosenberg, in his *Myth of the Twentieth Century*, specifically advocates polygamy for Nordic leaders, so as to improve the race.

IV.—Blood and Soil

Walter Darré, the Minister of Agriculture, carried the racial theory one stage further. A few years ago he won the ears of Hitler by joining the ideas of *Race and Soil—Blut und Erde* ; and he has spread his ideas so persistently that a regular cult exists to-day. Indeed, the twin ideas of *Blood and Soil* are now inextricably interwoven in Nazi political philosophy. They may almost be termed subdivisions of the wider entity of the *Volk*.

In Germany it is easy to underestimate the importance of the peasants, mainly because as a body they tend to be inarticulate. It is with truth that Riehl wrote : ' In the German nation there is one invincible conservative power, a firm, secure core resisting all change—and that is our peasant farmers.' He is not so apt in adding that, in their characteristics and individuality, their like cannot be found in any other country ; a thought of the French peasant alone would dispel any such claim. Nevertheless the basic fact remains—the peasant, wresting a hard existence from land and sea, is the fixed and immutable element in German society. *Blood and Soil* represents the vitality of the race, far more so than the banners and the bands.

The cult of the soil—of *Heimat* in general—is old in Germany. ' The love of Nature is the highest joy of life ', wrote Lenau, and there is no part of Germany without its strong local life and its legends. Even the monotonous regions of Lower Saxony and the Brandenburg Mark, even the eerie silence of the Luneburg Heath (which defied tradition until Hermann Lons revealed it to Germany) have a literature of their own. The science of *Geopolitik* started here, and the Germans are *par excellence* the apostles of geographical determinism. To quell the economic determinants raised by Karl Marx, they invoked the influences of the soil. The cult of *Blood and Soil* is not novel to Hitlerism, but a touching of the very soul of German history.

The German holds that he is the product of his soil. A race is kneaded by its environment over a long period of time— the original blood is tempered by centuries of contact with the local earth. Industrial cities obscure these cumulative traits and tend to reduce mankind to an international drabness and uniformity. Since a race, touched by industrialism, tends to become ' a mere dust of men ', Hitler declares war on deracializing cities and tries to stop the racial enervation they cause by turning to the land as a revivifying agency. He once said that the land gives unity to the German story right back to the original Germanic tribes who occupied the virgin soil. The first migrant tribes were, as he picturesquely said, ' the building stones of the nation ', and the edifice built from them has remained solid ever since, except when Jewry introduced an element of destructive rubble and when the cities brought in newfangled international cements.

Hitler thus preaches a most extreme form of racial reaction. But he recognizes the need of diversity within the wider unity. To him provincial differences are healthy variations from the Germanic norm—a sign of local virility and the influence of geographical mutations. In his camps, men from all provinces are mixed, not with any idea of breaking

down the differences between them, but in order to teach
them to respect and admire the ways of the other provinces
(always, of course, within the common framework of National
Socialism).

The *Führer* himself leans to the Bavarians, and it is said that
he has little sympathy for the typical Prussian attributes. He
looks south to Munich as his spiritual home—perhaps to
Vienna.   But he helps the cult of Nature everywhere, especially the Nature of forests and mountains.   He looks with a
kindly eye on the almost paganistic rites of his protégé,
Baldur von Schirach, and has sponsored the Youth ceremonies
that take place in the Harz Mountains—that nuclear land of
Germany, the *Stiftsland* or founder's country, the mystic heart
of the German nation.

It is significant that official propaganda draws a distinction
between the older and the newer regions of Germany.   The
West and the South clearly have the place of honour.   The
mountain-bound Thuringians provide the core, and round
them are grouped the Bavarians, the Franconians, the Lower
Saxons, and the Alemanni of the border mountains near
Switzerland, while farther afield a place of special pride is
reserved for the coastal Frisians, the purest of the Nordics.
Such a division, it will be noted, relegates the Prussians, the
dwellers on the frontiers, and the nondescript industrial races
to an outer place of subordination ; and it is constantly emphasized that the language, the folklore, and the traditions
come from the nuclear provinces.

This cult of *Blood and Earth* is not a cheerful one, despite
the songs of the *Wandervögel* and the jolly local festivals.
Regional writers have pointed out again and again that the
cult of the land finds its peak in the mysteries of twilight and
darkness, in the sadness of oak and juniper trees in the *Toten-
grund*, in dark tarns and hard rocks, in megalithic remains
that call up again the eeriness of prehistory, in the macabre
mysticism of medieval remains which make the Baroque
seem a podgily mirthful intrusion.   The cult is distinctly of
the *Walpurgisnacht* variety.

It is carefully tended, this cult of ' the days of long ago that
have no beginning '; and one seems in another world when

watching a group of adolescents in a Labour Service camp drinking in details of Diana Abnoba, the mythical goddess of the Black Forest. Indeed, the revival of pagan myth and prehistory in general is one of the most striking features of Nazi Germany. The bookshops sell large charts of pre-historic reconstructions for private homes, and in no other country have so many popular accounts of early history been issued in the last few years. The rush for works of this kind is as obvious as the demand for military books. To the German it is all very natural, for it symbolizes to him the ceaseless struggle for roots in a world in which moral standards are tottering. Moreover, it is to him the reaction against the obscuring foreign elements that have been introduced in modern times to confuse the fair Teutonic tradition ; so, in turning to prehistory and regional traditions, he is clearing away the dross which the negligent Republic allowed to accumulate.

This *Heimat* cult often descends into a bathos reminiscent of the worst excesses of tourist literature, but there is no denying its strength and importance in present-day Germany. Indeed, one of the main reasons for Hitler's survival is that he has sounded this note from first to last. He has identified a transient political movement with the age-old characteristics of the German people and in so doing has built better than he knew. Where these traits had been forgotten or had fallen into partial oblivion, the fierce light of his publicity revived them, but they were none the less real for the artificial methods he employed in their resuscitation. They are, in short, a political force of the first magnitude.

V.—The Community and the Individual

This, then, is the German philosophy of which Alfred Rosenberg and Walter Darré are the high priests, and the anthropologists and biologists and historians in every German university the acolytes. There is a Nordic *Volk*, triumphant over everything. This depends on unalterable facts of *Blood and Soil*, and the two combine over long periods of time to produce a race of supermen. Within the *Volk*, the naturally superior specimens come to the fore. Democracy is a historical accident of the last century, Communism a Jewish disease in debased Slav-Russia ; there only remains, then, a system of government in which the interests of the individual are cheerfully surrendered to those of the community or *Volk* as a whole. This system is National Socialism, and, within it, the *Führer* is the mouthpiece of the *Volk*, revealing its best interests by some kind of inspiration. As such, he must be accorded blind obedience, so that the *Volk* may prosper.

This means that the individual has meaning only as a member of the *Volk*. As a corollary, he must submit to many restrictions on his freedom. But the Germans accept this cheerfully, and even feel that they have gained thereby.

The strength of the nation—'folkic' unity—more than recompenses them. '*Wir sind nicht ganz frei*', the older Germans will say to you with a wry smile, but the younger sections will proudly retort—individual freedom is a myth, the only real freedom is freedom to serve as a member of a community. The older freedom meant unrestrained individualism—freedom to starve, freedom for agitators to continue their disruptive work, freedom to be exploited. It sacrificed the reality to the myth. In the early days of the movement, the Storm Troopers had a song : ' We spit on freedom, the Folk must be free', and this has remained true ever since. We may follow Jefferson in raising his everlasting plea for individual rights and in saying that no political organization can survive unless it is firm-based on individual liberties ; but the German of the new generation has had a surfeit of technical freedom. He finds his satisfaction in the strength of his community ; for the *Volk* he is prepared to die. It is the wider, the ultimate, loyalty. Just as industry is rationalized and controlled in the service of the nation, so, too, are the rights of the individuals. Moreover, the older theory was simply a political one that did not work, but the newer one—the doctrine of the Folkic State and the meaninglessness of the individual apart from his communal framework—relates to more than politics : it is a religion, the only practical religion of all time. This is the vital aspect of National Socialism ;

this is its core ; here is its real challenge to the rest of the world, and here it will live or die. Talk to an average German youth leader about individual freedom, and you will soon realize that here you have a completely new sense of moral values, held with such intensity that you will fear for the future, feeling that here are weapons which should never be used in any political struggle. Hitler has stolen the sanctions of religion for his own movement—that is the significance of National Socialism.

There is one last point. This political philosophy is acclaimed as the essence of modernity ; actually, it marks a reversion to the oldest state of affairs of which our anthropologists have any knowledge, for it is exactly the philosophy of the priests in savage societies. The Nazis have reconstructed the taboo system in its entirety—the system in which every part of the social structure depends on an unquestioning acceptance of the edicts of the priests : if a member offends against any part of the system, even in his innermost thoughts, the whole structure will collapse. This is Nazi philosophy—the taboo system of savages plus a warped mystical interpretation of modern history. The community counts for everything, the individual for nothing ; and every device of patriotic propaganda is employed to keep up the emotional backing, to sublimate it on the plane of sacrifice. And the last irony is that, with all its crudity, it gets back to something deep-rooted in human nature. The Nazis in Germany have probed back into the subconscious and removed the accumulated obscurities—some people outside Germany call them advances—of centuries. They have resurrected tribal instincts and the mystical sanctions of a savage society.

PART II

FOUR YEARS OF POWER

Chapter One

THE TECHNIQUE OF REVOLUTION (1933-7)

I.—*The Conquest of a Nation*, 1933

At noon on January 30th, 1933, Hitler's Government was installed. It is true that Hitler was 'a Chancellor in Chains', manœuvred into power by the Junkers. Von Papen thought to make him a puppet Chancellor—to discredit him by allowing him a few months of nominal power until a purely Conservative Government could come into office, with its main rival—Hitlerism—henceforth a declining power. But the scheme was turned against its founder. By one of the most daring moves in modern politics, Hitler swept off his chains and became in truth 'the People's Chancellor'. Von Papen was rash enough to cross swords with Captain Göring in Prussia and found himself ousted from real power.

Hitler was given his opportunity by the political miscalculations of the Junkers. Hindenburg was convinced that the bribe to Hitler of the empty title of Chancellor was the only way of saving his own class, those East Prussian landlords whose corrupt use of public relief moneys von Schleicher had threatened to expose. Sixty-six million people were delivered over to save the face of a few thousand Junker landowners. It is doubtful if the dotard of Neudeck was in a mental state to understand anything. He could only read what 'nephew Oskar' had written for him in four-inch-high letters on huge sheets of cardboard. All that he was made to realize was that the very existence of his beloved Junkers was at stake, and he was told that, after all, 'the fellow' would be powerless—with all his aspirations crucified on the cross of nominal power.

The Junkers thought that they had made a master stroke—

at one blow, they had saved themselves and had squelched the menace of Hitlerism. They thought that they had bamboozled Hitler and that he had, in effect, betrayed his followers by accepting the insignia of office. They had caught him, this simpleton corporal, by the oldest trick in the history of political manœuvring.

But the joke was entirely on the other side. It was the *Junkers* who were caught. Never had they shown themselves so out of touch with the new era. They had thought to catch the man who had ultra-modernized the political tactics of the Nazi Party—by an outmoded political trick that savoured of the eighteenth century. They had assessed wrong values to almost every element in the situation, and they paid the penalty, for ' the Chancellor in Chains ' at once began to throw off his encumbrances.

Hitler announced that he had three aims—national unity, prosperity, and equality with other countries. These constituted his first Four Year Plan, and he said that he would render account on January 31st, 1937.

In the early stages he concentrated on two phases—the occupation of key-posts and the assimilation of the provinces to the central Reich. He dissolved the Reichstag and announced new elections for March 5th, thus living up to his plea that he would keep within the letter of the constitution. He has, in fact, kept the Reichstag ever since, although his transformation of that body is far more insulting than its abolition would have been.

Then began the purge. The weeks after January 30th saw the most thorough clean-up in modern political history. Every one who expressed an individual opinion, everybody who had ever opposed Nazidom, was ousted from office. The ' cleansing ' leaves one staggered by its very audacity and no less repelled by the numerous cases of petty revenge. On the other hand, Hitler's political opponents probably deserved their fate, because, even while Göring was engaged in his destructive works, Social Democrats were howling down Communists, and members of the Centre Party were quarrelling with the Social Democrats. But there can be no excuse for the purge of officials who had never dabbled in politics, or private individuals whose only offence was to have criticized the Party years before. 'The integration of National Socialism', Hitler called these early days of power ; in reality they were a revelation of the essential pettiness of the Party leaders.

It was Göring who set the pace. As ruler of Prussia he soon made clear his idea of the relations between Party and State. All officials antagonistic to the Party were to go ; the police were to become completely Nazified ; all meetings criticizing the Government were to be broken up, and the police were to do everything possible to make Nazi meetings a success ; and the local Party leaders were to be consulted in all matters of administration. 'Shoot first and inquire afterwards, and if you make mistakes, I will protect you '—that was the gist of one of his first instructions to the Prussian police. In his famous Dortmund speech of February 26th, he was even more explicit. 'The faults which my officials commit are my faults ; the bullets they fire are my bullets.' He surpassed himself in his Essen speech on March 10th. 'I am in the habit of shooting from time to time,' he declared, 'and if I sometimes make mistakes, at least I have shot.' This is quite the most sordid avowal by any politician in modern times.

Göring proceeded to make himself Dictator of Prussia by means of police rule—incidentally freeing himself from the Sindbad burden of the S.A. masses. From the moment he came to power he mistrusted and feared his old comrades of the Brown battalions. One of his first measures was to prevent police officers from belonging to S.A. or S.S. units ; and then he began a long campaign to keep the police predominant over the Black Guards in Prussia, a campaign with the wily young Himmler which throws a flood of light upon rivalries within the Nazi circle. Göring's henchman was Victor Daluege, the former Brownshirt leader in Berlin, who was now made special commissioner of the Prussian police.

While Göring was making Prussia a model Nazi State, Hitler was fighting the wider political battle. His first ministry was an uneasy alliance between several political groups, each of which was resolved to climb to ultimate power over the shoulders of the others. In the scramble Hitler won, for a variety of reasons. The President's clique found their hands tied by the scandal of the East Prussia relief; von Schleicher's men were cleared out of their key-posts; the Reichswehr could not move against a 'National' Government of so many parties; von Papen's political wiles were too involved (it was said that even he, trained to a lifetime of wiliness, could not understand his own twistings and turnings!), and he had no answer to the bludgeoning tactics of his rival Göring; Dr. Hugenberg's Nationalist Party were too concerned with their own petty economic profits; and—most important of all—Hitler's henchmen brutally ousted all possible opponents, while Goebbels's propaganda secured the vote of March 5th to endorse the new 'national unity'. All of these factors combined to help Hitler. It is an amazing story, in which the most arrant forms of political freebooting succeeded.

All other parties went to the wall. The Communists, of course, were attacked at once. The Social Democrats, lulled into a false security, allowed the ground to be cut from under them by Hitler's promises never to go outside the constitution. For the mirage of becoming a safe opposition party, they sacrificed everything—ultimately their very existence. They looked ahead to a period of constitutional guarantees and political quietness, and accordingly did nothing in the first crucial days when the Nazis were taking over the realities of power as quickly as they could sign the necessary ordinances. They chattered at their headquarters in the Lindenstrasse while Göring's men acted. The Communists at least tried to hit out in their despair, but the Social Democrats—the most typically futile of the Weimar parties—actually bared their own throats for the killer's knife.

Next came the Centre Party—the strong moderating influence under Catholic control. Hitler had made up his mind before he came to power to get rid of them, but he negotiated with them for the sake of appearances. Within a week they gave up the fight and resolved not to act as a parliamentary opposition. They even voted for the Bill that gave

Hitler dictatorial powers, not having the courage of some of the Social Democrats in this regard.

Hugenberg's Nationalist Party had representatives in Hitler's first ministry, but their day of reckoning soon came.   Hugenberg strove desperately to cling to the Ministry of Economics and sacrificed even his loyal henchman, Dr. Oberfohren, to further his own aims.   Six weeks later Brownshirts murdered Oberfohren without any provocation, and still ' Hugenberg the Fox ' manœuvred.   But he was out of office in less than five months, regretted by nobody.

The parties received their final blow on July 14th, 1933, when a law decreed that the only party legally constituted in Germany was the National Socialist organization.   Promoters of any other party were liable to all kinds of penalties, even death under certain circumstances.

At the same time, the Storm Troopers dealt with the private armies which had sprung up within each political party.   The Communists soon fell ; and the republican Reichsbanner followed them.   They kept up their demonstrations until the March elections, but the police, acting under Göring's instructions, invariably took the side of the Nazis.   The Steelhelmets—the *Stahlhelm*, the old front-line fighters whose leader Seldte had accepted a ministerial post under Hitler— were a more difficult problem.   In March, after numerous clashes, they were disarmed in Brunswick ; and then dissension spread within their ranks.   Seldte, the one-armed distiller, was very anxious for office and took over most of his men as Brownshirt reserves ; Colonel Duesterberg, his second-in-command, was ignominiously discharged ; von Morozowicz, hitherto one of Hitler's mortal enemies, underwent a miraculous conversion and crossed with Seldte.   The old Steelhelmets had indeed fallen on evil days and, to all practical intents, had gone the way of the Red Front and the Reichsbanner.

Meanwhile Goebbels had been preparing for the election. A *Law for the Protection of the German People* was passed on February 5th, giving the Government control over the written and spoken word.   Despite the terrific propaganda, however, the outlook for the Nazis was not bright as March 5th approached. The provinces were too resentful ; there had been too many dismissals, especially in Prussia, and every village had seen a miniature social upheaval in the later days of February. The Nazis were in such a difficult position that Berlin even feared some kind of a *coup d'état*. But Fate or design provided a better idea. On February 7th the Reichstag was afire—in many places. This was at a crucial moment, and the people swallowed the story of ' Communist arson '.

Even so, despite all the official propaganda, despite the publicity of the fire, and despite the most blatant forms of pressure by police and Brownshirts, Hitler gained only 43·9 per cent of the votes. It would be stupid to call this a free election, but it was the last election in which other parties had even the semblance of competing. From every point of view, it was Hitler's worst defeat. Twelve million votes for the Left, 5,500,000 for the Catholics, 3,000,000 for the Nationalists—the truth about ' the National Revival ' is in these figures, and no subsequent ' consolidation ' can ever alter the fact. Hitlerism at the outset did not represent the nation. Discounting the official pressure at this last election, there can be no other conclusion than that Hitlerism was a minority movement—the largest movement in Germany, it is true, but in no sense a great national upwelling without any rivals. The Nazi Party was only one political group among many, and the revolution consisted not of their accession to power, but of their subsequent extermination of all opponents, and, later still, the achievement of a new sense of national greatness.

The way was clear after the election. The Party alone had no majority in the new Reichstag as it stood ; but, if the eighty-one Communist deputies were deprived of their seats, the Hitlerites would have a clear majority of ten over all other parties combined. The Communists were therefore declared incapable of sitting, and the Reichstag met in the garrison church of Potsdam on March 21st, ready to vote anything Hitler asked for.

On March 23rd, then, his 288 Brownshirt deputies passed a *General Powers Bill*, a Bill of five short articles which effectively destroyed parliamentary government in Germany. The

Cabinet was given the power of law-making for a period of four years. Reichstag and Reichsrat were no longer needed. Article 2 even said : ' National laws enacted by the National Cabinet may deviate from the constitution as long as they do not affect the position of the Reichstag and the Reichsrat.' The law was to last for four years unless the Government fell before that time ; in that case, its provisions were to lapse. When Hindenburg signed this Bill next day, the constitution —legally but very effectively—was shattered, and the Brown dictatorship henceforth had no limits. Only some of the Social Democrats voted against the measure. Hitler bitterly assailed the poltroons in the opposition, and his scathing words were justified when he contemptuously cried to them : ' Germany shall be free, but not through you ! ' One need be no admirer of Hitler to despise the last bedraggled standard-bearers of Weimar ; their final acts betrayed the greatness of their cause and they sank without a protest into oblivion.

II.—*The Fall of the Provinces*

In his first speech to the Reichsrat as Chancellor, early in February 1933, Hitler promised to respect the provinces, for they were ' the historical corner-stones of the Germanic Empire '. The only interest in recalling such a promise is to ask : Was Hitler honest at the time in saying this ? He made a great point of being a Southerner and was thus temperamentally opposed to centralization in any form. Within a month he was cutting away the very roots of the provinces, even of Prussia. The only conclusion from the facts is that either he was deliberately lying in February, or else was displaying an almost unbelievable ignorance of a vital matter of his future policy. Neither conclusion is flattering to him— for either he was a knave or a fool in his Reichsrat speech.

Göring took the initiative in the race for centralization, although here again the Nazis merely extended the devices of the Republicans themselves. The real ' rape of Prussia ' had taken place in the previous July, when the President had invoked Section 48 of the constitution to make von Papen

Federal Commissioner of Prussia, thus replacing the legally constituted Socialist Government of Otto Braun. Another decree suspended liberty of person and speech and assembly, so that the Nazis simply had to maintain the state of emergency already existing. Von Papen was left in office as Federal Commissioner, but Göring, acting as Prussian Minister of the Interior, reduced that office to a mere shadow. The duel between the two men ended in Göring's appointment as Premier of Prussia early in April.

Göring acted with his usual abruptness. He set to work to 'clean up Prussia', dismissing officials in hundreds—most of the police chiefs, most of the chairmen of provincial councils, most of the presidents of provinces. The ranks of the political police were purged, and selected Nazis were enrolled as armed 'special police' throughout Prussia—that is, throughout two-thirds of Germany. The Supreme Court declared many of these acts illegal, but Göring carried on. He banned first, then lifted the bans when the courts descended on him (but only after the occasion no longer needed them). Göring himself admitted that his actions conflicted with Federal and State law as it then stood, but boasted that his policy was to act first and clear up the legal position later.

On May 18th, the Landtag transferred all its power of legislation to the Cabinet until April 1937. Göring used this power to create a new Council of State, for the most part composed of Nazis. Its functions were to be purely advisory, as were those of the twelve new provincial councils that replaced the older democratic bodies in Prussia. All local administrative groups lost their powers. Everywhere, even in Berlin itself, nominated commissioners took over all authority. No fragment of the admirable system of local self-government that had for long commanded so much respect in Prussia was allowed to survive Göring's first six months of frenzied activities. He had indeed showed Germany what the Nazis meant by the process of *Gleichschaltung* —co-ordination.

Prussia's fall was followed by that of the lesser provinces. Early in March, Hesse fell. Frick, as Reich Minister of the Interior, sent Müller as Federal Commissioner, and armed

Brownshirts occupied all Government buildings. A day or so later, other States were assimilated. Wagner cleaned up Baden ; Bremen and Lübeck surrendered, and the others toppled like ninepins. In each case the technique was similar. Frick merely handed over the police to the Nazis—they did the rest. The legal basis for these usurpations was provided by the law of March 31st which provided for the ' assimilation of the provinces ' and authorized the State Cabinets to take over all power. This was supplemented a week later by another law authorizing Hitler to name a Regent or Statthalter for each of the provinces, with power to nominate and dismiss Cabinet ministers and to control all officials.

These laws ended the question for all the provinces except Bavaria, which presented special difficulties. Dr. Held, who had been Premier of Bavaria for nine years, contemplated resistance to the central administration, and there was some talk of a localist government under the Wittelsbach Prince Rupert. Held proclaimed that a new Hitler *putsch* would meet the same fate as that of November 1923 ; the head of the Catholic Party threatened to arrest any Federal Commissioner at the frontier ; and the Catholic militia—the *Bayernwacht*—resolved to stand to arms. The other States were looking to Bavaria for a lead, now that Prussia had fallen, but the elections of March showed that the southerners had little faith in their existing government, and, on March 10th, Ritter von Epp, a hatchet-faced diehard of the Freecorps period, a freebooter out of his century, was sent to Munich as Reich Commissioner. No resistance was offered ; the Government, despite its loud boastings of a week before, meekly accepted dismissal, and von Epp appointed three commissioners to govern Bavaria under him. The army—the last hope—stood quietly by, for von Epp, a former commander of the Seventh Bavarian Division, was not unpopular.

The States were thus doomed. Federalism disappeared that spring, although the formal proclamation of a unitary system for the whole Reich was, oddly enough, postponed again and again. It was expected when the Reichstag assembled after the overwhelming vote on leaving the League of Nations ; but nothing was done beyond passing a series of laws abolishing all representative institutions in Prussia (December 18th), a series which obviously only recognized the work done by Göring. A more extensive gesture was expected when the Reichstag met again on January 30th, 1934. It was just a year since Hitler had taken over power—a fitting occasion for the proclamation of a unitary system of government. Next day the last vestige of Bismarck's Germany disappeared. A short law of six articles destroyed all representative bodies in the States, transferred the States' sovereign rights to the Central Government, and made the State Governments and the Statthalters subordinate to the Reich Government. It was devastating in its completeness. Hereafter there were to be no local rights in Germany and no representative institutions. 'Co-ordination' was complete, for Germany, formerly a federal democracy, now became a completely centralized autocracy. All of this had been achieved within a single year and, as 'Legality Adolf' insisted, by purely legal means. The political face of Germany had been changed beyond recognition. Democracy had gone, regionalism had gone ; in their place, all power was in the hands of one man. Germany had delivered herself over to him for a period of four years ; before one of these had elapsed, he had evolved a system of centralized dictatorship unequalled in the history of the land. In every sense of the word, the political events of 1933 constituted a revolution—almost a miracle.

III.—*The Voice of the Prebiscites*

The rest of the story is told by a succession of plebiscites. The first took place on November 12th, 1933. It had been preceded by brilliant strategy. Germany had left the League of Nations and the Disarmament Conference on October 14th, and Hitler now asked the people if they approved of his action. Naturally the whole nation was united in supporting a policy which, in their eyes, restored Germany her freedom in foreign affairs. 'Peace and Equality' was the slogan,

and the nation voted that Hitler had restored Germany's
' honour '.   No less than 96·3 per cent of the voters were
for him ; a large majority of the prisoners in the concentration camps at Dachau and Oranienburg answered in the
affirmative.   He would indeed have been a strange German
who voted against Hitler's question that Sunday ; and Hitler
naturally construed the vote affirming his foreign policy as an
endorsement of his internal policy as well.

The next prebiscite was on August 19th, 1934, when Hitler
asked the people to uphold the action the Cabinet had taken
in making him *Führer* and Reich-Chancellor when Hindenburg
died.   Over thirty-eight million people voted for him.   It is
true that this total was two and a quarter millions less than in the
previous plebiscite, and that the Rhineland and Hamburg still
remained centres of opposition.   But the obvious fact was that
the people, especially in the country districts, were for him.
And so he began his life *Reichsführerschaft*.   The one man—
the visionary of 1919—had indeed become the nation.   In
his own words at the time : ' Ever since I first stood in the
thick of this political battle, I have been actuated by only one
motive—so help me God !—only one thought, Germany !'[1]

---

[1] For the last plebiscite, see Part V, Chapter I, *infra*.

Chapter Two

THE GROWTH OF PARTY ORGANIZATION

I.—*The Underlying Principle*

It would require a lifelong study of administration to understand the complicated political structure of the National Socialist Party, and even an expert would be driven mad if he tried to unravel the relationships of Party to State. The trouble is that the organization has always been in a state of transition. It grew out of nothing, and developed as it grew. When some new activity came within its purview, a new department was formed, and yet those already existing yielded none of their powers. Something was added here, new officials appointed there ; each one was jealous of his powers, and all created work where there was very little to do. A distinction must thus be drawn between the essential kernel of the organization (where most of the vital work is done) and the latter trappings that were added until the Party to-day is one of the most complicated, disorderly, overlapping, amorphous organizations in the world. It is impossible to represent it diagramatically or analytically. Indeed, its unwieldiness is a cause of mirth in Germany. Only one man ever understood the complicated machinery, it is said, and he suggested so many reforms and prunings that he was sent to Dachau concentration camp. Hitler knows what a mess it all is, but prudently does nothing. Indeed, he actually adds to the muddle, because it is one of his pet theories that unemployment can be relieved by increasing the number of official or semi-official administrative posts. Every man attached to Party Headquarters, he maintains, takes somebody off the dole—indeed, many people, because every official will acquire a typist and will commence ' organizing ' until he has a department around him. The stark truth is that *the Party* has been a happy hunting-ground for job-seekers. The 'departmentalizing' has often been so absurd that it recalls our own worst efforts during the war.

I was staggered when I was shown how the system works at Party Headquarters in Munich, until I realized that everything depended on 'finding something to do'. A staff at headquarters clipped foreign papers for items about National Socialism ; a few streets away, a still larger staff at an official records office clipped the same cuttings from the same newspapers ; and a Nazi staff officer from Berlin laughingly told me that 'that is the system', and, to take this instance alone, enough people are clipping newspapers in Germany to-day to fill several ministries ! Since there is not enough work to go round, it has to be invented.

I still think that the palm goes to the department at headquarters at Munich which has the most elaborate filing system I have ever seen, and a staff of trained historians and other experts delving into medieval records to find the first recorded picture of a butcher or a baker or a candlestickmaker. This department has searchers without number, copyists, photographers, and recordists. I must add that they offered to do anything possible to aid my own researches, even to supplying photostatic copies and reproductions without charge, either for my immediate work or for any other purpose. Notwithstanding this, I still fail to see what place such admirable historical labour has in the central buildings of the Party Headquarters. The director told me that his job was to prove the worthiness of Labour through the centuries and to show that the democracy of Hitlerism was to be found as far back as recorded German history goes. As I left, the main office was wildly excited—an engraving of a German baker had been found, some decades earlier than anything hitherto known. In the same building, other officials were busily collecting all anti-Nazi literature. There were rooms and rooms of it, even down to the most fugitive leaflet. It prompted one to the reflection that opposition is far from dead if it still can produce so much printed matter, despite Hitler's repressive laws. The custodian could not see this point, and dryly remarked : 'There must always be sin in the world.'

II.—*The Evolution of the Party Structure*

The present organization dates from 1925, when the Party was reconstituted after the Munich revolt.   While Hitler was in jail, Alfred Rosenberg kept together as many Party documents as he could, although most of them were burned by order of the authorities.   That is why, even at headquarters, very little survives about the early days of the movement.

At first there was a simple organization.   Hitler was chief, with the young student Hess as his secretary ; Franz Schwarz kept the funds, Philip Bouhler was business manager, and Max Amann supervised publications.   This little group had come together in February 1925, and in the following June were bold enough to open a new Party office, a dingy apartment in Munich's *Schellingstrasse.*

Headquarters arrangements naturally had to become more intricate as the Party grew.   Hitler counted on having fifty thousand followers by the end of 1926, and called a general meeting on May 22nd of that year to decide on the future organization.   Such matters were handed over to a corporation called the National Socialist Workers' Union, which was registered as a company in Munich from June 30th, 1926.[1]

The existing departments were kept, and, whenever a new activity was adopted, it was simply tacked on to the old structure.   Thus, 1926 saw the foundation of the Hitler Youth (but with headquarters at Plauen) ; the dreamer Gottfried Feder was playing with a new department which was to issue a National Socialist library ; while Goebbels descended upon Berlin (naturally with an organization of his own).   From the beginning of 1928, Gregor Strasser, from whom Hitler derived so many of his ideas but whose pretentions to leadership were already becoming rather trying, took over the work of organization ; and two key-posts fell to Goebbels and Major Buch.   Goebbels became propaganda

[1] It lasted until March 29th, 1935.

chief for the whole Reich, with Himmler (the astute and ruthless young Black Guard) as his deputy, while Walter Buch organized the terrible disciplinary body known as *Uschla*, 'the Investigation and Adjustment Committee' as it was known, whose function it was to crush out the dissidents and chastise the tactless within the Party. About this time, too, the ambitious Alfred Rosenberg was tiring of his newspaper work and began to dabble with a 'Fighting Department for German *Kultur*', and later with his foreign policy department, although he was prevented by his personal unpopularity from entering the most powerful inner organizations.

In July 1928, Goebbels had a further triumph, when the system under which he had mapped out Berlin in his fight for the capital city was adopted as the model for the whole of Germany. From early in 1929, a new department grew up, one rendered very necessary by the increasing mortality amongst the Brownshirts—the department built up by Martin Bormann to provide pensions for the families of Nazis killed and disabled in the fight. This was the *Hilfskasse* to which every Nazi in the land contributed. It soon became a Party insurance fund, which paid even for damages done to drums and trumpets in the hurly-burly of street fighting. At Nuremberg in 1936, I was even offered compensation from this fund for a raincoat torn in the crowd at the Zeppelin Field on the occasion of a Nazi review !

The next important addition took place in June 1930, when Hitler, newly obsessed with his twin ideas of Race and Soil, brought Dr. Darré to headquarters to organize the peasants and work out an agrarian policy for the Party. For a time after this, Hitler was more concerned with rooting out the Socialist heresies of the Strasser brothers than with expanding his office arrangements, and he did not rest until the organization was purged of 'Strasserism'.

This was roughly the position when the Nazis moved into the Brown House. By the middle of 1930, there were 200,000 names on the Party rolls, and Hitler had long been of opinion that a more imposing centre was necessary. So he bought the former Barlow Palace in one of the choicest positions of the Briennerstrasse and changed it into the Brown House. Redecorated and largely rebuilt, this was opened as Party Headquarters on January 1st, 1931.

Thereafter expansion was very rapid. The move into the Brown House coincided with a great drive to capture the industrial workers. Indeed, Otto Wagener was ordered to form an Economic Policy Department on the very day the Brown House was occupied, and, a fortnight later, Walter Schuhmann began to work out a department for a Factory Cell Organization—the famous N.S.B.O. (*Nationalsozialistische Betriebszellenorganisation*). Spasmodic efforts had been made in this direction in the previous three years, notably in Berlin, but with little success ; hereafter two departments at Nazi Headquarters were to see that the fight for the workers was intensified. So successful were they that almost a million workers were enrolled in the N.S.B.O. by the time Hitler became Chancellor.

No major changes occurred after this until the Strasser purge of 1932. Attempts were made to increase central control by the institution of Inspectors in June of that year, and by the formation of the P.O. (Political Organization) under Strasser. Unfortunately for himself, Strasser became too Socialistic and had his hands on too many of the key-posts in the organization. After months of intrigue, he was displaced on December 8th, 1932, and the organization then took the form it retained until Hitler became Chancellor. Dr. Ley became the main Organizer of the Party in Strasser's place, but Rudolf Hess was officially named Deputy Leader and, as such, took charge of a ' Central Political Commission ' which was henceforth to have paramount control over the political organization of the Party. This meant much more centralization, especially because of the merging into one efficient organization of the two separate Political Offices that had grown up.

It was fortunate for Hitler that the Party structure had been purged a month before he came into power, because this meant that he could face the problem of ' co-ordinating ' Party and State with a newly efficient organization behind him. A few months earlier the position would have been very different.

He was always fortunate in his subordinates. They provided the administrative capacities he lacked. They built up the remarkably efficient Party system behind the outside façade of his personality, and this organization was so truly erected that it remained even after some of the persons responsible for it were displaced.

Gregor Strasser, for instance, was mainly instrumental in winning over Prussia and the Ruhr for Hitler ; and, in the early days, Hitler owed much to Röhm (for organizing the Storm Troopers) and to Goebbels (whose mordant bitterness did not prevent him becoming the most striking propagandist of modern times). The machine, it is true, carried much dead weight, and organization in certain provinces was notoriously lax ; but, on the whole, the Party came to provide a definite shadow State.

When I was admitted to the Party archives at Munich and shown some of the earliest documents, I was struck by the breadth of the point of view behind the system, even in the infancy of the Party. Here were no hasty pencillings and fugitive scraps of paper. Even when the Party had only a single stenographer, its files were handled as if they were the archives of a great nation, and the most insignificant details of meetings were minuted and checked and counter-checked. They were treated as State papers, and it is quite clear from the documents themselves that there has been no retrospective building up of a system that did not exist at the time. It is beyond doubt that the men who organized the Secretariat of the Party in the first few years acted as if they were managing a nation. The inculcation of such an outlook over a decade made the ultimate transference of power much easier than it would otherwise have been.

III.—*The Party Organization when in Power*

Party and State are not synonymous, despite the verbiage of various decrees. The Party organization remains distinct from that of the State, and it would be entirely erroneous to think that the nominal holders of power are the strongest men in Germany. Some of the most powerful dictators have scarcely been heard of outside Germany, and yet, within the wheels of the Party machine, they effectively control the leaders of whom we hear so much. Power in Germany does not reside, for instance, in most of the members of the ordinary Cabinet. With the exception of Hitler and Göring, there are many men without Cabinet rank who have more real authority than any Cabinet minister.

The Central Directorate of the Party—the *Oberste Reichsleitung*, or O.R., as it is commonly known in Germany—is the key of the whole organization. It has nineteen members, and one would be safe in saying that nine out of ten people outside Germany have never heard of half of them. Who knows anything of Frank, Dietrich, Amann, Fiehler, Bouhler, Grimm, or even Schwarz and Buch? Yet they have a majority in the Party Cabinet. At present, that Directory comprises Rudolf Hess (Hitler's deputy); Franz Schwarz, the fat bald little man who has been the Party's Treasurer from the beginning and whose unobtrusive presence is never very far from the *Führer* himself; Goebbels; Darré (the Minister of Agriculture); Alfred Rosenberg; Ley (the head of the Labour Front but a member of the Party Directorate in his capacity of Organization Leader for the Reich—he organizes the Party Rallies, amongst many other things); Frick (the Minister of the Interior); Lutze and Himmler, leaders of the S.A. and S.S. respectively; General von Epp, the tyrant of Bavaria, but present because he leads the colonial and military departments of the Party; and a number of lesser-known men, Major Buch (in charge of Party discipline and chief of the espionage system); Willy Grimm, his assistant; Baldur von Schirach (Hitler's pet young man, who is in charge of all youth organizations); Karl Fiehler, censor-in-chief and labour leader; Otto Dietrich (the Party's Press chief); Max Amann (Hitler's old sergeant-major, who is in charge of the Press bureau—why he and Dietrich are both there is not clear); Martin Bormann (Hess's right-hand man, who has vague but very important powers within the Party); Hans Frank (director of the Party's legal section); and the mystery man, Philip Bouhler (the business manager of the

Party and one of the inner ring known as ' the dictators of the dictators '). These go to make up an odd combination. Only five of the Cabinet Ministers[1] are included, and such well-known figures as Göring and von Blomberg and, of course, Schacht, are absent. In dealing with this O.R., we are getting very near the realities of power.

The Party itself has changed curiously little since Hitler came to office. New departments have sprung up haphazardly to meet the new conditions or sometimes merely to provide employment for Nazi stalwarts ; but, while there have been many additions, there have been few replacements. The Party organization of to-day, then, remains in essentials what it was four years ago, except that it is even more cumbrous and complicated.

The central administration remains at the Brown House in Munich. Hitler is Leader, and Hess Deputy Leader, although Wilhelm Keppler is Deputy Leader in Economic Affairs, with offices in the Wilhelmstrasse in Berlin. Next in the list comes Hitler's personal adjutant, the hefty Wilhelm Bruckner, a beautiful physical specimen of Nordic mankind. In a somewhat lesser light are the two adjutants, Julius Schaub and Friedrich Wiedemann, who are the personal attendants of the *Führer*. The Chief of Chancellory, a kind of official private secretary, is Philip Bouhler, a mild-looking bespectacled young man of thirty-eight. At the age of sixteen, he was standard-bearer to a Bavarian regiment on the West Front ; five years later he left a Munich bookshop to become a reporter on the *Völkischer Beobachter* ; three years later again, he was made Reich business manager of the Party and has remained at Hitler's right-hand ever since. What spare time he has is divided between motor-racing and acting as Commissioner for the Protection of National Socialist Literature. A type of the new Germany is Bouhler, with enormous power behind the scenes, because the term ' business manager ' is by no means identical with ' treasurer '. Schwarz looks after that side of Party affairs ; Bouhler's idea of ' business ' is everything pertaining to Nazi organization.

Both Hitler and Hess, as I have said, have staffs at the

[1] Hitler, Hess, Frick, Darré, Goebbels.

Brown House. Hitler, for instance, has a director for Party matters (Victor Brack), a director for charity (Hubert Berkenkamp), a director for social and personal affairs (Albert Bormann), and an administrative director (Hubert Jaensch). Hess is more ambitious in so far as administration is concerned, for he has control of at least nineteen departments. He starts with two adjutants, a chief of staff (still another Bormann), and a staff executive. Then come separate directors for Internal Party Matters (Friedrichs), for Public Law (Sommer), for Personnel (Wulffen) and for Art and Culture (Schulte-Srathaus). The Chief Archivist (Dr. Uetrecht) and Press Director (Alfred Leitgen) come next, each of them with large staffs. Next among Hess's charges are three offices in Berlin—the Foreign Department Office under Ernst Bohle, whose task it is to supervise Germans abroad and to have a finger in the general propaganda pie; the department usually called the Ribbentrop Bureau, that shadow Foreign Office which the ubiquitous ambassador to the Court of St. James's has built up in his role of 'Deputy for International Political Affairs', and which is far more important than its place in the list of Nazi organizations would lead us to believe; and the Department for Technical and Organization Questions, directed by Dr. Todt, who is best known as constructor of the Reich motor roads, but whose office in the Pariser Platz has tentacles that stretch out far into German industry.

The next department under Hess is a very important one in Germany. It rejoices in the rather doubtful title of the Department of Hygiene. Its leader is the old fighter Gerhard Wagner, who, not content with four years of active service with the Bavarian infantry, fought in the Free Corps in Munich and Silesia and organized the medical branch of the Party. His bureau has two sub-departments, the department of Race Politics in the Robert Koch Platz, under Walter Gross (do they ever think of Koch's concept of medical science as an aid to humanity?), and the department for the Investigation of Kinship, under Dr. Kurt Mayer (he is also in charge of the department of Higher Education).

The queerest name of all is the department for the Uplift

of the Reich, which is under the charge of Adolf Wagner, the ruler of Upper Bavaria. What he does as ' Deputy for the Uplift of the Reich ' cannot be ascertained ; but he is an upright man, in the inner councils of the Party, and genuinely concerned with the development of art. His most striking achievement has been the ' House of German Art ' in Munich.

The remaining leaders who have departments at the Brown House under Hess are not so important. Theo Croneis is Director for Practical Technical Questions ; Fritz Reinhardt (whose main task is permanent head of the Ministry of Finance since the revolution) acts as Party Director for Unemployment, Financial and Tax Policies, a task that cannot be too onerous in view of the masses of publications he issues on financial matters ; Wächtler is Director for Schools ; Heindrich Stran is Director for the Party Congress ; Herbert Stenger acts as head of the Liaison Staff, surely the most difficult task in Germany if properly done ; while the former naval officer, Gustav Oexle, who describes his hobbies as ' politics and organization ', brings up the rear as ' Special Deputy for the Deputy of the Leader '. With all of these departments on his hands, it is little wonder that Rudolf Hess usually appears rather subdued.

At first sight, this range of departments would seem to run the whole gamut of administration, especially since the Party is only a shadow State and theoretically has not taken over any of the work of the permanent Civil Service. But we have barely started. Scattered round Munich and Berlin are a number of distinct ' offices ' or departments, fifteen in number. Some of them perform essential functions, either for the Party or the State ; others are triumphs of theoretical inventiveness.

It is difficult to group them in order of importance, although from the Party point of view, priority must be given to the Political Organization Office—the famous P.O. in the Barerstrasse in Munich, where *Reichsleiter* Dr. Robert Ley, lord of the Labour Army, spins a web that covers the whole of Germany and reaches out in most unexpected places. Ley's office simply bristles with adjutants and sectional leaders, and maintains a mysterious connexion with what is called

the ' Main Organization Office ' in the same building.   The
leader of the latter is Claus Selzner, the ex-machine-gunner
who was deputy leader of the Factory Cell Organization
and acted under Ley as organization leader for the Labour
Army.   It is far from clear which tasks fall to ' Political
Organization ' and which to ' Main Organization ' ; but
without doubt the two departments in the Barerstrasse mean
that Robert Ley keeps a rigid control over all matters affecting
Party structure.   There is also a Party Congress Organization
which Kropp runs at Nuremberg, but here again ' the hand of
Ley ' (which has become proverbial in Germany) reaches
out, and, as the Germans say : ' When Ley comes, others
make way.'   It is extraordinary how powerful Dr. Ley is
in Germany and how little known he is outside the country.
In reality, this man, *bon viveur* and Jew-baiter, is one of Hitler's
oldest personal friends, and enjoys licences that make him
stand out even in a land of dictators, although his behaviour
is often a sore trial to the more puritanical *Führer* himself.

A most vital office is the Reich Treasury, where one of the
oldest Nazi leaders, the sixty-two-year-old Franz Schwarz,
controls Party finances.   A Party member since 1922, he has
achieved much in his unobtrusive way and, for sheer constructive ability, ranks amongst the few first-class Party
leaders.   His department has always been a miracle of efficiency, and he holds an unqualified power of attorney from
Hitler to act in all financial matters.   The Treasury naturally
works in close contact with the main Chancellory, which
Otto Marrenbach controls from his room in the Brown
House.

The most feared of all departments is the Chief Party
Tribunal in the Karolinenplatz in Munich—the dread *Uschla*,
which is directed by the mild-mannered Walter Buch.   The
extension of this body has been amazing.   It has no rivals
as a Secret Service department, and its records are probably
unparalleled anywhere in the world.   At the moment,
Major Buch employs Ludwig Schneider as chief presiding
officer, and has so many calls for his service in maintaining
Party discipline and morale that he has set up three distinct
chambers, under Walter Knop, Wilhelm Grimm, and Eugen

Lusebrink. Of these, the tight-lipped Grimm, a *Reichsleiter* who has belonged to the Party from the outset, is the most drastically efficient, and is usually looked upon as Buch's successor as terrorist-in-chief.

Equally drastic in their actions, although in another sphere, are the two Press departments—the Reich Press Chamber under Max Amann (Hitler's old comrade-in-arms in the List Regiment, who seems to have slipped by the way in the apportionment of rewards), and the Press Directorship under Dr. Otto Dietrich, a forty-year-old Rhinelander whose journalistic abilities have stood him in good stead in writing ' inspired ' accounts of Hitler and the Party. Dietrich's department has headquarters both in Berlin and in Munich, and has an offshoot in the Press Policies Office in Berlin, the title of which explains its functions.

These departments naturally work in close contact (although not always close co-operation) with the well-known Reich Propaganda Leadership, the Party organization founded by Dr. Goebbels many years ago and now practically a part of the Propaganda Ministry, although technically apart. In this field, at least, Party and State are completely merged. Goebbels's main assistants in the Party organization are two young men still in their thirties, Karl Hanke and Hugo Fischer. They are keen-eyed salesmen of a new type of commodity ; rather needlessly they describe their hobbies in the official *Who's Who* as ' political propaganda '.

There is another remarkable department within the Party, the Foreign Politics Office in the Margaretenstrasse in Berlin, where Alfred Rosenberg employs a large staff to hatch his Eastern eggs. This department is described as ' the ghost of something that died long ago '. In the early days of the Party, Rosenberg made use of his experiences in the Baltic border-lands and in Russia, to build up a reputation as the Party's expert in foreign affairs, but his schemes were too wildly imperialistic, and he found himself gradually supplanted by the Ribbentrop Bureau and relegated to ill-defined posts in connexion with ' national culture '. A man of many enemies, the embittered Rosenberg managed to survive, although his tasks became more and more nebulous. He is still, however, a *Reichsleiter*. It is said that Hitler's loyalty to him keeps him within the inner circle of the Nazis, despite the open hostility of many of the Party leaders. His Foreign Politics Office is certainly one of the most redundant parts of the Nazi structure, and its main interest to-day is in demonstrating how fortuitous has been the rise of the Party and how difficult it is to dispose of a department once it has been established.

The remaining Party offices are more straightforward. Walter Darré, the Minister of Food and Agriculture, still maintains the office for Agricultural Policy within the Party, the office that gave him—late-comer to the movement though he was—such a spectacular opportunity of rising to power. Dr. Hans Frank also manages to make his Reich Legal Office in Munich a living entity. His difficulty has been to win over the Ministry of Justice, but the resignation of the Minister of Justice (Dr. Gürtner, a survivor of the Papen and Schleicher ministries) early this year cleared the way for a more rapid adoption of the peculiar legal concepts of Nazidom. At first Frank was a kind of advocate-general for all Brownshirts who came into conflict with the law ; but, as time went on, his office became a hatching-ground for entirely new theories of law, such theories as resulted in his formation of the People's Courts three years ago.

Two purely industrial departments exist within the Party, both of recent formation. The one is the Factory Cells Organization—the N.S.B.O. which Claus Selzner controls ; the other is the Office for Trades and Commerce, under Adrian von Renteln, a young man who made a name for himself at industrial conferences at Geneva. Joining the Party only in 1928, he was tried out as leader of the Hitler Youth but was soon transferred to industrial matters and, when the Party assumed power, worked up a great organization to further National Socialist ideas in factories. This organization was later taken over as a branch of the Party, and Renteln is to-day the Party's expert on factory organization, with an important post in the Labour Front as well.

The status given to the last of the Party offices affords a peculiar sidelight on Nazi affairs. The three schools whose task it is to train young men for Party leadership form a separate ' office ', an extraordinary privilege when one looks over the list of organizations that are merely ' affiliated ' and denied full Party status. This fact alone shows how strong is the *Führerprinzip* in the Party, and what importance is attributed to training the dictators of the future.

Such are the departments within the Party proper. But, closely associated with the central organization are the affiliated bodies, whose offices for the most part consist of magnificent old buildings along the Barerstrasse in Munich that have been converted into official departments and that, some day or other, will be centralized in the great Nazi City that Hitler is at present constructing in the heart of Munich, round the nucleus of the monument of the dead of the Feldherrnhalle.

A mere list of these affiliated bodies shows their scope. There is an office for Communal Affairs ; an office for Civil Officials ; an Educational Office (which appears to form an excuse for its director Wachtler to go to the Barerstrasse when he is tired of the office in the Briennerstrasse which he occupies as Party Director of Schools) ; a department for War Victims ; a department for Public Health (still another office for the ubiquitous Gerhard Wagner) ; a Technical Office (with Fritz Todt in control, although how he distinguishes his functions as Deputy for Technical Questions from those as leader of the Technical Office, is far from clear) ; a Welfare Office ; the National Socialist Students' Organization, and a kindred National Socialist University Professors' and Lecturers' Organization (does its leader Professor Schultze ever think of the 1,500 exiled teachers who were his colleagues ?) ; and, last but by no means least, the National Socialist Women's Organization led by a little statistician named Erich Hilgenfeldt, but really controlled by one of the most outstanding personalities in the whole of Germany, Frau Gertrud Scholtz-Klink, the Reich Women's leader and a great friend of the *Führer* himself. To all intents and purposes, each of these bodies is part of the Party organization.

To complete the picture, one must mention the thirty-three *Gaue* or administrative districts, each under a dictator appointed by the central authorities ; and the senatorial body

of *Reichsleiter*, of whom at the moment there are eighteen.
In each of the local districts, the confused structure of Munich
headquarters is duplicated, nearly always with superfluous
additions that reflect local conditions. The great national
organizations that I have mentioned at Munich have their
branches in each *Gau*, and, where these do not provide enough
rewards for zealous Brownshirts, new offices are created.
The load on the people is greater in the regional districts
than in the case of the nation as a whole, and the Party organization becomes so overpowering an incubus that outsiders
(like Dr. Schacht) have repeatedly protested against the
warping of the country's life and the breakdown that will
inevitably come if a halt is not put to the process of administrative spawning. And so down to smaller units—to each
Kreis and each *Ortsgruppe*. With Hitlerism in power,
Germany is literally weighed down by a vast machine to
which fresh parts are for ever being added, and which has
long passed its utmost efficiency. Size is the only criterion ;
and, if a stop be not made, the machine will soon include as
its working parts every living German. Whether Nazis or
not, they are becoming the slaves of a machine, and it is said
that even Hitler dare not tinker with the amorphous mechan-
ism. He must simply stand aside and watch it grow and
grow, even though it may ultimately collapse through its
own weight.

IV.—*Check and Counter-check within the Party*

An essential feature of the Party organization is the special
court which waverers have to face. Two hard-faced Badeners,
Walter Buch and Emil Danzeisen, supply the evidence on
such occasions, and a Nazi, however blameless he may be,
usually puts a Lüger pistol to his head when one of Major
Buch's ' Black Hundred ' begins to make inquiries about
him. Hitler believes in a régime of periodic purges to keep
up the morale of the survivors.

Walter Buch, who attracted world notice when he conducted the clean-up of June 30th, is an old machine-gunner,

and one of the band of '23 rebels.[1] Hitler appointed him to the command of the curiously named *Untersuchungs-und Schlichtungsausschuss*, generally known as *Uschla*. This is the body which keeps check on all Party workers, ostensibly with a view to preventing discord, but actually working as a dread punitive organization. The Nazis call it ' the Cell ' or ' Cell G '.

It is odd that a movement that makes so much of comradeship and joint sacrifice should have resorted to such a policy of check and counter-check ; loyalty rests on the suppression of disloyalty, faith is rooted in fear. So keen is Hitler's belief in this method of rule that he does not even conceal the checking bodies. Rather does he give undue publicity to them, for they are one of his strongest weapons. Every pamphlet on Party organization explains and boasts about them, and ordinary members do not appear to resent them in the slightest.

I have heard Black Guards themselves—possibly the next victims of a purge—boast about the efficiency of the checks imposed on them. What would be intolerable in English eyes is for them only a sign of efficiency. There is no sympathy for the waverer who falls by the way or the plotter who is found out ; and there is no resentment at the constant espionage and suspicion. ' If I weaken I must be shot, and it is the *Führer's* job to find me out before I can do any damage,' one dapper young officer of the S.A. said to me when I protested that the very existence of the ' Black Hundred ' would be regarded as an insult by any English organization. To him, however, it was perfectly natural and desirable if the officer standing next to him was a spy from ' Cell G ' in Buch's service. The motto is ' Be loyal or be shot '. Black Guard officials have said to be : ' That is the kind of system we can understand. There is no namby-pamby about it. We all feel the whole time that the *Führer* can read our every thought. There is no organization in the world as efficient as that by which he controls us ; and we welcome it, because it does us no harm as long as we remain loyal to him, and we know it is weeding out traitors and spies the whole time. I am loyal in thought and deed, so it does not hurt me, and it

[1] He was later ruler of Upper Bavaria and is now a *Reichsleiter*.

strengthens the movement by keeping the ranks pure.' How many waverers it has struck down we will never know, for Buch works in secret behind the scenes, and it is only on spectacular occasions (such as the murder of Dr. Bell at Kufstein or the executions of June 30th) that attention is directed to him. No records are kept of the *Sondergericht*— the summary court martial which hustles an offender away to a firing-squad.

This *Cell* works for the Party ; a similar role is played for the whole people by the political police. We have seen how Hitler used the police forces in seizing power in 1933. At first Göring stiffened the ranks of the ordinary police force by bringing in men from the *Hilfs-Polizei*, the advance guard of special police that had grown up within the Brownshirts. Finding these insufficient, he created a new body in Prussia, the *Gestapo* or Secret State Police.[1] This body was disciplined along military lines and really became a body of spies in the service of the Government. They could arrest and punish without trial. Once in the hands of the *Gestapo*, a man had no possible means of defence. No body of political police in the past has had greater power than theirs. Since early last year, they have been entitled to do in law what they had hitherto been doing in fact—to issue orders on any subject direct to civilians. Their position was consolidated at the end of April 1934, when Heinrich Himmler, the head of the Black Guards, was given control of all the political police in Germany.

The career of Himmler is an epitome of Hitlerism. Nothing distinguished him in his youth. He studied agriculture at a technical high school in Munich and is said to have served in a Free Corps in that city against the Soviet government. He was with Hitler in the first *putsch* and then retired from the public eye as an assistant in a Bavarian fertilizer factory. He lacks any distinction of appearance and is modest in manner. His very indefinite features and his glasses make him look rather insignificant, more of a student than an agitator ; so that his fellow-Nazis made the mistake of underestimating

[1] *Geheime Staatspolizei*, formed on April 27th, 1933. It was made an independent department under the Premier in December.

him and thinking that he could not stand up to the hearty manners of freebooters like Röhm and Heines. Hitler, however, had no illusions about Himmler's beaver-like capacity for quiet and effective work, and made him Party manager in sections of Bavaria and Swabia. In 1925 he joined the S.S., and within three years he had become commander of that organization throughout Germany. He is probably the best organizer the Nazi Party has produced and, whenever a ticklish job presented itself, word was sent out for this young man. When Hitler became Chancellor, Himmler was one of the ' three paladins '—von Epp and Röhm were the other two—who were sent south to overthrow the Bavarian government. This task accomplished, he devoted the next twelve months to building up bodies of secret police in no fewer than thirteen States. In 1934, as we have seen, he obtained command of all the political police in Germany, and the climax of his power came in June 1936, when he was made chief of the entire German police force, political or otherwise. His henchman, Heydrich, who had been so energetic on the night of June 30th, 1934, became head of the ' Security Police Department ', which includes all of the secret and plain-clothes and detective police.

With ten years of administrative experience behind him, Himmler is not yet thirty-seven years of age. He is rightly regarded as one of the key-men of the new régime. Foreign opinion usually looks upon him as a bloodthirsty ogre, a kind of German Yagoda, the slayer of his friend, Gregor Strasser, the ' cleaner-up of the Night of the Long Knives '. Undoubtedly it was Himmler's job to have a leading part in these events, but it is ridiculous to view him as a young man carried away by his inordinate power and revelling in his lust for blood. Actually, he sets an example of quiet dignity and simplicity of life that is often lacking in Nazi Germany, and remains entirely unspoilt, living like a clerk in a simple Berlin flat.

Personally I found him much kindlier and much more thoughtful for his guests than any other Nazi leader, a man of exquisite courtesy and still interested in the simple things of life. He has none of the pose of those Nazis who act as demigods.   He joins lustily in the songs of his Blackshirts, and is as natural at a camp *Biwak* as he is uneasy at formal public functions.   No man looks less like his job than this police dictator of Germany, and I am convinced that nobody I met in Germany is more normal.   Many people behind the scenes believe that he is the man who will ultimately succeed Hitler, and to this view I subscribe.   His proven capacity for organization, his control of the police, his command of over a quarter of a million loyal S.S. men, and the political cells he has painstakingly built up all over Germany lend support to this view.   Hess is too characterless, Goebbels too unpopular ; so that his main rival is Göring, a blunt man of action who would fall readily into the snares of a more subtle thinker like Himmler.   Göring has before this had trials of strength with Himmler and has never emerged the victor, and there is every indication that the rivalry is to be fought out on a far wider battlefield.   Himmler, ' diploma of agriculture ', lord of a million men—is he to be the second *Führer* ?   The years and events are with him, and he shows no hesitation in using harsh methods.

A man of this kind is a justification of the wildly empirical methods of Hitlerism.   Extravagant success has not spoiled him, unknown experiments have left him undaunted.   He seems to me to have the simplicity of true greatness and yet balances this by an astute mentality which quickly realizes the complexities of any political question.   The superficial see in him only a brutal opportunist.   To them he is the Bavarian who ground down his own State, the Catholic who became an apostate to keep his leadership of the Blackshirts, the protégé of Gregor Strasser who betrayed his master, the man who makes use of every confidence he has ever received.   I would rather describe him as the man who has built much out of nothing.   While not approving of his methods, I see in him capacities for leadership that may change the future of Europe, provided that he overcomes his failing of considering problems only in so far as they affect Germany.   His eyes become myopic where the rest of the world is concerned.

His faithful aide, Reinhard Heyrich, has also had a record possible only in Nazi Germany.   As a boy of fifteen he was a fighting member of the Halle Free Corps of irregulars. After two years he entered the navy as a serving officer for nine years. Then, in 1931, he resigned to become a Storm Trooper, rising rapidly and taking over the political police in Munich when Hitler assumed power. At this time he was barely twenty-nine years of age—a saturnine-faced young man with cruel slits of eyes and a distinctly Mongoloid appearance. Soon all of the political police of Bavaria were under his control, and he moved upwards with his friend Himmler. To-day he is his second-in-command and is unquestioned ruler of the dreaded political police or *Gestapo*, with a nation-wide reputation for ruthlessness.

These are the men who are the real terrorists or disciplinarians of Germany. The Party could not survive without the constant vigilance of Buch and Himmler. Their henchmen watch every household in the land and pounce on opposition before it is organized (and unfortunately sometimes before it is even thought of). They override the law and punish as they think fit. In short, they are as untrammelled a race of young autocrats as the world has ever seen, and the very necessity for them, and the extraordinary range of their powers, throws much light on the real nature of Hitlerism.

V.—*The Party and the Form of the State*

From an administrative point of view, the Nazi problem has been to reconcile the Party with the existing States. On the one hand was the heterogeneous collection of kingdoms, duchies and principalities, precariously welded by Bismarck into a confederation, with the local units fighting tenaciously for every last privilege. There were seventeen such States, with the ex-kingdom of Prussia comprising two-thirds of the area and population of Germany, and with its power accentuated by reason of its superior organization. Prussia was a free State of 38,000,000 people, two-thirds of whom were Protestant; Bavaria, another free State of whose 7,000,000 two-thirds were Catholic; Württemberg was a *Volksstaat* of

2,500,000 people, mostly Protestant; the former Grand Duchy of Baden had 2,250,000, with slightly more than half Catholics; Saxony was a free State of 5,000,000 people, almost entirely Protestant; Thuringia, the first State in which the Nazis had power, consisted of seven units, with just over 1,500,000 people, for the most part Protestant; and then there were the minor States—Mecklenburg-Schwerin, with 674,000 inhabitants; Hesse, with slightly under a million and a half; the free States of Oldenburg and Brunswick with 500,000 each, Protestant strongholds both; Anhalt and Bremen, the one a free State, the other a Hanse State, with a third of a million each; Hamburg, a free Hanse State with 1,250,000; and the tiny entities of Mecklenburg-Strelitz (110,000), Lippe (163,000), Schaumburg-Lippe (48,000), and Lübeck (128,000), some of them with the population of an ordinary provincial town. Half of these strange units had less than a thousand square miles each, and, taken together, they formed the strangest collection of historical survivals.

As against them, was the Party organization of Germany. As soon as the Party was re-founded in 1925, Hitler divided Germany into tribal districts or *Gaue*. At first there were twenty-three of these, each under a *Gauleiter*. Oddly enough, the only members of the original rulers of *Gaue* who have risen to eminence in the Party are Ley, Rust, Wagner, and Julius Streicher, the organizers of the Rhineland, Hanover, Baden, and Franconia respectively. As Party membership increased, so did the number of provinces. When the Party came to power, they numbered thirty-two, and, by this time, the organization was so perfected that each *Gau* was practically a shadow Government in the area under its control. Each *Gau* was divided into *Kreise* (circles); each *Kreis* into *Ortsgruppen* (local groups); and, in the case of urban districts, each *Ortsgruppe* was divided into *Zellen* (cells) and *Blöcke* (street-blocks). A pyramidal organization covered the whole country with an entirely new framework. Starting on a geographical and electoral basis, it had become systematized as a result of fluctuating experience during the years. It was, of course, the Russian system of Soviets transplanted wholesale into Germany, but Hitler chose to

overlook this fact and viewed his territorial organization as
the most novel of his ideas. Certainly the system was efficient, far more so than the archaic network of free States
and duchies and cities bequeathed to the German people
by a Bismarck who was not strong enough to insist upon
political unity. And yet it was odd how the Nazis could
never cut themselves away entirely from the historical units.
Most of the *Gaue* were named after the older provincial
units and, even to-day, the traditional localist element in the
Party organization remains very strong. It is believed that
newfangled systems cannot stand unless they are linked on
to the old historical life of the provinces. Nobody has
realized this more than Hitler, and that is why he has always
considered regional influences, as long as they do not act as
disruptive influences undermining the Third Reich.

In 1933, one of his main problems was the question of
future administrative organization. The actual political life
of the States was quickly ended ; but the issue then arose,
which were to be the National Socialist units—some revived
form of the old provinces, the Nazi *Gaue*, or some inter-
mediate structure ? Hitler has never satisfactorily answered
this question. The *Gaue* remain and are nominally concerned with the organization of the Party in each district.
In the first confused days of the régime, the office of the *Gau*
was the source of all local power, especially if the *Gauleiter*
was a strong man. As the months went by, however, the
Gauleiter received higher posts in the Government, and it is
significant that, to-day, not the name of a single *Gauleiter*
would be recognized by an intelligently informed foreigner.
There has been a steady drift of power away from them.

This was particularly the case after Hitler chanced upon
the device of *Statthalters*. Once federalism was swept away,
Hitler passed a law providing for the appointment of a *Statthalter* or Regent in each State. They were to appoint the
provincial Governments. They had power to appoint or
dismiss all officials, and, in general, were dictators of their
provinces, especially charged with carrying out the ideas of
Berlin. It was announced at the time that the boundaries
of their districts were in no sense to be final. Each of the

larger provinces had a *Statthalter*, for the sake of convenience, but some of the smaller ones were amalgamated under a single man.

There has been a striking continuity of power in the hands of these Regents. Of the original twelve, eleven remain in charge of a province. Hitler himself is the titular *Statthalter* of Prussia, but has delegated his functions to Minister-President Göring ; the old soldier von Epp, ' Mother-of-God's general' as he is called, rules Bavaria with an iron hand ; Martin Mutschmann and Wilhelm Murr, two business men, hold Saxony and Württemberg respectively ; Robert Wagner, the trusted confidant of the Chancellor, keeps a tight hold on Baden from his seat in Karlsruhe ; Fritz Sauckel, a bald-headed young sea captain with a rough voice and aggressive manners, contrives to act both as *Statthalter* and *Gauleiter* in Thuringia, and is not renowned for his gentleness ; Jacob Sprenger, a middle-aged postal inspector, is rewarded for being one of the earliest members of the Party and especially for aiding it surreptitiously in the days when it was suppressed, by being made Governor of Hesse ; Karl Kaufmann, soldier at sixteen, freelance in Poland at twenty, sabotage-leader against the French in the Ruhr at twenty-three, a member of the Prussian Upper House at twenty-eight, became Regent of Hamburg before he was twenty-eight—one of the strangest histories in a movement noted for oddities ; Friedrich Hildebrant, an unknown farmer, was placed over the two Mecklenburgs and Lübeck, an upstart dominating lands whose every inch reeked with history ; Karl Rover, fat and jovial, with the tiniest moustache in Germany on his round visage, sits in the town of Oldenburg where he started work thirty years ago as an office boy in a coffee-house, and ruminates on the round of life that led him, by way of a factory in the Cameroons and the Propaganda Office of the War Department, to Hitler's camp in 1923, and then ever upwards until he is now *Statthalter* of Oldenburg and Bremen, *Gauleiter*, and hosts of other things in addition (life is good for humorists like Rover if they happen to be on the winning side in Germany) ; and Alfred Meyer, a cultured lawyer with an extensive military experience, rules over Lippe and Schaumburg-Lippe, while the rightful princes of those regions join the army or become Goebbels's secretary or sink into political oblivion. Such are the local Pashas of Hitlerism. All of them combine a multiplicity of offices. Five of them are *Gauleiters* as well as being *Statthalters*, and all of them are members of the Reichstag, little though that means nowadays.

The problem of administration is easy when the leader of a *Gau* is also Regent of his province ; where they overlap, however, or where a Regent has to consider the suscepti-bilities of a local *Gauleiter*, the difficulty of compromise is evident, and very often the services of the doughty Major Buch and his disciplinary *Uschla* have to be called in, for no Nazi official however high in rank can refuse to appear before the Party tribunal. Some experts think that Hitler made a mistake when he insisted that each *Statthalter* should be a citizen of the district he was appointed to administer. Hitler thought that he was pandering to local pride in that way, and that his Regents would be fully cognizant of local conditions ; but some of his advisers feel that the Regents constitute the one important breach in his structure of centra-lization, and they fear that too much local power may go to a man's head. That is why Berlin has always kept such a strong rein on the local Regents, especially since the move-ments that led to the massacres of June 30th.

A *Statthalter* is far more than a formal governor—especially since the law of January 1935. He has absolute control of all legislation and executive matters ; his word is unquestioned ; he may call out all police and military forces in his district ; he is immune from criticism ; he can create or remove local legislatures as he thinks fit ; he can, in short, do anything he pleases as head of his State, as long as he enforces the in-structions he receives from Berlin and pursues the policy of *Gleichschaltung* (co-ordination) with a sufficiently heavy hand. Each province must remain quiet, whatever the cost may be and whatever methods are adopted.

Hitler does not intend to leave the matter at this stage, however. He insists on recasting the entire face of Germany, and has made many speeches insisting on a uniform adminis-trative structure. When the difficult times of transition are past, he will turn again to his first-born, the *Gau* or tribal district, and will remove every last vestige of the old States. The simplest plan would be to make the administrative regions coincide with the territorial *Gaue* of the Nazi Party. Each provincial governor would then have control of 2,000,000 people, instead of the present unequal system under which one *Statthalter* may have 16,000,000 and another 1,500,000 people under his control. It is known that Frick, the Minister of the Interior, welcomed such a change, although naturally Göring fought any proposal that took over 30,000,000 of his charges from him, and Ritter von Epp, himself a Catholic, did not want to divide his beloved Catholic Bavaria into three nameless regions. In other words, Hitler was already confronted by the opposition of vested local interests.

One of the greatest difficulties was moved when Göring was placed in charge of the Four Year Plan at the end of 1936, with the unofficial title of 'the Minister-President'. Thus, above competition and in a class by himself, he withdrew his opposition to a uniform territorial organization of *Gaue*, and there is little doubt that the change will come, although with probably fewer *Gaue* than at present. Twenty seems to be the favoured number.

Reform in this direction has been much slower than expected. It seems obvious in a totalitarian State to remove the last remnants of historical localism and to substitute regions based on economic or political foundations, especially when the Party has already worked these out to its satisfaction. But localism dies hard in Germany, and at times Hitler takes steps to encourage it, as when he issued a special set of regional postage-stamps two years ago, and when he fosters competition between the various provinces in certain ways, the better to achieve the national end.

All that Hitler has done so far is to leave the large federal States alone (after taking over their government) and to merge some of the smaller units, while still keeping their old historical names. Dr. Frick, however, has clearly outlined future development on more than one occasion. He wants twenty regions corresponding to the military zones and to the territorial organizations of the Party. Each will have

3,500,000 inhabitants. The smaller of the old States will be allowed to remain : Württemberg and Baden are models of what the ultimate *Gau* should be ; while larger States, like Prussia and Bavaria, will have to be split up. Even in Prussia, the existing division into provinces, each under a governor, foreshadows the ultimate development, and it is noteworthy that, when Hitler defined the place of the *Statthalters* in 1935, he adjusted their position to that occupied by the heads (*Oberpräsidenten*) of Prussian provinces. The final form of the Nazi State is thus clearly indicated, and all that is needed is to put an end to the farce of the Reichstag and have, as Frick wants, a Senate representing all departments of national life, artistic and economic as well as political. Then the Third Reich will shake off the last lingering trammels of Bismarck's confederation, and the fine old provinces, if their very names are not lost, will continue an emasculated existence as parts of *Gaue*. But not all the administrative centralization, not all the forces of the *Gestapo* in Germany, can take from the people their strong local consciousness. Regionalism is too virile in most of Germany for that. A Bavarian will always be a Bavarian, a Prussian a Prussian and a Saxon a Saxon, despite the forces of Hitlerism. Hitler's only chance is if he finds a way of carrying on the old regional names. He may divide the free State of Bavaria into the *Gaue* of Upper Bavaria and Lower Bavaria, but he cannot remove everything for which Bavaria stands. It is a striking fact that, after four years of centralization, healthy regionalism is stronger in Germany to-day than ever. The provinces were not very concerned about the loss of their political privileges, especially if the nation gained thereby ; but their traditions and distinctions are a question of their very soul.

VI.—*The Party and the Civil Services*

The relationship of Party and State is almost impossible to define. It is quite erroneous to say that the Party is the State. The famous law of December 1st, 1933, although it is called 'the Act for securing the Unity of Party and

State ', achieves collaboration but not identity of the two bodies. It is often misunderstood. The first words run : ' After the victory of the National Socialist Revolution, the Party is the bearer of the idea of the German State and is inseparably connected with the State.'

But this does not mean that the Party has taken over all State activities. Hitler has defined the relationship by saying that the Party is the mainspring of all public activity. It is the spirit behind the State, and its main function is educational. Indeed, on one occasion, Hitler predicted that the complete conversion of the State to Nazi principles would take at least a century. In the interim, there will be only one Party— National Socialism. Germany is a single-party State (an *Ein-Partei-Staat*). But this does not mean that the Party will hand over all State functions to its own members. Indeed, Hitler violently repressed those extremists who followed Röhm in wanting an immediate identification of Party and State. To the dissatisfied followers who kept on complaining that not enough positions in the Civil Service were handed over to Hitlerites, Hitler replied (at the Party Congress of September 1935) that such positions would be given to the Party if there was inefficiency or sabotage by their holders. The inference was that otherwise the position would go on as it is at present. On the whole, the services were not to be submitted to the same process of *Gleichschaltung* as were the States or the local administrations.

There is at present no parallelism between Party and State, and certainly no identification. The thirty-two *Gaue* or Party regions, for instance, do not coincide with the administrative or military regions, or even the twenty-one divisions of the S.A., or the ten regions (*Oberabschnitte*) of the S.S., or the twenty-three zones of the Hitler Youth. For a race with a passion for organization, such discrepancies are the more remarkable, because there is no reason for them. Nor do the departments within the Party correspond with the various Government departments in Berlin, either in functions or in personnel.

The revolution did not mean that the heads of the Brown House departments automatically took over the corresponding departments in the Civil Service. The Party had evolved a 'shadow State', it is true, but, when the time came, the shadow was not converted into reality. The Party structure was retained, and even added to, but the old Government departments went on as before, with certain purges. A law of April 1933 allowed Civil Servants to be discharged 'for the simplification of the administration'. This applied to non-Aryans and to all who 'because of their previous political activity do not offer security that they will exert themselves to the utmost for the National State'. This legislation was used to rid the Civil Services of all who were deemed undesirables. The process was completed within the first half of 1933, and its limitations proved a great disappointment to the mass of Brownshirts who expected the services to be handed over to them as the spoils of victory. On the whole, the great mass of Civil Servants (other than Jews, Communists, and Liberals) continues as before. The structure of the departments was not touched. There were no revolutionary changes of function. The purge was a purely personal one. Indeed, most of the persons displaced received pensions. Hitler even passed a law in June 1933, warning his followers that the State was not going to be weakened by a wholesale promotion of Hitlerites simply as a reward for their political services. The law specifically said that 'only such persons may be appointed as national officials who have the prescribed education or customary training or who have special qualifications for the office about to be filled'. The 'old fighters' of the movement had expected soft Government jobs; but, save for the leaders, they were given—a right of priority at all employment offices!

The amount of displacement varied in each department. The ranks of the police were thoroughly and drastically purged and the commands given to Nazis; and the postal department declared membership of the Party compulsory for all employees (since the ranks of the Party were closed, this meant the displacement of all non-Nazis). In the technical departments, most of the staffs remained, except those dismissed under the racial laws or those who had been obviously anti-Nazis in the past. The Ministry of Justice and the Ministry of the Interior, because of their key-positions, saw an extensive clearing ; but the Foreign Ministry was left alone, except for the dismissal of a mere handful of its officials.[1] A high official in the Foreign Office explained this to me by saying : ' A purge of undesirables was not necessary with us ; we saw to it ourselves in the past.' It is impossible to say with any accuracy how many Civil Servants were dismissed. The main point is that the German administrative structure emerged unscathed in its fundamentals, and retained all of its old efficiency.

Naturally this is far from meaning that the Party has no influence. The hold of the Ministers is particularly strong, and no departmental head could survive a week if he tried to obstruct Nazi ideas. In most cases, there are links between the Party and the State administrations—for example, Goebbels in propaganda, Darré in agriculture, Frank in law, Todt in public works ; and yet in the vital matters of finance and foreign affairs the links are purely personal.

The case of foreign affairs is particularly informative. The old Foreign Office continues to live its life in the Wilhelmstrasse as before, and the Foreign Affairs Department within the Party (under Rosenberg) survives in a half-hearted way ; but there has emerged a separate bureau (directly under Rudolf Hess in the Party's scheme of things) known as ' the Ribbentrop Bureau ', because its head is Joachim von Ribbentrop, the present Ambassador to the Court of St. James's. Ribbentrop was known as ' ambassador-at-large ' and played an important part in deciding the Chancellor's foreign policy. This bureau is very active. It can do things that would be against the traditions of the old Foreign Office, and yet it is not tied down by the same feeling of responsibility. There arises, then, a curious dualism in the determination of foreign policy. Some authorities looked on the Ribbentrop Bureau merely as a transitional organization, but it has not

---

[1] Early in 1937, Bohle, leader of the Foreign Organization within the Party, was placed in charge of a new department called the ' Foreign Organization in the Foreign Office '. This was the first Nazi incursion into the sphere of the Foreign Office. The translation of Dieckhoff as ambassador to the United States was a move in the same direction.

disappeared, even after its head became an ambassador abroad.

On the whole, it can be said that the Ministries have not been ' assimilated ' with the Party departments. The distinction between State and shadow State remains, and Hitler obviously leans towards increasing the duplication of functions rather than merging the two sets of bodies.

The inquirer soon notices one peculiar point. The Party departments or the Ministries taken over by Party leaders are far and away the most formal. The amount of *paperasserie* involved in entering Nazi strongholds is formidable. Even when one's entrée has been secured from the highest authorities, underlings of various grades insist on filling in endless forms. There is an elaborate system of chits and counter-chits—of forms to be filled in duplicate and of halves that must be minuted and returned and filed. One cannot enter without stating one's business, and one cannot leave without returning a bilious-coloured form that one's business has been completed. The Propaganda Ministry, Goebbels's own stronghold, is easily the worst offender in this regard. Goebbels has certainly done much to solve the unemployment problem by the amount of red tape he has introduced into his Ministry, and perhaps that explains why his offices, already the largest in Berlin, have had to spill over into another street. The Munich archives show that this red tape and formality applied in the earliest days of the movement, but it is significant that it has not spread to the older Government departments. Entry to all of them was much less formal than it would have been in London, the Foreign Office in particular treating its visitors much as an old-fashioned departmental store receives distinguished customers from the counties. The self-conscious officialdom of the purely Nazi organizations may pass in time, but at the moment most of it is merely purposeless and inefficient—on a level with the duplication and overlapping that one finds everywhere in their administrative structure. They have systematized even the slightest aspects of routine work, but their systems apparently have no method of registering waste or duplication. No Tweedledum is allowed to be without a Tweedledee in Germany.

VII.—*The Problem of Local Administration*

At first the revolution involved administrative chaos in the local districts. The weeding out of suspect officials was on a far. larger scale here than in the case of the central civil services ; and in most cases the towns and villages witnessed miniature social revolutions. It was here that a larger intrusion of Nazis occurred, although it became obvious after a few months that prowess in street fighting was not necessarily the best training for administrators. One of Hitler's main problems was to reward persons who had supported him in the early days of the movement. In practice his friendships have frequently outweighed his objectivity, especially in the matter of local appointments, and so we find that in Germany ' many an honest Indian ass goes for an Unicorn '.

The *Gauleiter* of each Party district, and later the *Statthalter* of each province, continued this policy of favouritism and displacement. Hitler seized the opportunity of June 30th to get rid of the most glaring cases of this new form of *Particularismus* ; but the process continued, until the local administrative machine became hopelessly cluttered up by zealous Nazis.

Hitler was hampered by his inability to create uniform administrative districts, despite his frequently repeated intention of doing so. He could easily appoint *Statthalter* as despots over the twelve provinces and, after some delay, he subordinated them completely to the central authorities. It was equally easy to install Nazi Burgomasters in the towns. The real difficulty was to erect a uniform system of government in each local area.

The problem was faced in the new Municipal Code, passed in January 1935. This was a simple measure clearing up all the existing confusion—that was due to the first days of Nazi rule as well as the old historical confusion. Hitherto forty or more different codes had dealt with local government, and many forms of self-government existed. In their place, the new law created a single uniform municipal law for the whole country.

This system was soon enforced. At present the Burgomaster is responsible for local administration. His council is purely advisory. Each Burgomaster is appointed by the *Statthalter*, or, in large cities, by the Minister of the Interior. It is thus certain that he will be a Nazi. He has to consult the local branch of the Party, which will appoint councillors and jurors and members of school boards. A wise Burgomaster will work in close co-operation with the local Party ; but if he falls out with them, the Minister of the Interior has the last word. In practice, the defaulter who is acting contrary to the best interests of the Party—whether Burgomaster or local Party man—will be chastised. The system aims at securing uniformity and centralization in the whole field of local administration. The old system has been swept away entirely. The emasculated local authorities of the old States have gone, and so, too, have the transitional bodies set up by the Nazis in their early days.

The necessary complement to this occurred last November, when Dr. Frick announced that in the future political and administrative questions would be separated. Each district would continue to have its Party political leaders, but administration (as distinct from political questions) would be in the hands of the local authorities set up under the Municipal Act. These authorities would be responsible, not to the local political leaders, but direct to Berlin. This gets rid of the very objectionable confusion of political and administrative functions that has done so much harm in the local districts in the last four years.

Thus administrative order is emerging out of chaos, and the complications due to the accidents of history are being removed in each province. Germany is becoming one great administrative machine, each part dependent on the other, and all controlled from the master-switch at Berlin. The theory of a totalitarian State is there ; the enabling laws have been passed ; and henceforth the administrative practice of totalitarianism will grow up as well.

Chapter Three

THE ECLIPSE OF THE BROWNSHIRTS

I.—*Brownshirts Versus Black Guards*

Germany is a land of uniforms. He is indeed a lost soul who has not the right to sport some uniform or other. The designers appear to have plunged into a competition for splendour. They soon departed from the *Führer's* simplicity and, as the more obvious symbols became exhausted, lost themselves in a search for ever more unusual and colourful emblems. Putting aside the permanent forces, one finds that there are no less than three hundred and fifteen distinct types of uniform, each of which a zealous Nazi is doubtless expected to identify at sight. In addition to these, there are hundreds of more or less unauthorized variations. Recognizing them is like fitting together a gigantic jigsaw puzzle, but woe betide the man who confuses an *Obersturmbannführer* from Hesse with a *Hauptstellenleiter* of the *Politische-Leiter* of Berlin. It is idle, of course, to attempt to disentangle the chaos of the Brownshirts, because their uniforms have been changed so often, and one finds relics of every previous system, even to dyed specimens of the original blue-grey tunic of the days before Hitler was sent to Landsberg fortress.

In striking contrast to this medley of the original Brownshirts is the severe and simple uniformity of the S.S. men, the Black Guards. No gaudy district variations are given to them, no multi-coloured insignia adorn their sleeves or shoulders. All of them are clad alike, whether they hail from Bavaria or Silesia. Tiny little stripes of a fiftieth of an inch in thickness, in discreet blue or green or red, show their *Sturmbann*. For the rest they must be content with the white stars and oak leaves on the black background, and the only note of colour on their uniform is the vivid red arm-band with the swastika in the white circle. They are an army whose duty it is to serve rather than be resplendent. Nevertheless, with this Spartan simplicity, they contrive to be the most impressive body of men in Germany, with their sombre black service-jackets, black tie, and black cap with its skull and crossbones. Their austerity befits their position as the spearhead of Hitlerism, and Himmler has succeeded in disciplining them thoroughly.

The motley Brownshirts look like an amorphous force in which each platoon has tried to evolve a uniform of its own. There is something pathetic in the pell-mell mixture of Brownshirt uniforms, something that shows how they belong to the past and how their leaders realize that it is futile to try and discipline them, even in the matter of uniform. They belong to the early days of struggle, whereas the grim-visaged youngsters of the Blackshirts are Hitler's own army, pledged to unquestioning obedience, and as disciplined as the Reichswehr itself; they are men on the serving list, while the raggled Brownshirts are the ghost of the past—the tired middle-aged veterans who are almost as antiquated as men in other countries who fought in the war. They bring out their old uniforms occasionally, they meet once in a while; but the spirit has departed from them. They recall the old days of street fighting and the struggle for recognition, but the youngsters of the Black Guards are concerned only with the present and the future.

Two Brownshirts slumped wearily into chairs opposite me in a café, after the great march past at Nuremberg. ' We have been on duty for fourteen hours,' they said, ' we are old, but ' (pointing to dancing young Black Guards) ' they can still dance. We were their age at Coburg and the Feldherrnhalle fourteen years ago, when they were in the kindergarten.' That day, Hitler had praised his ' old comrades ', but he had praised still more the *élite* corps that had been formed within the Black Guards, themselves already an *élite*. Even inside the Nazi Party, there is thus a real conflict of the generations, and the spry young Black Guards are viewed almost with resentment by the ' old guard '. But such a conflict was inevitable, and Hitler, if he wished to keep his position, had no alternative but to choose as he did, for no man could ever have moulded the mass of Brownshirts into an organized fighting unit. A national movement had served to bring him into power against other Governments, but he now wanted a disciplined Praetorian Guard to maintain his own Government.

II.—*The Twilight of the Brownshirts*

When Hitler became Chancellor, the Brownshirts thought that they would receive immediate rewards. With child-like faith, they expected jobs, especially the first 500,000 of them, ' the old fighters'. They also expected to be incorporated in the army, or even to replace the army entirely.

They were soon disillusioned. It soon became obvious that jobs could be found only for a few leaders ; while the ranks of the army were closed to them. The Reichswehr leaders would not take individual officers, and certainly not Brownshirt formations as a whole. The promised Elysium failed to eventuate, and those who insisted on the old programme were soon disciplined. Some of the Bavarian Storm Troopers, for instance, tried to enforce a few of Hitler's Twenty-five Points, and were staggered to find their efforts disavowed. Criticisms began to spread amongst their ranks, especially when the S.S. men secured the best jobs. It was felt that Göring in particular had declared against the old Brown Army. They became so bitter that, in a broadcast on April 8th, 1933, Hitler specifically pledged himself to their interests. ' I will be true to you to the last drop of my blood.'

But the bitter truth was that the S.A.—the Brown Army— had become superfluous. Hitler no longer needed their aid, for he had the political police and the S.S. everywhere. He no longer relished the difficult task of keeping them in order. He no longer wanted the possibility of a revolt of disillusioned Storm Troopers. Indeed, he no longer liked to be reminded of the methods he had used when in opposition.

Henceforth he was the State, and it was undignified to have to play up to old comrades whose only recollections were of fighting in the streets and bashing policemen on the heads. Worst of all, many of the Brownshirts still believed in the Socialistic side of National Socialism and were grumbling that Hitler (in power) was doing nothing to implement the promises that Hitler (in opposition) had made so repeatedly.

There was a further point. The S.A. were a mixed body, mostly workers or students or lower-middle-class tradesmen ; whereas the S.S., from the outset, were more definitely *bourgeois*. Not only were they of a better social and educational status ; they were more ruthless and less critical. They accepted any sacrifice and performed any unpleasant duties. Stark efficiency was their goal, and they acted unquestioningly. The older S.A. men, on the other hand, could never forget that they were primarily civilians with an interest in politics ; they were militiamen only secondarily, and they remained local politicians in all of their actions. They had to have their orders explained to them, and justified ; and at least implicitly they demanded a right of discussion. While they were thus admirable subjects for the hurly-burly of local street fighting, they were only a great mass of unmalleable material when Hitler came to want a corps of determined and ruthless instruments to dominate a whole nation. After all, the S.A. *were* the nation (at least, in section) ; while the S.S. were a caste of executive tyrants, blindly carrying out the orders of a central oligarchy. The two bodies had nothing in common, and it was soon obvious that they could not exist together without coming into juxtaposition. At first there was a difference between them—then a rivalry —and finally a fight for supremacy, a fight which relegated the old Brown battalions to the task of reminiscing in the local beer-halls.

For months before the clean-up of June 30th, 1934, Hitler had made up his mind to deal with them in some way ; and in this he was strongly supported by Göring, who always resented unpleasant voices from the dead past. The first step was taken at the end of April, 1933, when the Cabinet passed a proposal to place the Storm Troopers under military law. The deluded Brownshirts thought that this was an honour for them, and that it gave them equality with the army, but in reality the law gave power to Hitler to deal with the S.A. with the utmost severity at any time he chose. Henceforth he simply had to await a suitable occasion to stifle their whole organization.

The discontent became so vocal that Hitler issued a drastic warning early in July 1933. Speaking to a great assembly of leaders at the Bavarian health resort of Bad Reichenhall, he screamed : ' I will suppress every attempt to disturb the existing order as ruthlessly as I will deal with the so-called Second Revolution, which could lead only to fresh chaos.' At least he did not temporize. He definitely flung out a challenge, and those Brownshirts who went away to grumble and plot should have realized that they were gambling for their lives. If they did not stop, they must either win the day or face a firing-squad.

In the first months of 1934, Hitler met the criticism (and, the composition of the Brown Army being what it was, the criticism grew in proportion to the decline in trade in those months) by a series of purges. A new and more severe method of inspection from headquarters was evolved. Special campaigns were launched ' against grumblers ', but even Goebbels could not triumph over stark economic facts, and the campaigns failed.

The next stage was to order a general holiday for the Brownshirts throughout the month of July—nominally as a reward for their strenuous past services. Already there were rumours that the Brown battalions would never march again, but Röhm made a public announcement from Munich on June 8th that their duties would recommence on August 1st. ' If the enemies of the S.A. hope that it will not be recalled or will be only partly recalled after its leave, we may permit them to enjoy this brief hope.'

So the June days passed. A provocative speech by von Papen at Marburg, and conflicts between Brownshirts and Stalhelm served to confuse the issues, but there was a general impression of cross-currents at work. Nobody knew what was going to happen, but it was clear that something unusual was developing. Then the pace quickened. Goebbels announced that no meetings of any kind would be held in July ; Blomberg published a declaration of the army's loyalty to Hitler, and the grim-faced Arthur Görlitzer, Goebbels's deputy, predicted that undesirable members would soon be purged from the Party. All of these events took place in the last week of June. In the same week, Edmund Heines, who had been frantically busy amongst his Silesian Brownshirts, defiantly declared at a review : ' Germany will be eternal because the Storm Troop organization is eternal.' On the Saturday of that week the blow fell, and the Brownshirts were beaten into oblivion.

III.—*The Night of the Long Knives*

It is needless to delve into recondite explanations of ' the Night of the Long Knives '. Some commentators have seen in it the final victory of the army over the middle classes in Germany ; others the triumph of the capitalists of ' heavy industry '. While there is some ground for such interpretations, the events can be explained more simply as a ruthless quelling, if not of an actual plot, at least of tendencies towards mutiny—always assuming that numerous private scores were paid off at the same time.

The official story is that an actual conspiracy was planned for the first days of July. I heard in Germany many circumstantial accounts of plans to seize the Berlin Arsenal and occupy headquarters in Munich ; but, by the nature of the case, the truth of this will never be known. Hess, Hitler's deputy, also stated that Hitler ' relieved certain sections of the people from the petty oppression which had been exercised over them by a clique of moral degenerates '. This was an amazing statement in its damnation of various aspects of Nazi rule over a period of eighteen months, a staggering flaw in the story of Nazi perfection, the only one before or since. The plea of moral degeneracy becomes the more remarkable in light of the character of certain Nazi leaders who survived the fateful night.

The true explanation obviously lies elsewhere, for the stories of a plot and moral obliquity do not dovetail into each other. It goes back to the early days of the movement, when Hitler attracted a race of political freebooters, either professional soldiers of fortune like Röhm or, more often, unbalanced youths who had fought in the war or in the numerous volunteer free corps which kept on fighting after the war was over ('Feme' murderers like Heines, Schulze, and Hayn, or secret leaguers like von Killinger and Rolf Reiner). Such men were killers, and thought in terms of blood and force. They were the gangsters without whom Hitlerism could never have fought its way to the fore. Once Hitler was in office, they expected spoils. Many of them obtained good offices and have kept them. A small minority of them were dissatisfied and joined forces with a few honest zealots who wanted to accelerate the pace of the revolution. Behind them were the great mass of the Brown Army who had not received their due economic reward. More and more was heard of the 'Second Revolution', just as in the Russia of 1917 November succeeded March. To these men, Hitler had stopped half-way. He had betrayed the 'socialist' half of his programme and had fallen into the hands of the Goebbels-Göring clique. Röhm, the Brownshirt leader, was an old adversary of Göring. He had accused Göring of filching his position while he was away organizing the armies of Bolivia and Chile ; and he undoubtedly wanted to form a new cabal behind Hitler. Personal danger to Hitler was never intended. As everybody knows, some of the mutineers died with his name on their lips. All that they wanted was a different policy for Hitlerism and a different set of advisers in the key-positions—men who would find jobs for the clerks and peasant-boys and shopmen who had always been the mainstay of the Brown Army.

There was also much dissatisfaction about the relations between the Reichswehr and the Brownshirts. Röhm and his followers argued that some detachments at least of the Brownshirts should be incorporated in the permanent army as a reward for their services, while the S.A. as a whole should remain practically on a level with the army as a kind of second-line militia. This was no part of the plan either of the army leaders or of Hitler, although both were conscious of the discontent amongst the Brownshirt rank and file. Hitler subsequently explained this discontent as being due to officers misleading their men ; but the trouble lay far deeper than that.

It remains uncertain, I repeat, whether or not an actual revolt was planned for four o'clock on the afternoon of June 30th, although the ease with which the mutineers were caught rather tells against the idea. Karl Ernst, who held the key-post in the capital city, would have been on his way to Majorca at the appointed moment ; von Schleicher was idling, in country clothes, at his home twenty miles out of Berlin ; Röhm and Heines were at a mountain chalet some miles out of Munich ; and many other Brownshirt leaders would have been there at a conference summoned and publicly announced by Röhm. Strange behaviour indeed for conspirators !

The tale of von Schleicher's plot is incredible. There is not the slightest evidence that he and Röhm plotted together ; but Hitler said that von Schleicher, in planning high office for Röhm, only ' gave outward expression to the inner wish of the Chief-of-Staff'. Obviously men could die because others expressed their inward wishes ! Rather more to the point is the fact that von Schleicher was the stormy petrel of politics and that Göring hated him.

Nor has anybody ever been able to work out an all-embracing plot that covered von Schleicher, Röhm, Ernst, Heines, the Catholic secretaries of von Papen, Gregor Strasser (one of the oldest of Hitler's friends), the Catholic leader Klausener, the seventy-three-year-old von Kahr, the aged Stempfle (archivist of Hitler's own museum of Party relics), and scores of other men, of all ages and classes, ranging from mercenary *souteneurs* like von Alvensleben to quiet industrialists who had never dabbled in politics, from students' leaders and professional panderers to church historians. Admitting that there might have been two—or even more—groups of malcontents who opposed the Government on principle, the victims included many persons who belonged to no political group. Indeed, it is the wiping out of old personal scores that one finds so hard to accept.

However murky all these matters may be, there is no doubt about Hitler's actions. Together with Goebbels and his two faithful adjutants—Bruckner and Schaub—he left the Hangelaar aerodrome near Bonn at two o'clock on the morning of Saturday, June 30th. Two hours later he landed at Munich, made a few arrests at the Bavarian Ministry of the Interior ; picked up Major Buch and five carloads of policemen at the temporary S.S. headquarters in the Adjutantur and drove through the waning night out to Wiessee. There Röhm, Heines and a few other drunken leaders were arrested, some of them being killed as they slept. By seven o'clock the party was back in the Adjutantur. Röhm was left in a cell with a revolver and a single bullet, and finally, after two hours' stubborn refusal to take his own life, was shot.

Hitler went to the Ministry again, spoke to his leaders in the small council chamber at the Brown House, and sent out statements reorganizing the Storm Troops. As Hess said a week later—in one creative outburst, he formulated the Fourteen Theses which were to remodel the Brown Army. ' Not the smallest necessity escaped the attention of the Leader. He even issued the directions for publishing the news in the Press and through the radio.' That done, he took an aeroplane and landed in Berlin at ten o'clock that night.

The official story has been highly dramatized. It would almost appear that Hitler made a brave aeroplane dash and captured Röhm and Heines single-handed. In reality everything was planned. Part of the army was out ; the S.S. were out ; and Hitler's immediate friends and guards were out. Instead of being alone at Wiessee, he was accompanied by several carloads of men and even an armoured car borrowed from military headquarters in Munich. And he had with him his propaganda leader, the head of his Press department, and Röhm's successor. Hitler states that he came to his momentous decision only in the middle of the previous night at Godesberg ; but Göring, as usual, bluntly gave the show away. He told the Pressmen on July 1st that ' Some days ago he ordered me to strike as soon as he gave the word, and

he entrusted me with summary powers for the purpose '
Von Blomberg also knew about it, because he made certain
dispositions of the troops. If Hitler really made up his mind
at the aerodrome, then he must have dallied and procrastinated
until the last moment. But this is only one example of how
inconsistently the official accounts read. The times and the
dates they give cannot be reconciled, any more than can the
accounts given by the various Nazi leaders.

But we must return to the actual events, as far as they are
known. In Munich, Major Buch—as befitted his position
as chief of *Uschla*, the Nazi punitive court—supervised the
executions. The scene in the courtyard of the Stadelheim
jail that day defies description. Man after man fell—Uhl,
the man who knew too much and who was afterwards described as the chosen assassin of Hitler ; Ritter von Krausser,
ennobled for his gallantry during the war ; August Schneid-
huber, the Munich chief of police ; the one-armed Peter von
Heydebreck, leader of the Pomeranian Brownshirts, and a
legendary figure because of his military record (' Silesian
Hans ', they called him, because of his post-war fighting) ;
Hans Hayn, a fellow fighter of his in Silesia and one of the
earliest Nazis in Saxony (where he led the Brownshirts) ;
Willi Schmidt, the Munich Press chief who had become too
critical ; and scores of others, like Spreti and Koch and Rolf
Reiner who, according to a Nazi friend of mine, ' had become
politicians '.

Meanwhile, Göring had remained behind to clean up Berlin.
Towards midday, Dr. Klausener, a Civil Servant who occupied
the important post of Permanent Under-Secretary of the
Ministry of Transport, and who was also chief of the Rheinish
Catholic Party, was shot while working at his desk. In the
Vice-Chancellor's office, two of von Papen's secretaries,
von Bose and Jung, were killed at their work. In the afternoon, Gregor Strasser was taken from his home by men of
the *Gestapo* and killed. About the same time, General von
Schleicher and his wife were shot at their home at Neubabels-
berg by men in civilian clothes (incidentally at the very
moment when the conspiracy of which he was supposed to
be the leader was timed to break out !). A few hours later,

after nightfall, Colonel von Bredow, ministerial chief in the War Office under von Schleicher in the days before Hitler became Chancellor, was dragged away from his home to a waiting car and shot.

During the day, listless groups of Storm Troopers waited at their muster-stations. Nobody knew why they were there—whether they were summoned at Ernst's command to 'march on Berlin' or enticed out of their homes by fake orders. But they were left unmolested and gradually drifted home again. It was very different with the many leaders who were seized during the day by S.S. men or members of Göring's political police. Most of these were hurried out to the old cadet school at Lichterfelde, twenty miles to the south-east of Berlin, and there they were shot down against the red-brick walls of the central courtyard. Himmler was in charge of the hasty trials and summary executions ;[1] and scores of the 'old fighters' of the early days of the Brown Army—men like Karl Ernst, von Mohrenschild, Hoffman, and von Beulwitz—faced firing-squads. By mistake (not the only one !) the gallant aviator, Gehrt, was dragged in. When daylight failed, the ghastly work went on by the light of blinding army searchlights. The bodies were taken away in military forage-wagons to be cremated at Schmar-gendorf, a mile down the road.

Such seem to have been the facts of this 'Night of the Long Knives' (the name given to it by Hitler and taken from one of the earliest marching songs of the Nazis). Hitler claimed that he was a general confronted by mutiny in the field and also that, in a moment of dire peril, he was 'the Supreme Court of the German People'. On July 13th, he faced 600 of his own nominees, the so-called Reichstag, in the Kroll Opera House. To them he gave a confused and very emotional account of a conspiracy between von Schleicher and Röhm, a conspiracy that was said to include 'a foreign Power' and that had been hatching for months. Coupled

---

[1] Himmler, it must be noted, had been one of Röhm's men in the terrorist league known as the *Reichskriegsflagge*, and later had been Gregor Strasser's secretary. Now he played a leading part in killing both the men who had aided him earlier.

with this was the needless addition of the moral turpitude of what he called ' the Röhm sect ', the homosexuals.

In one argument he was sound. As he said : ' Mutinies are crushed in accordance with eternal and unchanging iron laws.' Counter-revolution is an accepted move in the revolutionary game, and the people playing it know that the penalty means facing a firing-squad. Nor can one blame members of a dictatorship taking stern measures against wavering brothers. It does not matter very much whether the plot was actual or an invention ; if certain tendencies existed which might conceivably have led to a rebellion, such a régime as Hitler's had to act. Discipline and uniformity are all essential, and a dictator's method is not to change his ministry. To quote Hess again : ' In those hours when it was a question of to-be-or-not-to-be for the German people it was not possible nicely to weigh the relative guilt of individuals in the exact scales of justice. There is a profound meaning in the ruthless principle according to which mutinies have hitherto been quelled among soldiers by shooting every tenth man out of hand, without raising the slightest question as to whether he was individually guilty or not.' This is a concise expression of a certain point of view, and needs no comment.

Hess's Königsberg speech of July 8th (from which this is taken) and Hitler's speech in the Reichstag of July 13th, leave nothing more to be said as to the moral standards of the German Government. ' The destiny of the nation stands high above the destiny of the individual ', runs their doctrine, but it follows as the night the day that any group of men in the position of the Nazi governing clique must periodically have recourse to such a purge. Identity of policy is impossible over a long period of time ; so too, personal conflicts are inevitable ; and, after all, it is the survivors, the men who get in first, who identify their deeds with ' the destiny of the nation '.

Hitler admits that seventy-six conspirators were killed that night. There are seventy-four blank spaces in the official *Who's Who* of the party, for the entries relating to the dead men were simply lifted out and white spaces left *pour encourager les autres.* But these were not all.[1] It is considered that at least 150 men were shot, and many authorities think the number ran into hundreds. Within the Party a remarkable callousness has developed about the murders. I heard a group of Nazis in Munich refer to several of the murdered men in these terms : ' Poor Edmund—pom-pom !' This phrase ' pom-pom ' is frequently heard as relating either to the past or the future of discontented members of the Party, and not once did I hear any criticism of capital punishment as the penalty for such discontent. The public complacently accepted the shootings. Indeed, as Hess boasted, the drastic steps taken against traitors made Hitler the idol of Germany, especially amongst the Hitler Youth. That a man should sacrifice his own friends for the well-being of the State seemed—and seems—to them the mark of the perfect hero. ' The Leader established an awe-inspiring precedent that redeemed the nation,' concluded Hess. The use of the word ' precedent ' seems a little unfortunate.

With regard to the known victims, opinion may be divided. One feels that Hitler can never be forgiven for shooting Röhm like a dog. Only a few weeks before, they had stood together at a function shouting the old soldiers' song, ' I had a comrade '. Now he was betrayed—Röhm, who had paid Hitler when he was starving, who had become No. 46 of the new Party, who had stood by Hitler in the Munich *putsch*, and who had done as much for the Party as any man, because he had built up the Brown Army that swept it to power. He had doubtless been plotting. Standing unhesitatingly as he did for the Brownshirts (' The S.A. are, and remain, Germany's destiny ', he said in one of his last speeches to them), he forced his Leader to choose between his old comrades and the permanent soldiers. He also wanted to rid Hitler of ' the talkers '—Goebbels and Göring and von Blomberg ; but reticence had never been one of his virtues, and everybody had known his views for months before. Similarly, his moral failings had been a matter of

---

[1] It should be noted that the *Who's Who* does not include many of the leading Nazis, and thus this evidence is far from final.

comment for years, and Hitler had allowed them to go on unchecked (his admission on this matter throws a wealth of retrospective light on the nature of the movement).   To kill one's oldest friend and then smirch his memory—these are not pleasant topics to dwell upon.

The attacks on Gregor Strasser were equally unworthy. The suggestion of his complicity in a plot against Hitler is merely silly—even Hitler had the grace to admit that he was dragged in.   Strasser was the last person in the world to plot with the Röhm section or with 'the black moles' (the Catholics of von Papen's circle).

The case of Karl Ernst is rather more difficult.   He was a typical product of the Nazi movement.   The twenty-seven-year-old son of a Berlin concierge, he had been trained for supreme command of the Berlin Brownshirts by his experiences as an usher in a picture-palace, as a waiter who was supposed to have served patrons at the notorious Eldorado night-club in an all-too-obliging manner, and then as manager of a café.   He owed his advancement to the favours of Röhm, and rumours were rife about his immorality.   But these were never proven (as they were in the case of Röhm and Heines), and Ernst was certainly neither a traitor nor a murderer like some of the others.   He was arrested on the way to Bremerhaven, where he was embarking with his wife on a trip to Majorca—strange behaviour indeed for a conspirator who was to launch a national revolution on the morrow. A freebooter he was, it is true, but the Brownshirt ranks were full of picturesque land pirates of this type.   A few short months before Hitler had attended his wedding and given him a present marked 'For ever united!'   Whatever his faults—and he was but a boy—he had commanded the Berlin Brownshirts, a whole *Übergruppe* of them, since the first days of Hitler's power, and he had kept Berlin loyal to his Leader.   Torn from his wife and dragged back half unconscious to the red-brick wall of Lichterfelde, he reeled before the firing-squad and could not understand what was happening.   Mutiny, revolution, he thought, and he fell shouting : *Heil Hitler !   Heil Deutschland !*

With Edmund Heines the explanation is very different.

Murderer and parasite, sadist and homosexual, he was a pervert if ever there was one. But even so, the blame must all go to Hitler for allowing such a man to attain a position of prominence in the Brown Army and for giving him executive positions long after he knew his real nature. For eighteen months Heines had terrorized tens of thousands of people with all the irresponsibility and whims of an Oriental despot, yet Hitler, knowing this, had done nothing. He had promoted him Brownshirt commander of all Silesia and had given him control of the Breslau police—this self-confessed murderer who, a few short years before, had been scrounging a living in the cafés of Munich, working intermittently as a waiter and between times begging or bullying people for drinks. Handy with his fists, he naturally became a platoon commander of the local Nazis and ultimately leader of 100 men, with a liking for fighting and plenty of time on his hands for political activities and discreet blackmailing. 'When Edmund came along,' one of his Munich intimates told me, 'the tradesmen paid up.' Caught in an act of flagrant moral delinquency in Röhm's villa, Heines, infamous Feme murderer, worst of all the Nazi types, was ignominiously shot, regretted by nobody. The very fact of his existence and power must remain an eternal reproach to Hitler.

To hold that June 30th was merely the paying off of personal grievances, or something in the nature of one of the recurrent State trials of Russia is to miss its fundamental significance in the evolution of Hitlerism. Hitler was indeed faced by a 'second revolution'. He had to choose between two sets of forces—those represented by the small *bourgeoisie* of the Brown Army and those that led him away from the Socialistic portions of his early programme in the direction of militarism.[1] Röhm posed the problem for him, and forced an early issue. Hitler decided without much hesitation. The facts of eighteen months of power all pointed in the one direction. Hitler wanted to break the hold of the unwieldy Brownshirts and free himself from the incubus

[1] The army even saw to it that the memory of von Schleicher was rehabilitated at a meeting of officers and Party leaders in Berlin on January 3rd, 1935.

of the lower middle classes who had been his main strength in the past. He chose for Nationalism against Socialism; and the Brown Army went to the wall. Its leaders were captured and shot without any resistance, and the Brownshirts disappeared from the German scene as a political force.

There was indeed a 'second revolution', but not that dreamed of by Röhm and the mass of the Brownshirts. The future destiny of Germany—and perchance of Europe—was decided that day. Hitler left his old comrades and, with the aid of Göring and Goebbels, decided for imperialistic nationalism, backed by the S.S. and the army. That is why the events of June 30th must be looked upon as of the greatest importance in the development of the movement. Hitler was at the parting of the ways, and, having chosen, had to go on along his new path. The next step was the reintroduction of military conscription—an inevitable corollary of June 30th. It is indeed the inevitability of the killings, as well as of the subsequent events, that emerges as the clearest feature of the whole business. They all form part of a sadly logical historical process.

THE ARMY AND ITS RELATIONS WITH HITLERISM

I.—*Hitler and the Army*

The twilight of the Brownshirts left the way open for a new emphasis on the army. Consequently it might almost be said that the dominant note in Germany to-day is not Hitlerism but a militant patriotism. The two are not the same thing. Many opponents of Hitlerism as a régime share with the Hitlerites that *Wehrbereitschaft* (readiness to bear arms) which is so obvious throughout the land. It is impossible to explain to any German that Britain could share this spirit. Throughout last year, Germans of all classes sympathized with me for belonging to a decadent nation like Great Britain. They were kindly disposed towards us, but their attitude was that a nation which called for 17,000 recruits in a time of grave international crisis and could secure less than 300 must of necessity be in decline. In their eyes it was bad enough to fail in ' technical preparedness ', but even more so to break down in ' mental preparedness '—that is, to lose the *Wehrbereitschaft*, as we were doing.

The Party from the first taught that the war had been forced on an unwilling Germany—that Germany had actually won in the field—that she was defeated only by a Socialist and Jewish ' stab-in-the-back '—that the Treaty of Versailles was a deliberate humiliation and in no sense a just punishment—and that the ' war-guilt ' clause was an unjustifiable insult. At no stage had the German people been to blame. They had always been morally correct and physically brave, and only the wicked Allies had been responsible for their ills. This was the comforting doctrine by means of which the Hitlerites gave new life to German pride.

Hitler is, and always has been, a militarist. He loves the army and enjoys military displays. He rushed into service in 1914 and has often said that the war was a fine experience. When peace came, he turned to the army for a living and was always pleased when he could attract the attention of the colonels and the generals. Once he started a party, he began to build up a militia body of his own, gave them uniforms, and organized them on a most intricate military plan. The hierarchy of his Brownshirts (and later his Black Guards) was as complicated as anything in the Reichswehr, and he liked to think of himself as the Field-Marshal of the Brown Army.

His entire political life has been characterized by attacks on the Treaty which broke German military power, and he promised his audiences that one of his first acts as Chancellor would be to enforce Point 22 of his programme—the creation of an army that would include the whole nation. But the truth goes far deeper than this. Some statesmen want a strong army because they can use it in implementing their policy, others accept it as a disagreeable necessity ; but Hitler wants the strongest army in the world for many other reasons. He wants it as a sign of Germany's greatness ; he wants the uniform of every conscript to remind Germany how he has retrieved the national honour ; he wants an army as the power which will enable him to pursue a policy of bluff in international affairs ; and above all he wants an army because he loves it and loves anything to do with uniforms and military life. He is obviously at his worst when he is deprecating war and equally obviously at his best when he is talking about the comradeship of military life and the benefits to be derived from a strong army.

He is quite clear in *Mein Kampf* on the point. ' We must be perfectly clear,' he wrote, ' that the recovery of lost provinces is not achieved by solemn invocations of the Beloved Lord, or through pious hopes in a League of Nations, but only through armed violence.' Nothing could be clearer than this passage, which still remains in the version of the book sold in Germany to-day. Goebbels, who is admittedly the brain behind Hitler, once said : ' The only instrument with which one can conduct foreign policy is the sword, the sword alone and exclusively.' As for Göring, the third of the trio, he was a born militarist. He loved his aerial fighting, and nothing could have given him greater pleasure than building up a new air force, first as a gigantic toy and later perhaps to try out his theory of ' a world war that would be a matter of days or even hours '.

Dangerous men, these, to be in charge of Germany at a time when the nation was reawakened and in a mood to accept any sacrifice for the sake of rearmament. Since Hitler became Chancellor, over four years ago, the entire life of Germany has been subordinated to building up the country's military strength, and this term has been interpreted in the widest sense, to cover every variety of economics and cultural militarism as well as purely military measures. Hitler has set the world a new *tempo* in the race for armaments, and has even risked economic disaster in his frenzied pursuit of military strength. The urgency for such a step existed mainly in his own imagination but, none the less, he produced a feeling of panic and fear in every other country. He achieved his beloved ' Equality ' and removed the slur of Versailles, but at the cost of bringing the world to the verge of war.

II.—*The Rebirth of the Army*

The Treaty of Versailles broke the old military machine of Germany. One of Hitler's most telling electioneering posters was that showing foreigners smashing German guns and burning the prized regimental records of certain German units ; and he plastered every village with the stark list showing Germany's losses under the Treaty—60,000 heavy guns, 130,000 machine-guns, 6,000,000 rifles, 16,000,000 bombs, 16,000 aeroplanes, 26 capital ships, 23 cruisers, 83 torpedo-boats, 315 submarines, and so on. The Germans had trusted in the guarantees of Wilson's Fourteen Points, and later in the promise of the victorious nations to disarm, only to be disillusioned in each case (as they saw it). Forcibly disarmed themselves, they had expected the rest of the world to follow suit; instead, they were surrounded by foes armed to the teeth and they were denied what Blomberg calls 'man's primitive birthright' of defence.

Two months before Hitler came to power, the German Government made a formal demand for military equality, but the acceptance of the demand in principle at Geneva produced no practical result. In protest against this continued degradation, Hitler fought for equality with the other nations and the abolition of the Treaties. This was Point Number 2 in his Party programme, and he lost no time in putting it into effect. Naturally he had to consolidate his own position before he could risk a move that might entail a retaliatory war on the part of the other Powers. So, for two years, he preached an endless campaign for 'Equality' and worked the nation to a frenzy of belief in his foreign policy. Then, when the moment was ripe, he launched the most spectacular coup of his career—the introduction of conscription on March 16th, 1935.

'The Law for the Reconstruction of the National Defence Forces' provided that all men had to serve in the army for a year. Moreover, the existing Reichswehr of seven divisions, was to give way to a truly national force of thirty-six divisions. Even the name of Reichswehr was to go, for henceforth all the armed forces of Germany were to be known as the *Wehrmacht* (Defence Force), of which the *Heer* (army) was only one part.

No time was lost. The armaments factories had been busy on Government orders for some time, and Germany had built up large reserves of war material. But the human element had been lacking, and the Government now set to work with a will to make up for 'the fourteen lost years', the years in which German youths had received no military training, whereas the neighbouring French, Russians, and Czechs had been intensively trained in the newer tactics that had emerged since the war.

When Hitler came to power, the Reichswehr included the 100,000 men (enlisted for twelve years) allowed by the Treaty. Despite alarmist stories abroad, the numbers were probably not much in excess of this, although the Germans had worked out an ingenious triple-unit system (three platoons to a company, three companies to a battalion, three battalions to a regiment, three regiments to a division) which really made the Reichswehr capable of easy and vast expansion, with every man in it a trained instructor.   The Hitlerites thought that the army would use this system to incorporate a large number of Brownshirts immediately, but the soldiers would have no swamping of this kind.   They stuck to their old point of view.   They were to be the striking force of the nation, with the million Brownshirts, if need be, as reserves behind them.

Hitler tided over his first two years with this awkward compromise, but increased the militarized forces directly under his command by getting control of the various police forces, by perfecting the training of the full-time units of the S.A. and S.S., and by infusing military discipline into his new Labour Service Corps.   By these means he brought the number of partly-trained forces up to a total of 2,000,000 men, although the General Staff repeatedly pointed out that such huge masses of man-power would be a positive danger in time of war, if the organization to use them did not exist. ' Every nought you add to your total in this way ', said one general, ' reduces your effective military power.'

The situation was cleared up by the decision of March 1935 to expand the army to 600,000 men and to give the Staff the power of choosing the best of the German youth by a system of conscription, although this meant changing the entire strategical conception on which von Seekt had built up the Reichswehr.   Von Seekt did not want a national levy ; he preferred a relatively small professional army to strike and large militia forces to occupy conquered territory, whereas Hitler desired to go back to the old pre-war idea, not realizing how great has been the change in military conditions even since 1918.   As the General Staff had no choice in the matter, they had to change their strategy and make the best use possible of the new reservoirs of man-power placed at their disposal, even if it meant sacrificing their old ideas of quality and mobility.

Their problem was a difficult one—to change a specialized

army of 100,000 men enlisted for twelve years into a national force of 600,000 conscripts forced to serve for a year or two. The necessary *cadres* could not be built up in a moment, and, even when the organization was provided, there was a shortage of everything—arms, equipment, officers, barracks. The greatest difficulty was the shortage of instructors, especially in the new aerial and mechanized units. At one stage, aeroplanes were lying idle for lack of trained pilots, because, despite Göring's efforts, Germany had been so poverty-stricken for years that there were few civilian pilots on whom to draw.

It became obvious, then, that it would take years to give practical effect to the law of March 16th. The thirty-six divisions did not exist even on paper when Hitler issued his decree on May 21st, and it was not until the misty morning of November 7th, 1935, almost eight months after Hitler's first announcement, that the first conscripts were called up and the new Nazi war-flag hoisted for the first time. The General Staff, which had been reconstituted in October under General Beck, fought valiantly to cope with the influx of recruits, although it was common knowledge that many of the professional soldiers still thought that a small well-trained army could be of more use in the war of the future than any collection of old-fashioned mass-levies. The first conscripts called up were the men born in 1914, and these were absorbed by the Staff in the skeleton organization built up in the first year of conscription. So slow was the progress, however, that not until October 1936 were even the headquarters of the last two of the twelve army corps organized. At that time only twenty-six divisions were complete, with a few others in an embryonic state. Innumerable difficulties of organization still existed, and supplies were short, despite the rush of the previous months. In particular there was a great lack in such vital matters as the provision of artillery support for the infantry.

Nevertheless progress was made, especially in 1936. The difference between the 1935 and 1936 manœuvres showed this quite clearly. In the former year, when only a single army corps was used, troops had to be taken from all parts of western Germany to get enough men. In 1936, however, the manœuvres were the largest since the outbreak of war. In each of the twelve corps areas, there had been preliminary exercises with, usually, a division on each side ; and, in the concluding ' grand manœuvres ' (which, incidentally, were designed rather to impress the world with Germany's new military might than to experiment in tactics), two army corps were employed. It was still significant, however, that, while the staff work was done by the Fifth and Ninth Corps alone, men to fill the ranks had to be drawn from a wider area, although not as wide as in the previous year.

I was in the region of the autumn army manœuvres of 1936 and was surprised at the mobility of the new army. One morning, in the Würzburg forest area, I drove about ninety miles through the hills. Detachments of extremely friendly and bedecked soldiers (whoever saw British soldiers at manœuvres garlanded with flowers ?) were at our starting point in the morning, and were awaiting us in the village where we had lunch. The only difference was that their orders had been to avoid all highways and keep only to side-tracks. What this means in mountainous country can be imagined, especially with heavy guns.

Special features of these manœuvres were the new types of anti-aircraft artillery (British experts told me that some of the weapons were of an entirely new type) and the use of small tanks of about five tons weight and much lighter in con-struction than those favoured in other countries. The Germans, oddly enough, have not gone very far in the develop-ment of medium or heavy tanks and they do not seem to have profited by the mistakes of other countries, although they may be concealing some new and improved designs. Mechanization, made much of in the *Wehrmacht*-day at the Nuremberg Congress and in the Press, is not nearly as far advanced as propaganda would imply, and we may dis-count such stories as that the mechanization of a third of the German Army is within sight of realization. It is said that she has three armoured divisions, and certainly a great fuss was made about 2,000 machines (supposed to be half a division) I saw at the Nuremberg Rally ; but the truth seems to be that, if all her armoured forces were put together, they would still come to less than a division. Although German military theorists lay great stress on such forces in the next war, there is no doubt that most emphasis is being placed at present on the air force and next on organizing the inchoate mass of her man-power. Her factories are busy pouring out aeroplanes, rifles, and big guns ; the time-factor alone would suffice to put mechanization somewhat in the background. Most of her field artillery and transport, for instance, are still horse-drawn. When all is said and done, Germany has had less than three years of open military preparations, and she cannot make up the gap of fifteen years in such a short time.

There is no doubt, however, about her strength in man-power. She has the largest army outside Russia. When completely organized, her thirty-six infantry divisions alone will include 600,000 men. Britain has just over 150,000 men, in five divisions, and had to call up her reserves even to put one division in the field in Palestine last year. France has a peace-time army of twenty-five divisions at home, and it would require all of her efforts to double them in time of war. In the matter of reserves Germany is also in a highly favourable position. In 1914, for instance, she had fifty active divisions, but these were immediately doubled by the mobilization of various reserves, and, in the end, she succeeded in putting no less than 240 divisions in the field. At the moment, most of her men in the reserves (the limit fixed at present is forty-five years of age) are without military training, although there is a strong nucleus of survivors from the last war who, in emergency, could train the younger ones who missed conscription. Moreover, many of them belonged to one or other of the political militia bodies, and it is very doubtful whether the training they received in them was as useless as the War Office would have us believe. On the whole, no reasonable observer can doubt that, if Hitler organizes his thirty-six divisions and trains 300,000 conscripts a year from now on, with two classes serving at any one time, in a few years he will have the finest army in Europe, with an admirable striking force of young conscripts and large reserves of older men for posts behind the lines.

Admittedly the French Army is superior at the moment in man-power, mechanization and leadership; and equally admittedly the Franco-Czech-Russian combination could overwhelm Germany on land; but these factors will not always apply, and every year that passes makes more possible Göring's plan of a sudden demoralizing dash against enemies before they have the time to come together.

Hitler announced in his Reichstag speech of May 21st, 1935, that 'in no circumstances' would he depart from the scheme of thirty-six divisions laid down in the Army Law. When the period of conscription was raised another year in August 1936, he again said that no extension was contemplated. It soon became obvious, however, how little his words were worth. His total did not include the new armoured divisions, the result being that, while foreigners thought that the thirty-six divisions would include all military forces, Hitler argues that they referred only to the infantry and that he might add as many armoured divisions as he pleased and still keep his promises. By the end of last year, three armoured divisions existed at Berlin, Wurzburg, and Weimar, and it was rumoured that three more were being planned, thus already bringing the German Army up to forty-two divisions. The limit fixed by the Army Law, already a very high one, is thus replaced by an indefinitely flexible one, and a new element of uncertainty needlessly introduced into European affairs.

III.—*Göring and the Air Force*

As soon as he came to power, Göring organized his Air Force—long before the relevant clauses of the Treaty of Versailles were denounced. He often boasted of his 'grey-blue boys', and expounded his theory that the war of the future—it should be noted this means an aggressive war—would be won in the first few days by bombing planes. Nominally his 'boys' belonged to an Air Sports organization, but it was obvious that they were the Air Force of the future, and, indeed, when conscription was ultimately introduced in

1935, entry to the Air Force was restricted to members of Göring's organization.

One of Hitler's first acts was to set up a new Commission of Air Transport, under Göring. Three months later, in April 1933, the Commission was changed into a Ministry, although obviously a country with no military air-arm scarcely needed a Ministry to deal with air matters. With his characteristic energy, Göring proceeded to build up the missing branch of the service. He called in pilots, he set up training establishments, he gave huge subsidies to the aeroplane industry, he fostered ' flying sports clubs ', and undoubtedly worked hand in glove with the Reichswehr while outwardly adhering to the terms of the Treaty. His *Luftschutz* campaign was carried on everywhere. Great placards even appealed to every able-bodied woman to enlist in a special Air Defence Corps. Periodicals were started, and huge sums spent in every kind of propaganda. No village was too small to escape the deluge, and the countrymen flocked to the *Luftschutz* nights, because, if the stories of invading hordes of enemy planes terrified them, they were repaid by the lavish entertainment the Minister gave them, a combination of cinema and vaudeville and tattoo.

His main organization was the Air Defence League—the *Reichsluftschutzbund*—which Göring founded the day before he was promoted to be Air Minister. The president of this was a retired artillery general, an old fire-eating Saxon, Hugo Grimme, who had been fighting for the air-arm for twenty years and who now proceeded to organize Germany down to the smallest hamlet. He called in a Steelhelmet major named Waldschmidt who had for long been wakening Silesia to the danger of Polish planes and who now transferred his activities to the whole Reich. Local State organizations which had grown up were absorbed by the end of the year, and Göring instituted a special air police for the whole country.

No method was too crude for this campaign. The laughable raid of June 24th, 1933, when foreign aeroplanes dropped leaflets over Berlin in the mist—oddly enough, only in the grounds of the public buildings in the Wilhelmstrasse so that nobody except Göring ever saw one !—was used to launch an unprecedented propaganda for 'Defence Planes'. It was argued that bombs could be dropped as easily as leaflets and that the only safeguard lay in making the people so air-minded that their howls of protest must make the Versailles powers concede their claims. The people rushed to join the Air Defence League—1,000,000 within six months, 2,000,000 in a year, 5,000,000 in less than two years. Hardly a work-man but gave his pfennigs to the appeals ; while the munici-palities contributed to air-training (of course, purely civilian !) and to the excavation of shelters from aerial raids. Fearsome-looking bombs, as high as a man, were erected in the streets and used as warnings of what might be expected, and also as signposts. Devastatingly real 'black-outs' and mock raids were held in most towns, and the average child was reduced to a state of terror at the thought of the thousands on thousands of French and Russian monsters that might come overhead raining death at any moment. 'Save your pfennigs for the R.L.B. and live to grow up !' ran one gruesome poster designed for the children. Whatever the methods em-ployed, one certainly has to admit that the continuous invo-cation of fear in the minds of the people was surprisingly well done, and every month of last year, even after Germany was openly building bombers, the campaign increased in intensity.

Meanwhile, the Air Minister was paving the way for an air force. The *Lufthansa* was reorganized from a military point of view, and an order issued that the old single-motored passenger planes were to be replaced by multi-engined Junkers and Heinkels and Dorniers that were obviously easily convertible for military purposes. The aeroplane industry was expanded, and great aerodromes built at strategic points. Special flying units of the S.A. and S.S. were set up, and aid given to other air sport bodies.

The result of all this activity was that Germany had an embryonic air force long before Hitler's denunciation of the military clauses of the Treaty in March 1935. Indeed, in that very month, the British Prime Minister had to admit that Germany already had aerial superiority over Britain, so rapid had been her surreptitious building. There was undoubtedly much panic at that time, and Germany's bombers seemed in our eyes to be as numerous as the leaves on Vallombrosa, possibly because the British Government wanted support for its building programme. The British Air Minister, five months before this, had placed the German strength at 1,000 front-line planes, a figure which, if correct, means that Göring has built only a few hundred more planes in the frantic expansion of the last few years.

Much controversy exists as to the actual strength of the German Air Force. At the end of 1936, it was suggested in England that she had 1,500 first-line aeroplanes, but German propaganda, officially inspired, claimed that the number did not exceed 950. As against this, it was understood at the Nuremberg Rally that the 600 planes we saw manœuvring represented about half of the front-line air force, and this seems a reasonable estimate.

Since then construction has been going on apace and to-day (September 1937) she must have about 2,500 machines ; and she claims that their striking power is greater than any equivalent number of foreign machines because of the new system of group-attack she has evolved. Russia has at least 3,000 planes and is said to be working up to the stupendous total of 15,000. The German scheme is said to arrange for 5,000 planes by the end of 1939, and it has to be remembered that German industry is working under conditions that are practically tantamount to wartime conscription. France and England together still have a marked preponderance, but it is a moot point how long this will last unless both countries give themselves over to a frenzy of construction. It is quite certain that Britain's argument that she must have parity with any Continental power within striking distance no longer holds. Moreover, Germany's machines are all new. In the early days of rearmament she claimed that she was handicapped by her lack of experience in the days when she was compulsorily disarmed, but, now that she has tided over the danger of war for a few years, this argument turns to her advantage, in the sense that she is not encumbered with a number of obsolete machines.

Her other difficulty—the shortage of pilots—is not so easy to overcome. Britain has 5,400 trained pilots, with years of experience, but Germany is backward in this regard, partly because (despite all the propaganda) relatively few pilots were trained in her ' lost years '. It is a notorious fact that Göring is straining every nerve to train flyers, even putting quickness of training before safety. The German Air Force has an exceptionally high number of fatalities every year. In a matter like this, zeal is not enough ; experience is far more essential, and the time-factor is against the Germans.

Meanwhile the preparations continue. Pride of place in German rearmament is given to the air force, and Göring owes his great popularity to his success as Air Minister and commander-in-chief of the air force. The Air Force Day, on the anniversary of von Richthofen's death, is the most popular of the many celebrations held every year ; and the gigantic Air Ministry opened last year in the *Französische Strasse* in the heart of Berlin is the largest and the most imposing Government building in Germany. ' It is almost big enough to house Goebbels's propagandists,' say the Berliners, and they have no larger method of expressing size than this. Every German believes that what goes on in the Air Ministry will decide the country's fate, and no branch of service is more popular than the air force. That air force is viewed as Hitler's greatest achievement, the outward symbol of Germany's new-found strength, and the most satisfactory method of protection yet evolved.

IV.—The New Navy

The navy has remained a bad last in Hitler's race for re-armament. In Imperial days, when German strategy was world-wide, an overpowering navy was essential, but Hitler is essentially a European. The army and air force are his playthings, and he needs a navy only to protect his coasts and close the Baltic, if need be. Nevertheless, the navy has a place in his scheme of things. His first task was to throw off the shackles of Versailles and allow Germany to build the type of ship she wanted. The pocket-battleships evolved after the war had their points, it is true, but Germany did not want to compress everything within 10,000-ton limits for ever.

Accordingly, in June 1935, an Anglo-German Naval Agreement was signed, limiting the German fleet to 35 per cent of the British (but with the significant exception of submarines). This gave Germany all the scope she needed for the ensuing five years and freed her from Versailles. She set to work with a will and immediately announced a programme that built up to half the limit permitted her under the agreement. She laid down the two 26,000-ton battleships allowed her, and launched the first, the *Scharnhorst*, last October—'the proud symbol of actual equality', as von Blomberg called it. From this she went on to a 35,000-ton monster still under construction. She has also launched three pocket-battleships since Hitler became Chancellor, although naval opinion no longer favours these vessels.

France raised an outcry against this German naval programme, but most experts believe that Hitler has been moderate in his arrangements. When his present programme is completed, France will still have an overwhelming preponderance, especially in cruisers and submarines. Moreover, Germany has adhered to those provisions of the Treaty of London which govern submarine warfare. On the whole, there seems no reason for alarm at Germany's new navy. Indeed, Hitler's moderation in this regard is very reassuring, because it shows that he has no thought of an aggressive world strategy of the kind the Kaiser desired.

It is obvious that he wants a fleet only for essential defence and as an expression of Germany's naval pride. There is an intense interest in naval matters in Hitlerite Germany. The old naval traditions are being revived, and most homes have books or calendars or models dealing with naval matters. Last summer I went to a special 'sea-sports school' on a lake near Berlin, and found groups of boys drawn from all over Germany to undergo a short course in naval instruction. Nowhere else in Germany did I see such enthusiasm (or so much admiration for England). The school was hidden on a lake in the dense pine forests to the south of Berlin. It was named after Gorch Fock, a popular poet who went down while serving as an ordinary seaman on the *Wiesbaden* at Jutland. To-day he is the people's naval hero and has been accorded a high place in the Nazi list of heroes. A genial cruiser-commander is in charge of the school, and I was told that the most intense competition exists amongst German boys to secure a place in it.

There also exists a Navy League, with branches all over Germany and with well over fifty thousand members, mostly ex-naval men. The new cult of the navy seems to me far healthier than the attitude of disdain which was all too prevalent in Germany in Republican days, when every proposal for a cruiser aroused snarls of opposition in parliament. To-day Hitler has definitely revived the tradition of the past. He has removed the neurotic disease which had led a sea-loving people to reject its own naval story and has restored a normal healthy interest in the sea. It is a good sight to see a meeting of the local Navy League in a southern inland town, or to visit a sea-sports school, or to witness the new cult of the sea in the old Hanseatic towns. One feels that Germany has cast off the repression which started with the naval mutinies just before the Armistice and has reverted to normality.

Chapter Five

THE SYSTEM *IN EXCELSIS:*
A NUREMBERG PARTY RALLY

The *Partei-Tag*—the Party Congress—has become an integral part of the Nazi movement. Its origins are obscure. Many congresses were held in the early days, a whole series of 'German Days' in particular, but headquarters assign the honour of the first Party Day to a meeting in Munich in January 1923. Little was done at this Congress, and nothing indicated that it was the precursor of a long series.

The intervention of the November *putsch* and the *Verbotszeit* of 1924 meant that the idea lapsed until the 're-founding' of the Party in February 1925. Even then seventeen months elapsed before a Congress could be held; and the second *Partei-Tag* at Weimar in July 1926 was a very minor affair. Hitler took over the 'Blood Banner', the shot-riddled flag that Andreas Bauriedl had held until he was struck down at the Feldherrnhalle nearly three years before. This relic hereafter became the centre of the whole ritual ceremony of the Nazis. A new flag was consecrated by its touch. It became, in short, the Host of National Socialism, the source of all holiness. Sixty thousand Storm Troopers marched past it that day, their outstretched arms pledging them to fight to the death. That day, too, the Leader founded the 'Hitler Youth' and set Feder to work on the task of collecting a 'National Socialist Library'.

The third *Partei-Tag* was held in Nuremberg in August 1927, but was not a great success. The city remained comparatively empty. I went there during the three days of its meeting and easily found hotel accommodation in the ordinary way. The townsfolk did not take it seriously. They enjoyed the torchlight procession—that was all. Hitler blessed twelve new standards and took the salute of 30,000 Brown-shirts in the Town Square, but not even the appearance of the banned Berlin formations or their subsequent alter-cations with the police could arouse much enthusiasm. Indeed, the gathering was so dismal and the people were so bored by Rosenberg's cultural campaign that it was resolved not to hold a Congress in the following year.

Numerous bloody clashes with the Communists gave added interest to the fourth *Partei-Tag*, held at Nuremberg in August 1929. A much more ambitious programme was attempted. The numbers went up—thirty-four new standards and 60,000 men this time, and 2,000 Hitler Youth for novelty. But failure lurked behind the processions. The speeches were dull. A new Legal Association was formed and there was much discussion of the methods by which future leaders were to be trained ; but the Party chiefs were too concerned with making a bid for actual power in some favourable state like Thuringia to trouble about the formalities of a Congress.

The result was that four years passed without a Party Day—the years of the rise and fall of Dr. Brüning and Hitler's own accession to the Chancellorship. A special effort was therefore staged to make the fifth Party Day (August 31st—September 3rd, 1933) a celebration of victory, a *Partei-Tag des Sieges*. Hitler acted as the pontiff of a Nazi Rome during the grandiose parades that ensued. He reviewed a platoon of each formation of S.A. and S.S. men who had fought for the national victory ; he performed the blessing rite over 316 banners ; he took the salute of 100,000 men of his militia ; he spoke to 60,000 Hitler Youth. From the doctrinal point of view this Congress launched the campaign for racial purity, and Hitler himself gave addresses on *Kultur und Rasse* and *Volk und Rasse*, reflecting the new influence of Darré and Rosenberg.

Hereafter there could be no question of dropping the Party Day. The ceremonial had to become increasingly impressive every year, and all the ingenuity of Dr. Ley employed to think of some new device of lighting or effect. The Congress thus became the outstanding example of show-

manship in Germany, and the people came to expect some
kind of super-circus and revue. But Hitler supplemented
it for more serious purposes. Every autumn he used the
Congress to outline the direction of Party policy in the forthcoming year, so that the world awaited some melodramatic
pronouncement of policy in those September days. Moreover, when Hitler found himself more and more encumbered
with official business, he took the opportunity of the Nuremberg Rally to meet his subordinates from distant parts of the
country and renew personal contacts which would otherwise
have been neglected. In all, then, the *Partei-Tag* came to be
a central institution in the New Germany, with a peculiar
practical and ideological significance.

The sixth Rally (September 1934) was held under difficult
circumstances. It was ' the Congress of the empty seats '.
In a body whose members occupied regular places, the clean-
up of June 30th left awkward gaps. An obvious depression
settled over the proceedings, and not all the drums and
bands could remove it. Hitler sought to end the tension by
newer and more striking displays. For the first time the
Labour Service Corps and the permanent army took part
in a Rally ; and thus entered the last of the elements that
go to make up a Party Day in its present form. By 1934,
Ley had worked out the programme that is now stereotyped.
Each day was devoted to a given arm of Nazidom. In this
particular year, 200,000 political leaders had their day at
the Zeppelin-field, 97,000 S.A. and 11,000 S.S. in the Leopold
Arena, 60,000 Hitler Youth at the Stadium, with 52,000
Labour Service men (not yet sufficiently important for a
day to themselves) very much in evidence.

The seventh Party Day (September 1935) followed very
closely along these lines. Named ' the Party Day of Freedom ', its main function was to celebrate the reintroduction of
conscription and the denunciation of Section 5 of the Treaty
of Versailles. Apart from the normal features (the 100,000
political leaders, the 86,000 Brownshirts and 18,000 S.S.
men, the 54,000 Labour Service youths and the 50,000 Hitler
Youth), most attention was paid to the new armaments.
Ten thousand men of the recently formed N.S.K.K.—the

motorized militia of the Party—passed noisily by as a prelude
to the army proper. Everything led up to the climax of
the *Wehrmacht*-day, when fighting planes droned overhead
and mechanized formations passed in review. Naturally
the key-note of Hitler's own speeches was to stress the identification of Party and State and the new realization of independence by the formation of the national army. In all,
'the Party Day of Freedom' would have been better described as 'the Party Day of the Army'. As compared
with this martial display and the adoption of the new flag,
the laws against the Jews attracted little notice. Nothing
could compete with the army—a shrewd move indeed,
because it reconciled to the new régime many Germans who
felt lukewarm towards the Party but who would accept
any form of government if Germany thereby secured a
position of military power.

The 1936 Party Congress (the eighth) was thus the culmination of a long series, in which a certain routine had
been worked out and in which the people as a whole had
come to expect striking ceremonial and some important
statement of policy. They were not disappointed. The
celebrations were bigger and brighter than ever before, and
Hitler now gave his messages, not to Germany alone, but
to the whole world. At this Rally he launched two new
campaigns—the Four Year Plan for economic self-sufficiency
and a crusade against 'the powers of disorder' led by Russia.

His *Ehrengäste* were a curious assortment, including an
official delegation of Italian Blackshirts ; a few lone Japanese
waving their national flag so that they could be identified ;
Hungarian Fascists and Scandinavian publicists ; many German
Americans ; English peers, parliamentarians, writers, and
publishers (and one man reflecting the trade union point
of view), French authors and Croix de Feu representatives,
and isolated Britons from as far afield as Australia and British
Guiana.

The Rally opened in the huge Congress Hall, where
60,000 people gathered to listen to Hitler's proclamation
on his achievements of the last three years. Hundreds of
swastika banners filed in, to the impressive music of the

Song of the Standards, and formed a solid mass of red and gold at the back of the stage. Every device of music and coloured light was used to keep the atmosphere tense, and the spotlight that played on the giant swastika behind the banners exerted an influence that was almost hypnotic.

Victor Lutze, head of the Brownshirts, solemnly read the name of every Nazi who had died for his cause. There were over four hundred of them, and the foreigner rather uneasily observed that the entries for the current year included the men killed in Danzig and the four Nazis who had fallen in Spain up to that date. Nobody knew what was going to happen, and we wondered if the Congress might not become a clarion call for intervention in Spain, as retribution for the last names on the Nazi martyrology.

Adolf Wagner, the ruler of Munich, next read Hitler's proclamation, ostensibly because his voice is almost exactly that of Hitler himself, even to the hoarseness and breaking. I shall not easily forget the roars that went through those crowds when Wagner dramatically declared that ' within four years Germany must be independent of foreign raw supplies '.

The atmosphere was most strained and unreal. The speakers deliberately played on the feelings of the people. At intervals, when something particularly impressive was read out, a curious tremor swept the crowd, and all around me individuals uttered a strange cry, a kind of emotional sigh that invariably changed into a shout of ' *Heil Hitler* '. It was a definite struggle to remain rational in a horde so surcharged with tense emotionalism. It was pitiful to see the stress of one young girl in the uniform of a Hitler Maiden, with the triangular badge on her sleeve bearing the name *Kap-Stadt*. I felt that, after all, Capetown is British and should be spelt our way !

The rest of the week consisted either of lavish displays or of meetings at which Party leaders spoke. The German excels in mass meetings. Not an hour of the day or night was quiet, and, when the official functions ended, zealous Nazis formed impromptu torchlight processions of their own. One day 160,000 men of the popular Labour Service Corps filed past, with their dark-brown uniforms and bright-polished shovels, and, on a bitterly cold morning, many thousands of them stood stripped to the waist for hours, listening to official speeches. On another day, a still larger number of Hitler Youth and Maidens and groups of the sea-scouts crowded a huge arena to listen to Hitler and von Schirach. On still another day, the Brownshirts and Black Guards formed a solid mass of humanity in the Leopold Arena—160,000 of them. One of the most striking ceremonies took place. Before addressing them, Hitler solemnly marched up to the sacrificial fires that paid homage to those who had died for the movement. It was the only moment of quietness in the whole week. For what seemed an interminable time, three men—Hitler, Himmler, and Lutze—strode up the wide path that clove the brown mass in twain and, after saluting the fire, as solemnly marched back. It was a superbly arranged gesture. Those three men represented individualism as against the solid anonymity of the massed Brownshirts ; they stood for leadership as against the blind obedience of the people. The silence became almost unendurable, and it was a relief when Hitler returned to the presidental stand and broke into one of his impassioned speeches that ' the Brown Army must march again, as it has marched in the past, if Bolshevism raises its challenging head in Germany or on Germany's frontiers '. The meeting closed with still another ritual—the consecration of rows of new banners by the touch of Hitler and the ' Blood Banner ' of 1923.

That Sunday afternoon every Brownshirt and every Black Guard in Nuremberg filed past Hitler in the central square of the town. For five and a half hours they marched in columns of twelve, and the whole time Hitler stood erect, punctiliously acknowledging every salute and never showing fatigue. Göring obtained relief by leaning against the side of Hitler's car, and the standard-bearers had to be relieved every half-hour, but Hitler went on to the end— and then dashed away to other lectures and a round of com- mittee meetings. Anybody doubting his physical strength need only look at his list of engagements that day.

The files seemed interminable—Brownshirts from the exiled

Austrians in the van, old Storm Troopers from all over Germany, the new Kraftwagen Corps with sinister black helmets (like figures from a future mechanical world), the permanent soldiers of the Brownshirt staff corps (bitter rivals, these, of the staff Black Guards, and superb soldiers, both sets of them), and S.S. men in their striking black uniforms. All of them goose-stepped past Hitler, the younger men with military precision, their elders more raggedly. In all that mass, the Bavarians alone retained some individuality. They were Brownshirts down to the waist; below that they had the leather shorts and white socks of their country. Even Hitler has had to concede something to the Bavarians' rugged localism and objection to discipline.

On the last day came the eagerly expected military display, the second of its kind. Ordinary Germans bought tickets for anything up to forty marks each, and the supply was exhausted days before the Rally commenced. Six hundred aeroplanes zoomed down to Hitler's box with deafening roars (but none engaged in any stunts or aerobatics), and then the great silver Zeppelin dipped its front in salute and rested motionless over the stadium. Mock aerial fights took place, the aim being to demonstrate the efficiency of the new anti-aircraft guns. Then a review was held of all ranks of the army, and with almost unpleasant realism a prolonged battle took place in the arena, to show how the new mechanized divisions could storm a defended post. The noise was deafening, the fight terribly real. But, even on a billiard-table surface, things could not go according to plan. The machine-gun nearest Hitler jammed; one of the two-men tanks dropped a piece of its armour; and there were many little confusions. It was odd to see the advancing infantry-men fling themselves on the ground, not naturally, but in so many precise movements, as on a parade-ground. For hours that afternoon, Nuremberg had all the experience of war, except for the ambulances and the burying-squads. A rally has no time for that side of war.

So the week closed—a triumph of organization and show-manship. A million and a quarter visitors were crammed into a town of 400,000 people, and every man—indeed, every guest—was moved about as if he were under orders. In fact, it was said that, amongst its many purposes, the Party Rally was a miniature mobilization. As a display of mass organization and as a colourful spectacle, the Rally could scarcely be surpassed ; but, as one left Nuremberg with Hitler's closing speech against the Bolsheviks ringing in one's ears, one wondered about many things. One felt deadened by the endless reiteration of a few simple motives. Everything was hammered in at a relentless pace, until one craved for solitude and quietness. Undoubtedly this was a new Germany one was seeing, with a new kind of patriotism ; but the values, clad with mysticism and pseudo-religious ceremonies though they were, made one conscious of an impassable mental gulf between Nazi Germany and the outside democracies. But Hitler is so certain of his movement that he has renamed Nuremberg ' the City of the Rallies ', and decreed in 1933 that the *Partei-Tag* was to be held there for all time. There he is building a special Congress City, and his latest plans include the levelling of a whole mountain to make room for his arenas. Nuremberg, with its fantastic medieval survivals, goes back to the beginnings of Germany ; Hitler plans to make it the permanent visible expression of the Party Rally. This linking of past and future is typical of the movement.

PART III

THE ECONOMICS OF HITLERISM

Chapter One

AUTARKY AND MARKETS

I.—The Doctrine of Self-sufficiency

At the background of everything in Germany is the economic problem. Even the ever-present drive for military strength is indissolubly connected with this, and it is a moot point whether economic matters are not considered primarily from the viewpoint of military strategy. It is realized on all sides that Hitlerism cannot hope to survive if it does not win out on the economic front.

Moreover, Hitler has elevated the economic question into a test case. His propaganda has made Germany believe that she is facing anew the situation of the Great War. Just as she was beleaguered at that time by the ring of allied armies and the naval blockade, so now she is facing a peacetime blockade that is no less serious. If anything, she views the present conditions as even more far-reaching, because they involve (in addition to the wartime issue of survival) the very continuance of National Socialism, which the Germans of to-day are taught to view as one of the greatest phenomena in all history.

To meet this pressing crisis, Germany has a simple economic theory—a theory on which she is staking everything, and to which she is subordinating every effort of her national life. This theory is the form of economic self-sufficiency or *Autarky*. It is argued that Germany must be able to stand alone economically. Otherwise her existence will be for ever dependent on the slightest whim of the foreign (and often potentially enemy) countries from whom she has derived her essential raw materials in the past. To obviate this weakness, she wants to make herself a self-sufficient citadel. She is always harping on the theme of *Encirclement*, and the people are convinced that a throttling economic encirclement by France, Czechoslovakia, and Russia can be just as devastating as an invasion. The result is that they now bring to the economic struggle the same emotion as they would to a war. To this degree Germany is a country suffering from a marked neurosis, and unfortunately, owing to the unnatural strains of the last twenty years, such a neurosis is singularly easy to implant.

But the German position has several obvious weaknesses. Geography has dealt meanly with her, and she still depends on outside countries for most of her essential raw materials.[1] If chemical processes cannot provide local substitutes, the struggle for self-sufficiency reduces itself into a constant effort to obtain funds with which to buy such raw materials from abroad. Although it is evident that it is contradictory to talk about self-sufficiency and at the same time rely on outside supplies, Germany still persists in her aim. While there has been some improvement of substitutes (*Ersatz* goods), the more immediate struggle has been to secure foreign credits (*Devisen*). When the full history of the last four years comes to be written, it will be seen how titanic this struggle has been. Dr. Schacht rightly says that his most important work has received no publicity.

At first the gold reserves were used, but these soon went ; and Germany then presented the amazing paradox of a country on a gold standard and yet with practically no gold reserves. At most the German gold cover is not quite 1 per cent, a fact which reduces conventional economic arguments to ridicule. Taking supplies of foreign exchange together with gold reserves, we see the story simply but drastically expressed in this table, showing the Reichsbank's holdings in millions of Reichsmarks :

November 30, 1929 2,637
1930 2,705
1931 1,175
1932 937

[1] See Section VI, below.

November 30, 1933	....	409
1934	....	83
1935	....	93
1936	....	72

Nothing could better demonstrate the economic plight of Germany in recent years.

When the emergency first became obvious, she tried to supplement her dwindling gold reserves by stringent acts to mobilize all available supplies of foreign currency. A *Law against the Betrayal of German Economy* was passed in June 1933, imposing severe penalties on all persons who concealed foreign assets. Such a threat resulted in the acquisition of 100,000,000 Reichsmarks in foreign exchange, but gold and *Devisen* were lost at so great a rate all through the rest of the year that the strictest measures were taken to prevent any flight of the currency and to reduce the amounts allowed to importers of goods from foreign countries. By the middle of 1934, imports were so controlled and rationed that only raw materials which were vital for Germany's rearmament were allowed to enter in as large quantities as were wanted. Similar conditions have pertained ever since, although at the moment there is a slightly more hopeful frame of mind in German trading circles.

Germany's next defensive measure was to lock up money already in the country. Great foreign companies, in particular, found it impossible to take away their profits. One American company even accepted several million harmonicas in an attempt to get its money out of Germany. But such evasions have obvious defects; and most of the companies with tied money preferred to put it into fixed assets or to embark on building programmes which they would not normally have started. As one German said, pointing to a hideous ultra-modern building erected by such a company : 'That is the way they are getting their revenge.' The drastic limitations on export of capital still exist, and to-day nobody is allowed to send more than ten marks a month out of Germany, and the expenditure of even that is closely supervised. A German sending money to relatives abroad must submit to the most detailed inquisition and have the amounts entered in his personal papers.

II.—*The Problem of Foreign Trade*

Such measures, however, were in the nature of safeguarding the already existing situation. They did nothing to improve it in the future. There were only two ways of doing this— either by cutting down imports or by increasing exports. It is the latter which has attracted most attention in the last three years, and which is to-day still in the forefront, despite the contrary theories of the Four Year Plan. The plain fact is that, if the wider movement of national regeneration is to continue, and if Germany is once more to take her place amongst the great nations under normal conditions, she must expand her foreign markets. The only alternatives are either a recourse to war or the complete success of the Four Year Plan ; and the Germans delude themselves into thinking that, even if the Plan succeeds, they can be self-sufficient in so far as imports are concerned and, at the same time, sell their exports to a gullible world outside. One arrives at the conclusion, then, that, either way, foreign markets are essential to her, since there is no other method of obtaining the foreign credits she wants so badly. As one cartoonist crudely but accurately expressed it : ' We must have markets or bust ' ; and if she ' busts ', the whole structure of Hitlerism is carried away as well.

Unfortunately for her plans, this effort coincided with the attempts of other countries to recover from the world economic crisis. It was a period of general restriction of world trade, whereas one of the basic premises of the German argument was that she should be able to pick her markets just as if the economic relationships between all outside countries were being conducted on a normal basis. Other countries had either evolved the idea of *Autarky* for themselves or taken a leaf from the German book, for, in these abnormal times, it fitted in equally well with their position and aspirations. If Germany could ruthlessly control her imports and check the trade of foreign countries with her (in the sacred name of National Socialism), they could just as easily close their markets against German goods (either for self-preservation or in pursuit of some will-o'-the-wisp theory) ; and this is exactly what happened.

Germany's export trade thus dwindled month by month. In desperation, Dr. Schacht introduced his famous *New Plan* in September 1934. The old method of restriction by quota and manipulation of foreign exchange had failed. It had led to a constant draining of the Reichsbank's resources, and the only way out of the difficulty was for some *New Plan* to reduce the volume of trade itself. By means of foreign-exchange permits, Dr. Schacht planned to restrict imports to the level of exports, so that there would be no drain on Germany's gold or on her holdings of foreign credits. In carrying out this policy there was to be a most comprehensive control of all imports. Expert bodies in Germany were to make careful monthly estimates, although they were to consider political and military factors as well as the purely economic. Licences were to be issued only for goods which could not conceivably be produced internally, and then only to carefully limited amounts. Simultaneously Germany concluded special clearing agreements with various creditor countries (twenty-six in all).

This restrictive policy was never viewed as the most desirable means of permanently satisfying Germany's wants ; it was only a makeshift measure to ensure survival then and there. At first it worked badly, mainly because the export trade from Germany failed to respond to the artificial stimuli, but also because the booming metal industries continued to clamour for foreign raw materials. In other words, the New Plan was based on an unrealizable harmony. Even within it the mutual parts were at variance with each other.

Month by month, then, imports kept up, while exports still dwindled. Finally, in March 1935, Dr. Schacht stated that all Germany's efforts had been nullified by the trade restrictions and currency tinkerings (with the resultant ' currency-dumping ' as he so aptly described it) of foreign countries. If Germany could not find markets for her manufactured goods, he went on, she would have to reconsider her entire position, because she could not continue to be a debtor to the extent of 25,000,000,000 marks a year—she who had been a creditor to that amount in the years before the war !

This desperate appeal led to a slight improvement in the situation, and, from March 1935 onwards, it was possible to keep imports and exports in equilibrium, although only at the cost of a great shrinkage in the total value of foreign trade. As her exports could not rise, she had to force down her imports, drastic though this was at a time of national rearmament and internal expansion of manufactures. But the ' necessary evil ' did at least convert the import surplus of 285,000,000 marks of 1934 into the small export surplus of 111,000,000 marks for 1935. This hardly-won valance saved National Socialism in Germany and opened up a more hopeful prospect of economic survival for the country, although the failure to win large export markets was still a limiting factor.[1]

Moreover, the improvement was more illusory than real, because the Reichsbank's holdings of foreign exchange had in no way improved. Exports were just paying for the absolutely essential imports, and were not sufficient to provide the additional raw materials needed to keep German workers fully employed or to cover the deficiency in food supplies. There was thus no great relief to be expected from ordinary exports ; and Schacht's other devices—such as barter—had not succeeded. No foreign exchange was derived from them.

Nevertheless, Germany has adhered to her policy of ' only buying what she can pay for ' and, by the strictest surveillance over imports, has maintained a consistent, but small, export surplus for every month of 1936. However this was not enough, because an analysis of the figures showed that the volume of exports was actually declining (a fact which was concealed by rises in export prices, and that the table was weighted in favour of imports, because the prices for many of the goods she had imported had fallen.

[1] Her export trade is still only a third of what it was in the years 1928–1930.

Despite the statistical improvement, the position thus became more and more threatening as the year went on, especially when Germany had used up the abnormal stocks of raw materials she had accumulated during the recent international crisis and found it necessary to replenish them. The dilemma remained, despite Schacht's *New Plan*. After all, that Plan only resembled the plight of a man who lacks money to buy sufficient food and who cuts down his purchases to the few pence he has. While his balance-sheet may be satisfactory, he must gradually starve. A realization of this led to the dramatic launching of a new policy at the Party celebrations of September 1936—the Four Year Plan which was to transform German economy, and which was to lead the people to the promised land of fat and plenty, under the guidance of General Göring with his peculiar method of mixed geniality and bullying. Its aim was to make Germany independent of imported raw materials within a period of four years.[1]

III.—*The Quest for Markets : The Schacht Offensive*

Another of Dr. Schacht's devices was barter, either the Stone Age system of direct exchange of goods for other goods, or the modern equivalent of barter, bilateral trade. Theoretically such methods had their points, but complications arose in practice. Various countries found it difficult to get the right kinds of goods from Germany in payment for the raw materials they had already handed over, a position which Germany has increasingly used for political ends as well as for her own economic benefit.

At first sight, barter arrangements would appear to mean the simple exchange of equivalent quantities of goods either between traders in different countries or through the medium of the respective governments. The Germans were the first to perceive that the matter could go far deeper than this. Indeed, this realization affords one of her main elements of strength at the moment.

[1] See Section IV, *infra*.

The working of the device is particularly instructive. The barter negotiations were aimed mainly at South America and (in accordance with Hitler's own wish) the countries of southern and central Europe. For a variety of reasons, imports from the United States and the whole of the British Empire[1] declined, so that Germany had to fall back on her traditional markets in south-eastern Europe, Spain, and South America (especially Brazil). Sanctions, of course, meant an increase of her trade with Italy, but this situation was exceptional.

The procedure has been similar in all cases. For a start, Germany would buy vast quantities of raw materials and agricultural produce from, say, Yugoslavia or Greece. When the Balkan growers began to press for payment, Germany retorted that payment could only take the form of goods ; and here came the rub. Since the middle of November 1935, Germany has imposed a series of embargoes on the export of certain manufactured goods, with a view to ensuring adequate supplies of these commodities for home consumption, especially if the international situation should become worse. That restriction left a narrower choice for the Balkan countries which had sold their crops to her and, in practice, often compelled them to take payment in the form of armaments or materials for public works. This meant that the Governments of those countries, in order to obtain some compensation for their exports, found themselves embarking on ambitious programmes of unproductive public expenditure which they would not otherwise have considered.

It is even asserted by many authorities that a political factor entered. If a Balkan country depends on Germany for its armaments, for replacements for those armaments, and for munitions for those armaments, it can be seen what an effective bargaining handle (to say the least) Germany has secured. Probably Germany at first did not realize that mere trading agreements could lead to such results, but she soon did so. I had this impressed on me from many quarters in Berlin, and several people insisted that this latest

---

[1] Except South Africa, where there was a special agreement to increase wool shipments.

form of commercial diplomacy, this inveigling of the over-seas flies into the German spider's web, was a marked contribution to international affairs, with Germany in a fortunate position, because she achieved so much before other countries realized what was in her mind. But such retrospective Machiavellism is rather forced, and it is probable that the position grew haphazardly.

As a result of such agreements with Greece and Yugoslavia, trade with those countries was diverted from other lands (incidentally their political allies) and given to Germany. France and the other Little Entente States became very perturbed, fearing that, rather than lose their 'frozen claims' in Germany, such countries as Yugoslavia might be inclined to follow economic ties with Germany by some form of political understanding. To give a fillip to German trade in these regions Dr. Schacht made a series of flights in the summer and autumn of last year, ranging over the Balkan capitals and going as far afield as Ankara.

The results he obtained were not as great as he expected. In August 1936, he laughed at the current suggestions that he had changed the economic face of southern Europe and insisted that he had merely made a rapid reconnaissance by air of very interesting country. He minimized the importance of anything that he had achieved, although talkative enough about his achievements in other fields.[1] I had the clear impression that the results of his Balkan peregrinations were potential rather than actual and that such peripatetic commercial diplomacy was not as simple as it sounded.

The Balkan countries apparently realized the drawbacks of the German system whereby 'influence follows trade', and Greece and Bulgaria in particular became restive about the ultimate results of such a system, far more so than Yugoslavia.

Nevertheless, Germany persists in the system, because it has worked so well in South America and Yugoslavia. It is the kind of *Realpolitik* that looks well on a map, and is perhaps the modern way of reviving the dreams of *Mitteleuropa*, with

[1] Dr. Schacht realizes quite well that the central and southern European markets take only one-tenth of Germany's exports.

the always troubled waters of the Near East farther afield. Carried to its extreme, such a policy means not only the securing of the raw materials she needs so badly at present, but also the building-up of 'tied markets' for the future, markets that are dependent at the least on goodwill and at the most on judiciously applied pressure.

Even if ultimate political pressure is ruled aside, Germany sees in such markets one of her weapons for preventing the crisis that would normally follow the bursting of the present internal boom. Of set purpose, she has deliberately speeded up production and created boom conditions. Normally, when the enlarged demands due to rearmament and the ambitious schemes of public works have subsided, she could expect a slump like the post-war crisis in Great Britain. The country's industrial structure would have been erected on an inflated standard of consumption, and, when the unusual conditions disappear, would have to be restricted, with all the depression and dislocation that this would involve—with all the outward failure that no dictatorship can bear.

Germany realizes that her armament activities cannot go on for ever, but she hopes, as these gradually subside, to replace the markets they have created by the new 'tied markets' she is obtaining in foreign countries by means of her barter agreements. 'Continuity of markets' is her present goal ; and she is confident that her methods will ensure these and that they will be of sufficient extent to enable her to stave off anything in the nature of a post-boom collapse. It is characteristic of her that she does not see that this is irreconcilable with the Four Year Plan.

Chapter Two

FINANCIAL JUGGLERY

I.—A Multiple-geared Currency

Lest this analysis should be thought somewhat far-fetched, and lest it should be imagined that foreign observers are reading too much into Germany's campaigns in the Balkans and South America, let us examine her currency position in relation to her export trade. Here again we have the same story, and in addition the clue to one of the most ingenious and amazing currency episodes, even in the history of crazy post-war finances. Germany has worked out a new device in currency control and, in effect, has carried the principle of currency management to its ultimate point. She has, in fact, rationalized it to serve the greatest variety of ends at the same time.

Briefly, the idea is to obtain what can be called ' a multiple-geared currency '. Having a currency with one fixed value is, in German eyes, on a par with running a motor-car with a single gear. It is far better if currency can be manipulated so as to provide the most suitable value for any given condition, especially if the State can benefit in the process. To obtain such elasticity, Germany has resorted to a most complicated series of manipulations of her banking structure and an elaborate system of blocked accounts. The result is that, on an analysis of the situation, one finds that there is not one, but a large variety of currency units in Germany ; and it would be most misleading to argue from the value of the mark as quoted at the ordinary foreign exchange rate and reckon German values in terms of that equivalent.

It is not a mere matter of a currency being over-valued or under-valued in relationship to other currencies. It is much more complicated than that ; it is a system whereby there is an infinite variation in the value of the mark ; the net result being that Germany pays as little as possible and gets as much as possible out of any given transaction. It is admitted that, in everyday German life, twenty-five differently valued marks are used ; and it has been asserted that if the investigator probes sufficiently deep into the German banking morass, and has the requisite technical knowledge, he can ultimately distinguish no fewer than two hundred and thirty-seven different values !

Quoting a simple example, one finds that the ordinary foreign exchange value of the mark is roughly twelve to the pound sterling. By the device of travellers' marks, however, the tourist obtains twenty-three to the pound, and he soon finds out that if his supply of registered marks runs out, he will have to pay just double for his expenses in Germany. Here, then, we have two different values for the same mark. Carry this one stage further and assume that I buy a book for a mark. If I buy it in Germany for a mark (obtained from a travellers' cheque), I pay a little over tenpence. If I buy it from London, with money purchased on the open market, I pay one shilling and eightpence. But if I buy it through official export agencies, I probably pay about fifteenpence, owing to various rebates, subsidies, the manipulation of foreign exchange for export purposes, and so forth.

Apply this system to the whole complicated structure of a modern State, and carry the system of blocked accounts to its logical conclusion, and you will see that there can be an endless variety of marks in Germany, each with a different purchasing power as applied to foreign countries. Germany first hit on this principle when she discovered in the early days of Hitlerism that certain of her holdings were quoted at varying discounts abroad. She soon used the difference between the external and the internal value of such holdings to improve her own position. By using various methods of persuasion, she would, in effect, buy at the external rate and sell at the internal value, pocketing the difference for the State. This was the way in which she made a profit out of the ever-increasing discount abroad on dollar bonds (ownership of which was concentrated in the Gold Discount Bank) and on blocked accounts standing in Germany to the credit of foreigners.

Then the principle was extended to apply to the various clearing and barter arrangements that have multiplied so rapidly in the last four years. The most important of these is the celebrated *Aski* device, a device ethically dubious but financially effective. This was applied to those countries which had no official clearing-house arrangement with Germany and which relied on barter. In such instances, special blocked accounts were set up in the names of foreigners, to be used in international payments. The foreigners at first acquiesced, because this saved them the bother of looking round until they could find a transaction that would exactly match the one they wanted, always the difficulty in an act of barter. They sold goods to Germany and received deposit credits from the special blocked accounts in Berlin. Then, in turn, they went on the open foreign market and sold these receipts to traders who wanted to import goods from Germany.

So far so good. But in the course of time, as Germany's economic position became gloomier, *Aski* marks began to depreciate ; and naturally, in a world cluttered up with varying customs and currency restrictions, such blocked *Aski* marks came to have different values in different countries. As Germany immediately realized, the existence of such discounts (often substantial) meant in effect a reduction in the selling-price of German goods which they are used to purchase. In other words, they became a stimulus to exports and thus a vital aid to the purchase of raw materials abroad. They gave her the advantages of devaluing her currency without any of the drawbacks.

In the end, German officials began to regulate the *Aski* market, until it came practically to mean a different value of the German mark for export purposes in every country. In this way she surmounted to a certain degree the great obstacle imposed on her export trade by reason of a currency which was over-valued in the ordinary foreign exchange markets. She came to conduct practically all of her foreign trade in marks devalued from 20 per cent to 80 per cent.

It is beside the point to argue that this deliberate diversification of the country's currency is of doubtful morality, because the German view is that, in the strained conditions of to-day, international trade is as much a battleground as any war could be. Indeed, she has made finely organized systems out of what were originally accidents favouring Germany. She has evolved an ingenious collection of supplements to the discount on *Aski* marks. Sometimes these take the form of varying barter premiums to importers of German goods in foreign countries ; sometimes they become special grants to certain imports into Germany, varying of course for the different countries. A complicated structure of Investigating Agencies exists to look into each particular case and, in effect, vary the value of the German mark for that particular case. That is why there are hundreds of values for the mark, even though it is quoted continuously at twelve to the pound sterling.

The final commentary on the whole system is given by the exclusion from *Aski* and barter arrangements of those goods in which Germany possesses some kind of monopoly. Since she can demand any price for these, they can be bought only for cash, not with *Aski* marks. Ingenuity can go no further than this, though whether it is the best way to promote economic goodwill between the nations is another point.

It will be understood from these instances, then, how Germany has evolved a currency system with an infinite degree of flexibility. It is complicated and abnormal, but it serves its purpose, although it must require a super-mind to unravel and piece together such a multiplicity of banking accounts. It is said that Dr. Schacht and Dr. Fischer (of the *Kreditgesellschaft*) are the only two men in Germany who can find their way through the morass.

Another result of the system is that there seems to be no reason for devaluation of the German mark at present. Most German authorities are agreed on this. On the surface, Germany has a grossly over-valued currency, and is tied to gold when in reality she has no gold backing. But this is far from being the truth. As a result of a flexible and managed currency, the main significance of the mark (standing at twelve to the pound sterling) is that she is able to buy her raw materials from abroad at a particularly advantageous rate. She can also meet her large interest payments abroad at a favourable rate.[1] Normally this would have involved getting unduly small returns for the goods she exported, as foreign buyers would have to pay in over-valued marks, but we have seen how she overcame this by her multiple-geared currency. This being so, and since she already has a separately valued mark to meet most contingencies, why should she upset the whole elaborate system by devaluation, when she has nothing to gain and when she would have to face a grave internal crisis because of the psychological fears that devaluation would mean a repetition of the inflation of thirteen years ago ? It would be different if there were any prospect of a large increase of her export markets, but the universal restrictions in other countries rule this out. Moreover, devaluation would deal a shrewd blow to Hitler's prestige at home. The head of one of the big German banks told me that, even if devaluation was economically desirable, a dictatorship could not introduce it without weakening its position. 'Every new proposal of a dictator must appear a national gain, and it would be impossible to present devaluation in this light.'

At the moment, then, devaluation would mean a positive loss to Germany. Hitler has apparently burned his boats in this connexion, for, when France devalued in September 1936, the inspired German Press construed this as a sign of French weakness and promised that the German mark, 'the soundest currency unit in the world', would never follow the French franc. The relief of the people at this was most marked, because the generation that had seen everything wiped out by uncontrolled inflation had no wish to repeat the experiment, and the people do not believe that such terms as 'reflation' or 'realignment' mean anything but currency collapse.

The only drawback would be if Germany had a large balance of payments in her favour, as in pre-war days, and if

[1] Her foreign debt is now thirteen billion marks. It was reduced by at least five billions when various of her creditors devalued their currencies.

she got only twelve marks for every pound that was owed her ; but, as we have seen, she is now a debtor country and is most unlikely to become a large creditor in the near future. Devaluation thus remains a technical question in Germany ; and the more localist her economy becomes (as with the Four Year Plan) the more the arguments for devaluation recede into the background.

Germany, then, must maintain a constant struggle. To get raw materials she must find markets ; to find markets she must resort either to bilateral agreements or to barter ; to make them pay she must manipulate the currency by such devices as *Aski* marks and must continue her policy of sub-sidizing exports within the country.[1] Coincidently with this she must constantly be altering the direction of her foreign trade to prevent any unfavourable balances, because her entire system is so precariously maintained that any large unfavourable balance will upset the whole structure. That is why she has to close down on purchases from ' bad custo-mers ' like Australia. If she needs Australian wool, as she does, she is forced to do what she did in the three years before 1936—buy it second-hand from Great Britain ; because she exports to Britain half as much again as she imports from her. It even pays her to incur the extra middleman's charges by purchasing partly manufactured Australian wool through Britain, rather than to make payments to ' bad customers '. There is no feeling about Australia in all this ; the problem is approached only as a part of Germany's general foreign policy.[2] In German eyes, she must have ' equal trade ' with each country or group of related countries, or she will break down and lose everything, Hitlerism included. Her argu-ment is that each country, even those producing raw materials like the British Dominions, must arrange a balance of trade. Ireland and South Africa were the first to do so. New Zealand followed, and Germany holds that it is up to Australia and countries similarly placed to do likewise. We may not

[1] This means that she is sacrificing her manufactured goods for less than they are worth. By comparison with 1921, she is giving away twice as many goods for any given number of marks.

[2] She started buying directly from Australia again in 1936.

agree with such an extreme bilateralism, but with Germany it is an ineradicable part of her whole programme of national regeneration.

II.—*Meeting the Bill*

In considering the general background of this peculiar condition of industry, one is confronted again and again by a single question : How is Germany able to keep going from month to month ? How is she averting collapse with her unconventional methods of finance ?

The main answer to this is that she survives because she is giving no reckoning. She is postponing the evil day as long as possible, and in the interim keeps people in the dark. She has no budget estimates, no discussions in Parliament, no presentations of departmental accounts, no annual stock-taking, no facing of criticism.

Her last budget estimates were for 1934–5, a year which closed with a deficit of 354,000,000 marks, bringing the total accumulated deficits up to 2,464,000,000 marks. Since then critics have lacked any information, and the announced intention of the Government is to present no budget until ' the great experiment' should allow a total summing-up. Even apart from the huge armaments bill, Government expenditure has been increasing in all directions, without any commensurate growth of revenue. The Government claims to have increased its annual revenue by 2,600,000,000 marks in the last three years, and at the same time to have reduced its expenditure on unemployment relief by 1,500,000,000 marks, but Dr. Reinhardt, the permanent head of the Finance Ministry, recently issued an urgent appeal to tax-collectors to be more stringent. Throughout 1936 it was felt that the ever-rising financial needs of the Nazi State would necessitate new taxation, and the subject became such a sore one that editors who mentioned it in their newspapers were punished. The Government was admittedly loath to lay any new burdens on an already overtaxed people, but Count Schwerin von Krosigk, the Minister of Finance, had to admit that, even with the increased revenue, expenditure was not being met ; and undoubtedly the situation has recently become worse.

The fundamental weakness of the position is that over 98 per cent of the Reichsbank's note-cover is represented by short-term State bonds which may easily become worthless. The Nazi State is being financed by short-term loans. Hitler was able to survive by doing so, because nobody in Germany could demand a reckoning, and he naturally refrained from offering one. The only information he has vouchsafed is that, between his advent to power in January 1933 and June 1935, the public debt of Germany increased sevenfold, from 348,000,000 to 2,640,000,000 pounds sterling. This, it will be noted, was before the greater part of the expenditure on armaments.

The theory behind this expenditure is that the new schemes (such as the absorption of the unemployed and, later on, rearmament) should be financed in their initial stages by State credits, the amount of which should not be disclosed lest the public become alarmed. As time went on, these would gradually be incorporated in the current national budgets, but no budget was to be presented until the time was ripe. Ultimately they would be consolidated in long-term loans.[1]

While the various official figures about expenditure and floating debt are obviously incomplete (and sometimes contradictory), it is clear that a start has been made in the direction of consolidation. Compulsory loans have been obtained from the banks and the insurance companies ($4\frac{1}{2}$ per cent loans of 2,000,000,000 marks for long periods), and several of the short-term loans have been converted into medium-term issues. All through 1935 and 1936, the big companies were induced to make so-called 'voluntary' loans, until the armament firms complained that they could no longer bear this burden in addition to the heavy increase in their costs already imposed by the activities of the new Labour Front (a charge estimated at 8 per cent of their costs of production).

[1] They are issued for three months, then turned into a commercial bank ; and then renewed indefinitely for further periods of three months, at $4\frac{1}{2}$ per cent interest.

In the end, the incapacity of industry to carry the burdens put an end to further conversions. Dr. Schacht had already met much opposition because of his levy on industry, a levy which aimed at 1,000,000,000 marks for the purpose of subsidizing exports; and it was claimed further that the initial levies which were imposed when new companies were formed (ranging from 15 per cent to 35 per cent and averaging 25 per cent) were stultifying progress. What the Government was achieving by expansion of credit, on the one hand, was being neutralized by excessive levies on the other. Companies were unable to maintain their net profits, and the public were losing faith in private industrial ventures. The bubble of the boom was being pricked by excessive Governmental levies, and Dr. Schacht was compelled to call a halt, even though it meant postponing his efforts to consolidate the financial position.

His problem then resolved itself into the question whether Germany could prevent a breakdown in the next few years, assuming that he could postpone his reckoning for so long a period. Industrialists and commercialists in Germany with whom I conversed are convinced that Germany *can* hold out during this interim period, provided that no additional expenditure on a large scale is incurred on the Nazi Party or Labour Service camps or similar institutions. They say that the gap between revenue and expenditure is diminishing, that the peak of expenditure on rearmament has been passed, that most of the town budgets have already balanced, and that the State finances are becoming more hopeful. On the whole, an investigation in Germany to-day shows that the towns have faith in this ultimate hope of redemption, while the country districts are not so sanguine. The countrymen are afraid of collapse and are inclined to hoard their products, pinning their faith to material goods as they did in the old days of inflation and mistrusting the paper jugglery both of the Nazi Government and of Dr. Schacht's financial wizards. The townsmen would risk everything on a more venturesome policy of industrial expansion; they think that the only way out nowadays is to career along on the crest of events; they prefer a dynamic policy to ruin. The country dwellers, on the other hand, look backwards to the bitter experiences of the past, and see in the present unnatural boom only a repetition of the false prosperity that preceded the previous collapses. Firm-rooted in the soil, they are unwilling to take risks and mistrust the newfangled theories. It must be admitted that, of the two attitudes, the sheer opportunism of the townsmen is far more in accord with the ideology of National Socialism, but, even in the towns, there is little conviction. Their attitude is rather the devil-may-care bravado of a man in inextricable difficulties than a moderate and reasoned pursuit of what is desirable. They are plunging desperately, believing that this chance of success, slight though it may appear, is the only alternative to collapse and chaos.

Chapter Three

THE INTERNAL BOOM : HITLERISM AND INDUSTRY

I.—*The Position of Industry*

The other side of the new German economy has been the deliberate creation of an internal boom, alike for economic, political and psychological reasons. For some years before Hitler came to power, Germany had suffered from a contractionist policy. The volume of credit had been steadily reduced, and this was accompanied by a decline in production and a staggering increase in unemployment. The only consolation was that Germany had the basic materials for stimulating activity afresh when the time was deemed ripe, because the expenditure of foreign loans some time before this had led to 'the rationalization boom' of 1926-9, the result of which was that Germany had probably the most up-to-date factory system in Europe.

When Hitler became Chancellor, it was decided that the time had come to reverse the policy of credit contraction and create an internal boom. Six million people were unemployed, and the new régime could not hope to survive unless they were given work.

The Government's plan was a simple and direct one—to use the Reichsbank for the steady expansion of credit facilities and to finance ambitious programmes of public works. The works were paid for by 'public-works bills'; the Reichsbank made these eligible for rediscount, took up a large number of them itself, and encouraged other banks to do so. To the end of 1936, anything up to fifteen billions of marks were thus used as liquid short-term investments. Credit was created, and yet the amount of notes in circulation tended, if anything, to decrease in the next few years. Within the short space of three years, the total volume of Reichsbank credit alone expanded by no less than 2,700,000,000 Reichsmarks, as the following table shows.

Reichsbank holdings of Treasury and other bills.

November 30, 1929	......	2,410	To these must be added
1930	......	2,109	bills of the associated
1931	......	3,957	Gold Discount Bank.
1932	......	2,766	 343
1933	......	3,027	 263
1934	......	3,856	 214
1935	......	4,151	 1,443
1936	......	4,909	

It must be remembered that the great degree of centralization in the German banking system helped this creation of cheap credit. The ordinary commercial banks do not require the high cash-ratio that is customary with us. They lean more directly on the Central Bank; and conversely any creation of Reichsbank credit eases the money market more directly and more rapidly than in a system where the private banks are stronger.

This new credit was used to finance public works, building schemes, and of course, the new rearmament programme. But the resultant boom was peculiar in this—that it was due to public investments rather than to any tremendous private enterprise; and its main result was more in the absorption of unemployed than in any large increase of ordinary share prices. Indeed, the private capital market has been rendered almost stagnant by the demands of public authorities, and that is where the present boom differs from earlier ones.

Nevertheless, it led to a tremendous growth in industrial activity. Germany has increased her industrial output far more than any other nation in the last four years.[1] Yet the increase was not a natural one. The greatest part of it was

[1] In the first three years of Hitlerism alone, the increase was 87 per cent. Compare Britain's 35 per cent and the United States' 49 per cent.

for capital goods, not consumers' goods. It was for armaments, machines, and cement, not for such products as textiles or food derivatives. That is why the recovery has
been such a limited and temporary one. The general share-
index of the *Statistisches Reichsamt*, for instance, showed a
marked annual decline for every year from 1928 to 1934,
and the figures have risen in the last three years only because
of the enormous rearmament programme.[1] The foundries
and shipyards are busy, but the community as a whole has
less purchasing power. Retail turnover has not increased
since the depression.

It is impossible to determine how much Germany has
spent on armaments in recent years, because no figures are
officially quoted. The Finance Minister, Count Schwerin
von Krosigk admitted, however, that the decision to rearm
changed the entire national economy. 'The rearmament
of Germany, viewed economically,' he said, ' has taken the
place of the original policy, which was to provide work
for the unemployed.' It has been rather wildly asserted
by some British politicians that Germany spent £800,000,000
sterling on armaments in the year 1935 alone, but an analysis
of the statistics used to support this claim shows that it is
untenable. The figure should probably be divided by three.
Even with the elasticity of credit provided by the structure
of the Reichsbank, it is inconceivable that Germany should
spend on arms in one year alone the total amount of the
British budget. Credit expansion cannot be carried to that
length. All that can be said is that the vastly increased expenditure has gone on unproductive works and armaments ;
under German conditions it would require a magician to be
more explicit.

It is difficult to write of the place of the industrialists in
the German system. Fantastic stories that Hitler came to
power as the nominee of the Thyssen group may be dismissed. Apart from relatively small contributions, Hitler
did not receive much support from the industrialists until
1930, when Fritz Thyssen of the Ruhr, badly hit by the

[1] The rise in 1936 was most marked—from 90.4 in 1935 to 104.7 in
December 1936, taking 100 as the figure for all shares from 1924 to 1926.

depression, swung into line behind him. The Krupp group did not come until later, for Krupp von Bohlen even opposed Hitler in the presidential election of 1932.

The truth seems to be that Hitler, in common with other political leaders, received subsidies from various industrialists ; but, once in power, went his own way. The industrialists found themselves checked in many directions. The cartel legislation kept prices down ; dividends over 6 per cent were ' held at the disposal of the Government ' ; levies were imposed to aid exports ; employers were forced to keep on unnecessary employees, and at times to scrap modern machinery ; and contributions for all kinds of Party purposes were imposed. Consequently, it was not until the armaments' boom of 1935 onwards that heavy industry revived and even then the lighter industries (such as textiles) and the commercial sections failed to benefit. If Thyssen had been the real power behind the scenes, the result would have been very different. On the other hand, Hitler has done nothing to break the power of the big industrial combines. Indeed, one of the striking features of his four years of power has been the rise of super-trusts in the heavy industries, especially of the Thyssen and Flick interests.[1]

The large industrialists have suffered from the rise of Hitlerism just as little as have the Junkers. Article 13 of the Party programme, demanding the nationalization of all trusts, thus becomes a quaint historical survival. The position, then, seems to be that most of the heavy industrialists have been saved from the aftermath of the depression by Hitler's armament programme. They are gaily careering along a path of expansion and, for lack of a more stable condition of affairs, acquiesce in a dashing but somewhat risky policy. In return for being allowed even this grace, they submit to the tributes Hitler exacts from them. But to say that Hitler is a puppet pulled hither and thither by the Thyssens seems inaccurate. The real test of strength will come when the armaments boom is ended.

[1] e.g., *The Vereinigte Stahlwerke A.G.*, of November 1933.

II.—*The Position of Labour*

In the first days of the boom, if the aim was to reduce unemployment, the Government's steps were undoubtedly successful. When Hitler came to power, at least six million of the twenty million workers of Germany were unemployed. Since that time the official statistics naturally tell only part of the story. They do not take into account the Marxians, Socialists, Jews, and Pacifists who have lost their jobs and are cut off from relief; such persons do not appear in the official figures of unemployment. The refugees are ignored. In addition, at least a million people have been absorbed in the Army, the labour-service camps, the Nazi organizations, and various partly paid forms of labour on public works. Half a million women have been taken off the labour market in the last four years by means of the marriage allowance paid by the Government to entice them away.

With these and many other limitations, the official figures show a steady growth of employment. Germany now has 1,000,000 people on her official lists as unemployed,[1] but the Government has constantly insisted that many of those who figure as 'employed' have extraordinary occupations which cannot be indefinitely prolonged. It is their point of view that only a return to normal trade conditions (including export trade) can really solve the unemployment problem. What they have done has been to introduce a series of emergency steps which have drastically reduced the number of unemployed; but such steps, by their very nature, are in many cases temporary. On the other hand, the reduction by 5,000,000, however artificially it may have been achieved, has had a tremendous propaganda value for the Government, and it is the fixed belief of most Germans to-day that Hitler has achieved wonders in providing employment. There is a ceaseless propaganda contrasting his efforts with the policy of drift in, say, France and Great Britain. On the other hand, another side of the picture is shown by the official

[1] End of 1936.

admission that no fewer than twelve and a half million people received assistance from the Nazi Relief Fund in the winter of 1935. The *Winterhilfe* campaign is a marked feature in the German year, and the highest Nazi leaders have been known to come out on the streets and jingle collecting-boxes. Even Hitler has been unable to cope with the seasonal increase in unemployment every winter.

Labour conditions remain in a most peculiar position in Germany. So many special local factors exist that comparisons with conditions in other countries are ruled out. Amongst these, to take a few of the more obvious, are the huge Nazi machine (which duplicates practically all Government departments and which sets up new ones like the Labour Front) ; the provision of all kinds of nation-wide organizations such as the Hitler Youth, with large permanent staffs ; the compulsory labour-service of all youth ; the concentration camps[1] ; the labour camps (for beggars and parasites) ; the new military conscription ; the Göring Plan to take youths from the towns to the farms ; the withdrawal of whole classes of the community (like Jews) from many sections of the labour market ; the enforced ' spreading of labour ' (and the consequent carrying of unduly large personnel) in offices and factories ; and, last but by no means least, the full-time members of the S.A., S.S., and the Party.

It is a very moot point what the conditions of labour are in Germany to-day. According to the officials, wages have remained constant for the last three years, but the worker receives much more in the way of additional benefits. The average return for manual labour in Germany (averaging all forms of skilled and unskilled labour) is 120 marks a month, for a working week of forty-eight hours. Every worker belongs to the new and interesting body known as the Labour Front[2] and, as a member, receives special housing facilities, cheap travel for holidays, reduced rates for sport and enter-

---

[1] Germany insists that only six concentration camps still exist, with 3,694 political offenders and 1,067 habitual criminals. But this does not include camps or prisons maintained by the State Secret Police or various local authorities.

[2] See Part IV, Chapter 3, *infra*.

tainments, and many other concessions.[1] Hitlerite Germany
is reviving the Bismarckian expedient of ' social oil ', the free
use of palliatives to keep the workers in a satisfied frame
of mind. Rents are controlled, so that the average worker's
flat costs from twenty-four to fifty marks a month ; and
the prices of foodstuffs are kept within fixed limits. All
the weapons of autocracy are used in this connexion, the
result being, according to the Government, an increase in
the real value of wages in the last four years. Labour newspapers, published in places outside Germany like Basle,
query this claim and assert that real wages have gone down
by anything up to 40 per cent—a claim which my own
investigations supported.[2]

An observer's impression is that the Government's policy
in this regard has been reasonably successful in cities like
Berlin and Munich, but that the standard of living remains
undoubtedly low in the Rhineland industrial regions, while
much genuine distress exists in such areas as Westphalia and
Silesia. There have been complaints even in some of the
model factory foundations, such as the motor-manufacturing
works at Rüsselsheim near Heidelberg ; and the claims that
the Government has removed all the grievances of the workers
of Hamburg are easily disproved. Certainly there has been
great progress here and elsewhere in the removal of slums,
especially in the areas of Berlin and Hamburg that were
formerly so notorious. The scheme to provide new houses
for workers has gone far. At the moment, Hitler favours
the erection of single-family residences in place of the barrack-
like aggregations of flats that sprang up a few years ago. In
his own words : ' The day when every German worker
possesses a house and a plot of his own, Communism will
disappear from the land.' Activity in this direction seems
recently to have been subordinated to the construction of
public buildings and armaments.

It is impossible to assess the true position, because strikes

[1] The workers, however, have to pay 900,000,000 marks a year in dues
to the Labour Front.

[2] The *Neues Tagebuch* in Paris is of the same opinion. Its economic
expert, Haniel, is, however, an anti-Hitlerite.

are forbidden and agitators are visited with all the penalties for sabotaging the interests of the Third Reich. The officials at the central offices of the Labour Front insisted repeatedly that there is no longer any need to use the instruments of autocracy, but the fact remains that they are always there in the background, and no survey of the German labour position can be complete without stressing them. So, too, the control of the Press prevents such discontent as does exist from becoming vocal. The official attitude is that no complaints exist anywhere, and that 20,000,000 workers, many of them well organized in private armies of their own, have swallowed the strong medicine of National Socialism without any demur. To talk like this is to insult one's intelligence. The many whispering campaigns alone would refute such a statement, even were it not so transparently at variance with the facts of human nature.

The most obvious feature of the whole stiuation is that the German labourer, be he Nazi or non-Nazi, is no longer free. The authorities admit this and glory in it. 'He is no longer free, that is true—no longer free to starve.' The element of constraint is everywhere. Labourers and employers alike are viewed as peace-time soldiers working for the interests of the nation ; and, in last resort, the same kind of sanctions apply to them. The State is everything. But this doctrine has its limits. The worker may be content to give up his freedom, he may make no demur about carrying a kind of labour passport and being forbidden to move from district to district ; but he at least expects efficiency in return, and he will not accept ration-cards (with the clear suggestion of failure that these imply) without complaint.

THE FIGHT FOR RAW MATERIALS AND SUBSTITUTES

Existence under modern industrial conditions reduces itself to a constant struggle for raw materials, and modern international history can be written in terms of deficiencies in such raw materials. There are thirty-four vital materials without which a nation cannot live, and unfortunately, Germany is worse off than any other great State in so far as these are concerned. Whereas the British Empire is largely dependent on outside sources for only nine of these, Germany has only two in ample quantities—potash and coal. That means that she must turn to the foreigner for all of her supplies of twenty-six of these and for part of six more. Yet this is the Power that sees fit to launch a plan for complete self-sufficiency. It is ludicrous, unless she looks forward to obtaining control of the vast raw materials of central Europe or the lands behind the Ukraine by some adventurous foreign policy. Even Italy, whose economic position is usually looked on as very weak, has a third of the essential materials. Yet the mass of Germans are so inflamed by official propaganda that they believe Hitler when he says that Germany must, and can, stand alone.

Germany relies on her chemists. She conquered nitrates, she conquered indigo, she conquered silk, and she holds she can conquer her other deficiencies by the same methods. So far her efforts have been mainly directed towards rubber, wool, and petrol. Since 1932 she has been producing *Buna*, synthetic rubber, in large quantities (although not yet on a paying basis), and Hitler claims that the artificial product is anything up to a third more durable than real rubber.

Her fight for wool is an older one and dates back to one

day in May 1921, when the Patents Office affixed its double-eagle seal on Patent No. 62613, which dealt with what seemed the chimerical proposal to convert wood into wool. Production began next year, and the Germans made no secret of their methods. Models of the complicated machinery may be seen working in the Deutsches Museum in Munich. Vistra was a glassy-looking substance that was not much use by itself; but in 1926 the mixture of Vistra and wool in equal quantities produced the substance known as Wollstra, which is to-day the basis of Germany's efforts to make synthetic textile materials. The production of this was en-widened in 1933, and I was told that important new cloths were to be made after this year.

The great dye combination—the I.G.—acted practically as a Government agent in controlling this artificial production, and several of their officials told me what progress had been made and what difficulties had been encountered. At first the technical obstacles were many. The new fabrics would not withstand rain. There is the story of a representative of a colonial government who had bought a substitute raincoat and boasted of it at the Foreign Office. The official there sent out an order: 'For goodness' sake detail somebody to look after him and at all costs keep him out of the rain!' This defect has been largely overcome. The substitutes can now stand showers, but not heavy soaking rain. A deplorable sight in Germany is to see a row of cheap German hats (made of artificial wool) after rain.

The chemists went a certain way and then stopped. Clever as they are, they seem to be able to go no farther, and German industry to-day must content itself with producing large quantities of artificial woollen products with all their present defects, unless, as one official said to me, 'we stumble on what we want'. It is admittedly easier to spin with Vistra than with real wool, because of the uniform length of the fibre, but the problem of 'scratching' still remains, and the experts have not been able to produce a curling fibre or to secure the necessary flexibility. The artificial cloths have a cold flabby feeling, like flexible glass, and most of them have no warmth. That is why Germans will rather have one suit of 'English cloth' than three of the mixed local material. Every shop in Germany distinguished between the local textiles and 'English cloth', which always had the place of honour. It is the mark of good tailoring with the young blood in Nazidom to have an English suit. An official concerned with production ruefully admitted to me that the whole scheme seemed to be breaking down on the rock of public taste. As soon as the people were getting more prosperous with the internal armaments boom, they were wanting imported cloths. The saddest man I met in Germany was a well-known Munich tailor whose clients were from the wealthy class, but who could not replace his dwindling supplies of West-of-England cloth, however much he was offered. 'I have only a few metres of Irish material for their white vests, and next month they will have to have dress vests made from wood,' he moaned.

In the last couple of years Germany has found that she has to mix an ever-increasing proportion of natural wool to produce a good serviceable cloth, and apparently the mixture most favoured at the moment is two-thirds wool and one-third Vistra.

For a time it was compulsory to dilute natural wool with a certain proportion of Vistra, but this is no longer the case, although it still applies to cotton goods. It is most significant that Germany has recently been considering Vistra as more suitable for mixture with other substances than wool, so far has she given up the fight. The I.G. combine has a great advertising campaign to show the advantages of mixing Vistra with cotton, linen, and other materials. One advertisement displayed everywhere shows flax and Vistra walking hand in hand along the road that leads to German salvation. That is, the substitute first devised to mix with wool is now found more useful in conjunction with other materials. 'We would solve wool,' I was told, 'if wool did not have such peculiar characteristics.' But, as it is, Wollstra seems no more successful (as compared with natural wool) than the Lanital which the Italians are making from the casein in milk. In both cases enormous quantities of cloth are being made, and in both cases the public will buy either because of suasion or cheapness ; but neither Wollstra nor Lanital can be compared with real wool. This is demonstrated by the fact that, when Germany had a trade quarrel with Australia (her greatest supplier of fine merino wool) she had to buy Australian wool indirectly through British middlemen, despite the extra charges. Even to-day, when all the emphasis is on the Four Year Plan, and when foreign exchange is so short, Germany is enlarging her purchases of wool. It is one thing for Hitler to say that Germany will be independent of outside supplies in eighteen months, but quite another when it comes to closing the outside wool markets, so much so that one wonders how far the Four Year Plan has been mooted for purposes of internal propaganda.

It is more difficult to ascertain the position regarding the production of local petrol. There are masses of propaganda on the point, and the officials concerned will readily give figures about production ; but it is almost impossible to ascertain the truth. Visiting statesmen have been told that it would be inadvisable for them to see the most modern plants, even in cases where they have been interested in buying German patents for their own countries ; and the ordinary investigator is put off by the excuse that the patents are under Dutch control and the applicant has to wait until assent comes from Holland.

The production of oil from coal is, indeed, looked on as part of Germany's military preparations, and the same secrecy applies. I know of one representative of an overseas government whose perfectly innocuous notes on coal were taken from him at the frontier. On two points the Germans are loquacious—on data that can be easily obtained from the British works at Billingham, and on estimates of future production that will make Germany self-sufficient in a couple of years, and that, if extended mathematically, will soon allow the German-made petrol to deluge the world market. Nobody ever doubted the mathematical ability of the Germans !

The ascertainable facts are as follow : The German efforts in this connexion go back a long way, even to before the war. At present, production is based on two sets of patents, one belonging to the *I.G. Farbenindustrie* (this is the set being used extensively in England, France, Russia, Spain, and elsewhere abroad), and the newer ones, known as the Fischer Process, a method developed by Dr. Fischer, the head of the *Kaiser Wilhelm Institut für Kohleforschung*. The dye combine is in practical control of the experiments, and it is said that no direct governmental expenditure is involved. But what happens is that the Government imposes a heavy import duty of almost twenty-two marks per hundred kilogrammes on benzine from abroad, as compared with a low excise duty of one mark for an equivalent amount of benzine from indigenous raw materials. The difference is really a subsidy to the local substitutes. In addition, the importers are subject to certain other charges.

The main centre of the German experiments is Leuna, two hours from Berlin, and the synthetic product is marketed through the Leuna pumps which the motorist sees everywhere in Germany. At present German cars run on a mixture of 40 per cent local benzol, 10 per cent alcohol, and 50 per cent foreign gasolene, and there is much inspired propaganda to the effect that this is better than foreign brands which, according to the propaganda, rely largely on cheap Rumanian products.

It is stated that no technical difficulties remain in the way of producing petrol from black or even from brown coal. Three factories belonging to the Brown Coal Company started production in payable quantities last April; and, while figures of production must be looked on with some reserve, it is an undeniable fact that, despite the great increase in consumption in the last two years owing to the formation of a new mechanized army, imports of gasolene from abroad have been stationary, in the vicinity of 3,000,000 tons. A year from now is the date Hitler has chosen for complete self-sufficiency in petrol, but, as against this, the international importing companies say that the time limit is too optimistic. Despite constant governmental threats to nationalize their industry, they base their continued expectation of life in Germany on a much longer period. On the other hand,

Leuna alone is said to be producing a third of a million tons a year without loss (if the Government diversion of duty on foreign benzine is taken into account), and it is claimed that five new factories will be producing by the end of this year.[1] If production figures are cut down to a third of the official estimates, they probably show the true situation.

On the other hand, officials state that there does not yet exist a process for the production of gas-oil at a reasonable rate. The main interest in this question is whether Germany's boast that she can become self-sufficient in so short a time will be justified, and especially whether, in the interim, costs of production will have so fallen that the present bonus will be no longer necessary. If this gap is not bridged, large Government subsidies will be necessary, because the price of petrol is already high in Germany and cannot be increased much more.

Germany is also experimenting with other forms of substitute fuel. Satisfactory results are obtained from wood-fuel, a delegate to a recent international traffic conference in London driving his car from Berlin to London on such fuel at a cost of only ten marks. Still more recently, it was announced that the Schichau process of using pulverized coal had passed its test, and high hopes are entertained that this Darmstadt process (which necessitates a special form of engine) will provide Germany with an important source of power.

It is still too soon to pass verdicts on such experiments, except in so far as they show Germany's fixed desire to make herself independent of foreign supplies. One of my strongest impressions of Germany was in the office of a highly placed executive charged with producing artificial petrol. Flourishing a document on his desk, he said : ' This is too important to be ignored or overlooked. It is an order from the *Führer* that Germany shall never again be in the position she was in once last year, when her whole foreign policy, at the

---

[1] If 600,000 tons are produced (the figures anticipated for 1937), this would supply the country's needs for motor transport ; but it should be noted that Germany uses 4,000,000 tons of petrol in all every year. In addition to gasolene, she produces nearly a million tons of crude wood alcohol and benzol yearly.

moment of reoccupying the Rhineland, was in jeopardy owing to inadequate supplies of petrol. This order is that self-sufficiency must be quickly achieved, whatever the cost may be.' It is indeed a topsy-turvy state of affairs, when one remembers that oil could be bought abroad and stored in Germany for one-fifth the cost of making it locally, but a fixed design of foreign policy is allowed to override all economic considerations, however much the normal life of the nation may be warped in so doing. While the rest of the world is talking of over-production and dumping of oil, Germany is arguing that her national survival depends on artificially producing her own oil, at any cost. She can doubtless do so, if she can find the five or six hundred million marks it will cost every year.

After all, this fight for *Ersatz* goods is bound to fail. Assuming that Hitler made Germany produce enough rubber, wool and petrol, she would in no sense be able to stand alone. The most vital matter of all—vegetable oils—would still remain unsolved ; and what of the nickel and tungsten for her army, the chromium for her armour-plates, the Yugoslavian bauxite for the aluminium alloys she uses so much, the antimony and the molybdenum, the asbestos and the vanadium ? In time of stress she would still have to resort to the time-honoured method of accumulating stores of these from abroad, for without them her factories would close, her air arm would be paralysed, and she could not use her mechanized forces over a long period. Since she can never hope to produce or replace these materials, her present policy is based on an untenable bifurcation of existence. It is on a par with making a country immune from air attack and yet making no provision against starvation. Cotton, jute, flax, manila, hemp—one might go on indefinitely in Germany's case. She has only a third of the iron she needs ; her copper comes from Chile, and she even has to import certain varieties of coal which she must have in her foundries. On the other hand, a sealed Germany would not harm the world. She leads in the production of potash, but if she closed her frontiers, no great hardship would be imposed on other countries.

From whichever angle one approaches the question, self-sufficiency for Germany in her present territories is a chimera, a dream impossible of realization, and I shall point out later that no redistribution of colonies which could possibly be acceptable to other countries would improve her basic weakness. In the face of her deficiencies of vital raw materials, her only sensible policy would be co-operation with other countries. If she rules this out, one can only conclude that, since her experts are no fools, she is relying on a sudden demoralizing thrust that will give her control of territories possessing the sources of supply she lacks. The facts about raw materials are all too clear.

Chapter Five

SCHACHT VERSUS THE EXTREMISTS

Practically every month of Nazi rule has been marked by conflict between the moderates and the extremists in economic matters. The moderates are led by Dr. Schacht, whose position in Germany is a most peculiar one. Briefly, he may be described as unwanted and unpopular, but indispensable. He makes no secret about what he thinks of many of the Nazi leaders, and realizes full well that he would be tossed out to-morrow if the National Socialists could manage without him. Indeed, he even goads them and takes pleasure in seeing just how much they can stand, for it is in his nature to be cynical, and he knows that he is the only German leader who can command the respect of banking circles abroad, a fact which is the more amazing because until Hitler came to power Schacht was generally regarded as an able but somewhat unstable banker, relying overmuch on hazardous experiments.

Nobody has ever doubted his brilliance and his amazing luck in playing risks. It was he who, as president of the Reichsbank, drew Germany out of the morass of inflation fourteen years ago ; it was he who took a leading part in negotiating the Dawes loan and in opposing the execution of the Young Plan. He resigned from the presidency of the Reichsbank early in 1930, as a protest against the weakness of the German Government in accepting economic terms laid down by the Allies, but Hitler recalled him as soon as he came to office, and next year made him Minister of Economics. The appointment was a temporary one ; Schacht still holds it.

He is a most amazing person. Amongst all the German leaders I met he stands out as the most distinct personality.

A slightly-built man of sixty, he looks and acts as if he were twenty years younger.   He is a mixture of nerves and brilliance.   He radiates an extraordinary energy and is extremely vivacious.   Speaking perfect English with bewildering rapidity, he dashes from place to place in his conversation and demolishes a conventional argument with a few epigrammatic cynicisms.   Nothing is sacred to him, except his belief in himself, and this is so overwhelming as no longer to seem personal.   He makes the most exaggeratedly egotistical statements without his hearer being aware of any personal boasting.   Nor are they boasting ; he is merely expressing his own interpretations of a world in which he does not doubt for a second that he is a leader, and indeed, the leader behind the nominal leaders.   One feels that he has little faith in human nature, and that he looks on the mass of people (the politicians in particular) as insignificant molecules whose destiny his super-hand can lead in given directions.   It irks him to find his intricate plans upset by the blundering interference of some ignorant Nazi leader or to have to listen to the half-baked economic ditherings of the Leftist sections of the Nazis ; for he knows that in the long run his juggling with State finances will be the dominating factor.   The interference of others he places on a level with the incapacity of most men to understand his methods or his aims.

I heard him say, with a disarming smile : ' There is no secret about what I have done.   Anybody could have done it.   I simply was governed throughout my career, whatever the actual problem was, by three cardinal principles—firstly, a profound realization of the difference between mine and thine ; secondly, never forgetting that two and two make four and never five ; and thirdly, never failing to profit by the mistakes of other men, and don't forget that Governments make mistakes as do men.'   He went on to explain how frequently the mistakes of others had helped him, and cheerily added that what they had done in the past they would certainly do in the future, concluding by a shrewd rapier-thrust (a warning, though subtly conveyed) as to the probable mistakes my own Government would make in the near future in her economic relationships with Germany.

The general impression of his utterances was of a cold-blooded detachment in dealing with finance and politics, but there was something distinctly likeable about his frankness of exposition, and his obvious joy in relating his past experiences and the discomfiture of those with whom he had had occasion to deal.

One phrase he repeated three times : ' Whatever they may say of me in the future, whatever they may do to me, nobody will be able to deny that I have saved my mark—I have saved my currency.' And twice more he used the phrase : ' I have saved my mark.' He obviously regards this as his greatest achievement, and the context made it clearer that saving the mark ('my mark', be it noted) was a much more difficult matter in the last three years than even during the earlier inflation.

He also said that he knew perfectly well what was going to happen in Germany, and that he had no doubts at all as to the outcome of the crisis through which his countrymen were passing, but that nothing would induce him to reveal that outcome, so that it would be of no use asking. With another man one might have felt that this was mere bluff, but with Schacht, one left the room feeling that he was merely stating an indisputable fact.

Schacht was not a member of the Party until this year, and at Party gatherings had a special seat reserved for him, alongside von Papen and Schwerin von Krosigk in the front row, looking up at the serried rows of Nazi leaders. None of these latter has the subtlety of Schacht. Their earnest sincerity stands poles apart from his scintillating opportunism, and their curious lack of expression (apart from their spate of fixed platform utterances, and always excepting Dr. Goebbels) contrasts markedly with Schacht's rapid-fire powers of exposition in at least three languages. He is of a race apart ; in fact, he seems to have stepped out of medieval Florence, a Machiavelli with a complete mastery of twentieth-century technique.

Of course, he is not popular. A man with his searing tongue, a man who voices the most devastating criticisms with a pleasant smile and a cultured voice, could not be popular; but it probably pleases him more to be forced on people despite themselves. He is a slippery eel amongst the thousands of identical herrings in the Nazi Party, and nobody knows what he will do next. It is reasonably easy to know how a Hitler, a Göring, a Goebbels will react to any given situation, and it is quite clear that none of them will ever say anything completely new. They have long since exhausted their mental stimuli, whereas, with Schacht, one has the feeling that, at any moment when conditions are favourable, he may come into the open with some completely new policy or theory. The potentialities of such a man are endless, and there are no signs that his mental control of the German economic situation is diminishing. It is commonly said that he is the only man who understands the position of German economics at the moment, the only man who can unravel the tortuous statements; and I believe it. A Schacht does not take his associates into his full councils unless there is some need for it, and he would be the last person to explain everything in detail to his unwilling Nazi colleagues, even if he thought they could understand complicated economics. All his life he has sedulously cultivated the tradition of 'Schacht magic', and he will obviously never destroy part of his stock-in-trade. Nothing would be further from the truth, however, than to conclude that Schacht is nothing more than an economic necromancer concealing a paucity of tricks beneath an outside cover of smart patter. I repeat, I have met nobody else with such an economic mentality or such a peculiarly commanding personality. Hjalmar Schacht, 'the slick Schleswiger', as he has sometimes been called, stands alone alike in personality, theory and practice. He has contributed a definitely new approach to the confusion of issues, half political and half economic, that have typified the post-war period. And I believe that he has clarified this confusion for himself and made it possibly more confused for others by introducing a third set of values—the psychological. His success in skating so often over thin ice that would have carried nobody else has probably been due more to his psychological analysis of the human factors than to any application of economic truths, despite his own deprecatory remarks that he has never done anything more than apply ' the A.B.C. of economics ' to every successive problem he has had to face.

Dr. Schacht's most prolonged struggle has been with the Left Wing economists within the Party. From the earliest days of the movement, when Gottfried Feder drew up the vaguely Socialistic programme of the Party, they had repeated meaningless phrases on a thousand platforms. The clean-up of June 30th was supposed to put an end to such pressure from the Socialistic elements, but this was not so, and the semi-educated sections of the party continued to dream of a Utopia when they would be freed from ' the slavery of interest ', whatever that may mean. Their idea was to hurtle Germany along the road of credit-expansion ; the note-printing machines were their solution for everything.

Schacht maintained that this could lead only to collapse, because Germany has already exceeded the sensible limits of credit expansion. He has been unpopular for some time with certain Nazi leaders, especially Dr. Darré (whose agricultural policy he opposes), and Dr. Ley (whose Labour Front he claims to be unduly expensive) ; and there is much feeling about the Party relying for its financial guidance on an outsider. Schacht refused to join the Party until a few months ago, and has often rebuked the Nazi extremists, even on matters that were outside economics. For instance, he has opposed their anti-Jewish policy, on the ground that it cuts right across Germany's plan for economic rehabilitation. He has also attacked them for alienating international capital and for neglecting the outside world, by subordinating everything to their theories.

Schacht, in effect, is an orthodox financier (at least, by comparison with his opponents), and he believes that, while the recent expansion of Governmental expenditure staved off disaster for an interim period (especially when coupled with a financial dictatorship), no permanent recovery is possible without a renewal of private enterprise. As against this, the extreme Nazis want to keep the existing Government control on economics as a permanent feature of their rule. Schacht's arguments that they cannot keep on expanding

the volume of credit by an unlimited issue of Treasury
Bills seem to them sheer reaction, and they do not feel disposed to have a doctrinaire banker putting a brake on their
beloved theories.   It was not for this that the Third Reich
was instituted, not for this that 400 men died in street fighting.
When Schacht argues that Germany must regain her international trade, not on to-day's basis of organized subsidies,
but by standing on its own feet, they invoke the doctrine of
self-sufficiency.

In August 1935, Schacht publicly condemned inflationary
schemes and all attacks on the saving public of Germany as
' suicidal '.   The Nazi economists thereupon demanded that
he must go.   As the year passed, he went further, and even
had the temerity to declare that the State could not carry
the burden of Nazi extravagance for ever.   The Nazi organizations had to be reduced in size, he said ; and even the
budgets of the military and the secret police had to be supervised.   This was the sheerest treason in Nazi eyes.   But
Schacht answered it by a still clearer exposition of his views.
He said, in effect, that Germany could not afford to go on
spending money at the present rate, and that she must econo-
mize at home and create confidence abroad in order to obtain
the credits she needed so badly.   He wanted to clarify the
budgetary situation and release Germany from the strangle-
hold of exchange and other restrictions, and then return to
more normal methods of trade and Government finance.
The time was coming, he went on, when Government expenditure would have to be fixed, not by the amount to
which credit could be expanded, not by *a priori* estimates of
what was desirable from the Party point of view, but by the
capacity to which the people could afford to pay taxes.

At the end of April 1936, the complaints of the extremists
against Schacht bore fruit.   They insisted that he was sabotaging the whole future of Germany by an adherence to worn-
out financial conceptions, and that his policy was at variance
with basic Nazi doctrines.   They were supported at this
time by many of the industrialists, who objected to Schacht's
proposed continuance of the levy on industry to subsidize
exports.   It was said that Schacht wanted not only to continue

the levy of 600,000,000 marks on industry, but to add to it 200,000,000 from commerce and another 200,000,000 from agriculture. Dr. Darré, as Minister of Agriculture, had always opposed Schacht ; hereafter, he had to face additional opposition from the industrialists, who would have preferred devaluation of the mark to any continuance of the export levy.

As a result of this conflict of views, Hitler decided to put an end to the public squabble by appointing Captain-General Göring to co-ordinate the activities of the various departments concerned with raw materials and currency questions. It was assumed that this meant the displacement of Schacht as economic dictator of Germany and a turn to Herr Keppler, Hitler's personal adviser on economic matters. Keppler stands for devaluation and credit expansion, and it was assumed that his advice would become effective at once.

Actually, however, Schacht continued in office. Göring used his well-known decision and energy to lessen the deadlock between Schacht and the Party. He kept 'the old fighters' of the Party (the Socialists) within check until the Nuremberg Rally in September, when they were offered the sop of the Four Year Plan, a policy which reduced the rest of the world to a fitting place of impotence in Nazi eyes.

Dr. Schacht remains unregenerate. He still maintains that Germany must act in harmony with other countries, and that she cannot go on having a price-level out of all relationship with world parities. He knows that German prices cannot be adjusted to those of the rest of the world as long as the present abnormal restrictions continue ; he knows that those restrictions cannot be removed until large foreign credits allow a normal export trade for Germany ; and he knows that such credits cannot come until foreign lenders have political confidence in Germany, and until the budget is balanced. In short, Germany is going round and round. She can get nowhere until she returns to normal economic conditions, but she is afraid to try and get back to those, because she fears economic collapse and social upheavals if she does so. Moreover, since the spectacular launching of the Four Year Plan, she cannot retrace her steps, and all that Schacht can do is to keep the new inflation within limits that can stave off a complete collapse. Last year's phase of a conflict between two ways now belongs to the past ; a course has been set, and Schacht, as pilot, must turn away from the safe channels he knows and attempt to steer the ship past the rocks and the shoals which are strewn along the route the politicians have chosen. But even such a good pilot has his aberrations, and Schacht (who has always been associated with colonial bodies) thinks that the mirage of tropical colonies is the safe coastline which will keep him on his course.

Chapter Six

THE AGRICULTURAL FIASCO

I.—The Rise of Walter Darré

The future of the German experiment depends as much on agriculture as on industry, because even if the industrial expansion succeeds and the necessary foreign credits are obtained by building up exports, there would be no gain if those credits have to be used in importing food supplies. This argument applies still more strongly in a time of crisis. Once we grant the assumption that a nation has to be a citadel, able to stand alone, it follows at once that it must be able to produce its own food, whatever the cost may be. However much Dr. Goebbels may claim that bullets are more important than bread, there is no more certain way of risking military defeat than by incurring a food shortage.

Not the least of Germany's difficulties was that, owing to the poverty of her soil, she was a large food-importing country. If she wanted extreme self-sufficiency, it was doubtful whether she could extend it to agriculture, and, even if she did so only partially, it meant that industry and commerce would have to carry still another burden, because any extension of agriculture was not economically possible with the world price of foodstuffs at the low levels of the last few years.

To complicate matters, one of the deciding factors in German politics has always been the conflict between industry and agriculture—between the aristocratic *Junker* estates of the east and the factories of the west. The position was even more difficult than usual when Hitler took over power, because of the scandals over the distribution of agricultural relief in eastern Germany. There had always been an unnatural alliance between State Socialism and feudal land-ownership in those regions, and the *Junkers* had come to accept large doles from the State as a matter of right. One of the reasons for Brüning's fall had been his courageous attempt to insist that the *Junkers* should attempt to make their farming efficient. He held that the remedy lay with themselves rather than with charity from the State, and he put forward a plan to take over those large estates that could not be made to pay, and distribute them amongst small peasant holders. There was a great howl from the *Junkers* at this proposal, and their influence was especially strong in the immediate entourage of President von Hindenburg, himself a *Junker* of the *Junkers* in training and mentality.

Hitler's position, then, was a very difficult one. He had frequently pledged himself to aid the small farmers, and he had to face the discontent of the people, who were sickened by the revelations about corrupt distributions of State money in East Prussia. On the other hand, he could not come out openly against the *Junkers* (there is no evidence that he wished to do so in practice), because he depended so greatly on the army clique which was associated with the *Junkers*. He thus had to balance on a greasy pole, and adopt a policy of opportunism, since he could neither enforce the Socialistic policy of his Party programme nor come out openly for the large estates with their aristocratic owners. He solved these two problems by keeping them distinct and never allowing them to come into clear juxtaposition, although some of his advisers wanted him to declare for the peasant proprietors alone.

His first step was to do what he could to extend small settlement, and here he had the support of his agricultural expert, Dr. Walter Darré, a young man with an extraordinary variety of experience. Born forty-two years ago in the Argentine, he was educated in Germany and England, and took specialized courses in overseas methods of farming at the German Colonial School at Witzenhausen. After serving in the war (most of the time in the ranks), he returned to his agricultural studies and later entered the Ministry of Agriculture. When stationed at posts in far eastern Germany, and when making inquiries in Finland, he became convinced that the salvation of Germany lay in a combination of a revival of agriculture and a strengthening of the Nordic type of peasant. *Race and Agriculture* became his cry, and he published several monographs urging the connexion between the two. A comparatively late-comer to the National Socialist movement, he attracted no attention until he outlined his theories at a meeting of Party Leaders in Munich seven years ago. What he did was to give a summary of his book *The Peasant as the Life-source of the Nordic Race*— so impressively that Hitler realized that this earnest young agriculturalist could fill a gap in his Party organization.

Dr. Darré was given the task of rallying the peasants, who had hitherto shown no inclination to swallow the Nazi nostrums. His peculiar theories had the effect of promising them better farming conditions, and at the same time tickling their racial pride, a most important matter in Germany, where the peasant's pride of family is often as exclusive as that of the Junkers. Darré built better than he knew in emphasizing the family aspect of German farming, with a people whose records often went back farther than those of the nobles in Gotha. His earlier treatises on such matters as *The Domestication of the House Pig* would have left them cold, and they would probably have remained sceptical of his practical experience on Oldenburg farms and keeping stud-books in East Prussia ; but they accepted him as a prophet when he told them that they were to be the nucleus of the New Germany, and when he wrote books with such titles as *The New Nobility of Blood and Soil*. The two agricultural papers which he founded achieved some measure of success ; and the peasants, while not being very interested in his fulminations against the Jews and his fanatical hatred of Walter Rathenau (on whom he wrote yet another book), followed him in his economic diatribes against the failure of capitalism to give a proper place to agriculture. Even if they could not understand him (and he popularized many of the haziest economic ideas of Gottfried Feder), they sympathized with his ultimate goal, and he did much to woo the countrymen to Hitlerism. They did not become enthusiastic, but they at least remained neutral and did not become open foes of the new régime.

Early in 1933, Darré became the agricultural dictator of Germany. In addition to being Farming Leader of the Party, he was now Reich Minister for Agriculture, and he soon obtained the leadership of the three biggest agricultural bodies in Germany—the body of farmers' leaders, the agricultural credit organization, and the German Agricultural Council. These bodies, which had hitherto been at loggerheads, were now unified by a common leadership, and hereafter the farming communities could find expression only through Nazi channels. He still found time to write, however, and, next year, produced a book entitled *The Struggle for the Soul of the German Peasant*. He also built up a strong Race Bureau within the organization of the Black Guards, and never for a moment relaxed his campaign for Nordicism.

Still one of the babies of the German ministry, Darré has come to be looked upon as rather an *enfant terrible*, not tempering his theories by any admixture of tact or practical considerations. He is frequently in trouble with the purely opportunist element, who are prepared to jettison any theory if it is temporarily a nuisance ; and he has become more and more associated with the economic policies of the Left section of the Nazis. His zeal for the farmers has led him to become a confirmed *Autarkist*, in the most extreme sense of that ugly word, and he holds that the Party should immediately declare its policy of State Socialism and go ahead with it, irrespective of the trammels of people like Dr. Schacht. He really wants an isolated Germany, achieving her goals by inflation (he calls it a social use of credit) if need be. In economic matters he stands perilously near those Left-Wing Nazis who wanted a second revolution and whose aspirations ended in the barrack square on the night of June 30th. If he lacks the personal magnetism of Goebbels and Göring, he at least has well-defined theories and is probably the most obstinate member of the Ministry and certainly the most sincere in his beliefs. Opposition comes to him from many directions, even within the Ministry, but so far nobody has been able to make him budge, especially because his agricultural plans fit in with the programme of the army, even if they cut athwart the interests of the big *Junker* farmers.

II.—*The Food Estate*

When Hitler made Darré a minister, it was definitely a gain for the small farmers.   Indeed, the subsequent development of German agriculture has depended on the extent to which Darré has been given a free hand.   In the autumn of 1933, a start was made when the famous Food Estate was set up—the Reich Estate for Food Production or *Reichsnährstand*.   This was a kind of agricultural guild, an autonomous public body, sitting in Berlin, and having wide powers to put agriculture on a sound footing.   It was the first of the corporative bodies to be set up by the Nazis, and its main idea was to remove agriculture as a whole from ordinary ' profit-and-loss conditions ' and make it strong, whatever the cost might be.   Everything to do with agriculture came under its control.   It could regulate production of all crops, it could alter or fix prices, it could organize distribution, it could reduce rates of mortgage, it could prevent industry making undue demands on agriculture ; and, not least, it could enforce its decisions by penalties of imprisonment, fines up to £8,000 sterling, and by forbidding guilty persons to work on the land at all.   It took over all associations, co-operative bodies, and trading groups in any way connected with agriculture.   Wide as these functions were, the Reich Food Estate went much further.   It was not only a form of protection that lifted German agriculture away from all external and internal competition ; it was also a sociological instrument by which Hitler could advance his peculiar racial and biological ideas.   He had taken over Darré's ideas about *Blood and Soil* and was for ever talking of them as the basis of German life ; and his idea henceforth was to regenerate the German race by a new contact with the land.   The Food Estate was thus to be a bureau of eugenics on a scale hitherto not attempted.

It was an instrument for building up a population of small peasant proprietors who were guaranteed their farms from generation to generation by an Hereditary Farms Law.[1] Hitherto farms were usually divided between the whole of a farmer's children ; but this policy was condemned as being uneconomical, and as opposed to the best interests of the race. After the new law, the farm was to go to the eldest son[2] (the law did not apply to Jews or to any family which had mixed with Jews since 1800). The proprietor, however, can never sell or mortgage his farm, and he must support his younger brothers and sisters until they are grown up. To be a peasant owner in Hitler's Germany thus has its drawbacks. All farms of a certain medium size—about a million in all—came automatically under the new law, and many larger estate-owners elected to come under it as well.

The first act of the Food Estate was to withdraw agriculture from the system of free competition and regulate it on the social basis of ' a just price ', even if this involved a complete departure from the world prices then ruling for farming products. Prices were raised in 1932 and fixed at remunerative levels. But this was not enough, because the farmers might easily abuse such a system. To prevent this, the law of June 1934 set up an elaborate control over every farm in Germany. Every farm that produced more grain than the farmer's family could use had to deliver a certain amount of grain, at a price fixed by the State, to one of the nineteen grain organizations in Germany. Every field in Germany came into the scheme, and each farmer received his orders as if he were a private in an army.

The farmers received other benefits. The moratorium which Hitler had imposed as soon as he came to office was continued by the Food Estate, and interest rates were reduced. The farmers also received certain exemptions from taxes and ' social contributions '. They received the service of ' land-helpers ', and were allowed up to twenty-five marks

[1] *Reichserbhofgesetz*, September 29th, 1933. It had in mind farms about 12 to 125 hectares.

[2] In some districts where local usage conferred the farm on the youngest son, this was allowed to continue.

a month for every extra hand they employed. And it could not be denied that, even if they had to restrict their production in some cases, they benefited from the fixed prices and the monopolistic selling boards set up by the Government.

The new control extended surprisingly far afield, and it was said that boards were set up for everything ever mentioned in connexion with agriculture from classical times onwards. Thus it was singularly unfortunate, said a wag, that Germany's Minister of Agriculture should have been an historian of agriculture !

III.—*The Results of the Drive for Agriculture*

Naturally, all these steps cost money, and Hitler asserted again and again that the other classes of the community simply had to carry the burden of agriculture. Loud complaints arose from the city consumers when they found the cost of living going up, and from the industrialists who now had to pay for the losses of agriculture in addition to giving large subsidies to aid German exports. Nor was the farmer too well pleased. He objected to the dictatorial powers of the Food Estate and to many of its ramifications. He did not like being told just how much or how little wheat or asparagus or barley he was to produce each year. He objected to delivering his products at fixed times. The planning, in short, was too extreme and was introduced too rapidly. Even to-day there is great confusion in many fields. Some of the marketing-boards (especially those dealing with eggs and asparagus) have become mere objects of mirth ; and many of the proposals to secure agricultural self-sufficiency are a trifle comic—the suggestion, for instance, that the use of rhubarb could obviate any importation of lemons. The main trouble, however, is in the overlapping and the complication of administrative machinery, for apparently nothing is too trifling an excuse for the institution of some fresh board or committee. A chart of the organization of the Food Estate is like the bad dream of a lecturer in administration, so many and so variable are the new committees.

More important from the national point of view is the criticism that the new policy, despite the hubbub of propaganda around it, has not been producing results. There has been no general increase in the area cropped or in total production. Taking the fundamental bread cereals, for instance, the annual figures of production (in thousands of metric tons) for each year after 1931 were 11,046, 13,522, 14,492, 12,284, and 12,341. The position last year, as the Government itself admitted, was still worse, because the crops were of poorer quality; and the inevitable conclusion is that Germany is feeding herself less now than before the Food Estate was established.[1] Fodder crops tell the same story. The pastoral situation has remained constant in the last three years, and the only conspicuous success has been in reducing the imports of milk and butter. So that, if the aim of the Food Estate was to increase production, it has failed. Not all the measures of regulation and control have succeeded in solving the problem, and in some vital directions (the provision of fats, for example) Germany remains more utterly dependent on foreign supplies than ever before. The armour of self-sufficiency thus not only has chinks in it—it is absolutely falling apart. Herein lies Germany's essential weakness. She cannot produce enough food for herself, and she has not sufficient foreign exchange to buy both food and raw materials for her armaments. So she economizes on the food, although it is a strange aberration that makes her go on perfecting armaments while her food supplies are dwindling (even the army reserves of grain have gone !) and while she suffers from a basic lack of fats.

There are other results, too. Owing to the growing scarcity of foodstuffs, the herds have not been able to get enough fodder. Cattle have had to be killed, and it is estimated that the German herds have dwindled by almost a quarter. A grave blow has been dealt to her pastoral industry, and naturally the effects of the decrease of the herds are cumulative. Last winter, the Germans lacked beef and veal and pork, and even cheese and eggs. Göring, in effect,

[1] Contrast the Republic's achievements. From 1925 to 1932 wheat production went up 43 per cent, cattle 10 per cent, and pigs 40 per cent.

was cutting into the reserves of the future by decimating the flocks and herds themselves in order to enable his system to survive month by month.

The position of Germany is indeed deplorable. Last year the masks came down, and Germany entered the world market to buy 1,000,000 bushels of wheat. Every year she is faced with a problem of bare subsistence over the long winter, and it is a very thin subterfuge that covers the shortage with the social veneer of a common struggle for the nation, a campaign for *Winterhilfe*. This is only an attempt every year to whittle down the use of breads and fats to the lowest level consistent with survival.

The record of the Food Estate is thus a very chequered one. Germany cannot feed herself, and the indisputable fact is that all the propaganda has produced no increase in rural settlement. On the contrary, despite the shortage of food all over the country, the area under grain has diminished —a staggering fact. Production of foodstuffs is much less than in 1933, yet food imports have gone down. The only inference is that Hans and Paul are tightening their belts. One cartoon I saw summed up the situation thus : ' We have tightened our belts so often that soon we will have to wear braces ! '

A reversion to open competition on world markets would make the situation far worse. The conditions under which the German farmers work are so artificial that such competition would immediately ruin them. Meanwhile, the consumers pay more for their food, and the industrialists have to bear heavy burdens in order that an uneconomic agricultural system may survive.

Hitlerism has periodical campaigns against profiteers ; but the truth is that the rise in retail food prices is due to the system itself, not to a few traders who evade its spirit. Since Hitler came to power, wheat has gone up 16 per cent in price, eggs 50 per cent, butter 40 per cent, potatoes $75\frac{1}{2}$ per cent, and most meats at least 50 per cent. It is little wonder that the townsmen are raising an outcry against the farmers. Just as in France, they are looked upon as ' the spoilt children of the State ' ; and the ordinary townsman has little sympathy, say, with Count Helldorf's periodic assaults on Berlin shop-keepers. With food so short, he is now blaming the men behind Helldorf, the men who decide agricultural policy.

But this is only one side of the picture. Other factors than mere production come in. In German eyes, since farming is conducted on a long-term basis, it is more important to lay the bases for future self-sufficiency than to achieve immediate increases in production ; and here the results are more difficult to assess. Propaganda asserts that Germany can provide enough cereals and meat for her population, and that ultimately she will provide sufficient fats ; but the reiteration is palling and the public wants facts of achievement.

In short, Hitler has settled none of the far-ranging problems that have so sorely beset German agriculture since the war. The long outstanding question of the *Junkers'* large estates has not been solved or even attacked. The scandals of the *Osthilfe* Relief have ceased, but that is all. Despite Darré's theories and the years of Party agitation against ' land monopolies ', Hitler has taken no steps against the large landowners. On the contrary, his measures to aid agriculture (tariffs, subsidies, mortgage-relief, and so on) have benefited the *Junkers* quite as much as they have the peasants. Their greatest difficulty (the securing of sufficient labourers) has been overcome by Hitler's edicts forbidding rural workers to enter factories or even to migrate to the large cities. The *Junkers* have in no wise suffered under Hitler ; the classes squeezed to the wall are the middlemen—the millers, the handlers of grain and the like. While the farmers, large or small, have received artificially high prices for their grain, and the consumers have not paid very much more for their bread, the middlemen have been made practically bankrupt. They have no place in the Nazi programme, for, useful as their services may be, no art of propaganda can make an ' *élite* of service ' out of them.

Hitler's main experiment has been the crusade of *Blood and Soil* ; and after all, this seems a poor exchange for an economically sound system of agriculture.

PART IV

THE BALANCE SHEET OF HITLERISM

SECTION I.—WHAT THE ONLOOKER SEES

Chapter One

THE YOUTH MOVEMENT : THE FIGHT
FOR THE FIRST EIGHTEEN YEARS

For the young, National Socialism is primarily a spiritual movement, a development through constantly renewed ecstasy to endless achievement. Why talk of past crusades and wars of liberation when they have before them the *Führer*, and behind him Schlageter, Horst Wessel, and the forty boys who died in the awakening of the nation ? In a great boys' camp in Franconia, I saw sentries on duty in front of a column, round which heaps of banners were piled. I moved to approach the monument to read the names of the boy-martyrs inscribed on it, but my road was barred. ' This is holy ground, untouchable,' said one of the sentries who stood there night and day. A week before it had been a run for cattle !

The Youth Movement is nothing intrinsically new in Germany. Many such movements existed before the war, and many of the political and religious organizations after the war had youth subsidiaries. The difference between the Hitler Youth Movement and the many that it superseded is that it is now nation-wide, and includes 6,000,000 young people in what is practically a State department.

Kaiserdom looked askance at the various Youth bodies and saw to it that the patriotism which caused them to throw themselves so eagerly into their country's service was rewarded by being allotted the most dangerous posts in the early months of fighting. After the war youth was broken, and it was a long time before the Nazis realized the importance of appealing to the very young. They used instead the cynical prematurely-aged youths who had borne a part of the actual fighting in the last years of the war. The children were overlooked until 1926, when, at the *Partei-Tag* at Weimar, Hitler made Kurt Grüber National Leader of the 'Hitler Youth'. Grüber had formed a cell of children in Plauen (Saxony), and now Hitler gave him an opportunity to spread his ideas throughout the nation. The name 'Hitler Youth' was suggested by Julius Streicher, the leader of the anti-Semites, and it was meant to include boys from the ages of fourteen to eighteen. Two years later, plans were made to have similar organizations for girls (the *Schwesternschaften*, after 1930 the 'German Maidens') and for boys from ten to fourteen (the *Jungmannschaften*, later the *Jungvolk*, as we know them to-day).

From its administrative centre in Plauen, the movement grew rapidly. It was soon banned in Bavaria, Hanover, Hesse, and elsewhere, but as usual it throve on persecution. By the beginning of 1929, steps were taken to link it on to the Storm Troopers. Henceforth the boy of eighteen passed from the *Hitler Jugend* into the Party and the Storm Troopers. At the *Partei-Tag* that year Grüber proudly led 2,000 Hitler Youth past the *Führer*, and received banners for each of his provinces. The children marching behind their red flags with the hammer-and-sword insignia were now definitely part of the movement.

A somewhat stormy period then ensued, in which there were quarrels about leadership and methods of organization. The seat of the movement was transferred from Plauen to Munich ; the whole of Germany was mapped out into ten Youth Groups ; and Grüber came to be overshadowed by Hitler's twenty-three-year-old protégé, Baldur von Schirach. Towards the end of 1931, Hitler made von Schirach chief-of-staff of each of the three Nazi organizations for young persons (not only the Hitler Youth but the Union of Students and the Union of Scholars as well). Grüber resigned, and his successor survived for less than eight months, making way for von Schirach as National Leader of the Hitler Youth (June 1932). At that moment, the Hitler Youth were under Brüning's ban, together with all National Socialist organizations, and there were only 35,000 members ; but von Schirach began to plan a great army of Germany's childhood, with himself as commander-in-chief.

Their organization henceforth duplicated that of the Brown Army, from the smallest band of ten comrades (the *Kamerad-schaft*) up to the *Gau* (or province) and the nation as a whole. Indeed, the Hitler Youth frequently thought it their main duty to follow the Brownshirts into the street mêlées. In one of these fights, the fifteen-year-old Herbert Norkus was murdered by Communists, and before Hitler came to power no less than twenty boys lost their lives in the street fighting.

A great expansion took place under von Schirach. Hitler himself claims that the 35,000 members of June 1932 had swollen into 1,000,000 six months later, when he became Chancellor ; but, however this may be, membership jumped up phenomenally once the Nazis were in office. One by one the other children's organizations fell into the Nazi maw. The Scharnhorst Youth, the Evangelical Youth, the *Bund der Artamanen*, and all the sports and gymnastic clubs were absorbed. 'Integration', it was called ; and, if any groups stood up for their own opinions, as the Bismarck Youth did, they were summarily disbanded. By these means and by the undoubted natural growth of fervour for Hitlerism, the Hitler Youth came to include 6,000,000 members by the end of 1934. Their formal parades were now heralded by 600 banners, while their camps had representatives of the fifty-three foreign countries in which Germans residing abroad had dressed their children in the brown shirts and shorts of the Hitler Youth. Statistically the movement left nothing to be desired by this time.

A word must be said about the leader. Baldur von Schirach is a plump self-satisfied young man of just thirty years of age. When he was an art student ten years ago, Hitler, his intimate friend, was able to discern exceptional qualities in him. He has one of the longest entries in the Nazi *Who's Who*, telling at length how frequently he communed with the *Führer* or how often he consulted the Ministers. Described as 'Journalist (Editor)', it is related how millions of his verses sold and how two of his books, *The Unknown*

Hitler and *The Triumph of the Will*, were the best sellers of
1932. His best-known poem is the song of the Hitler Youth,
Forward, which commences :

> Forward ! Forward ! Let the bright trumpets sound,
> Forward ! Forward ! Youth knows no peril ',

and goes on with this repetitious cacophony to the climax :
' We will march for Hitler through night and through danger,
With the flag of youth for freedom and bread ', and ends
with the line : ' The standard is better than death.' A
contrast of this with the really fine *Die Fahne hoch*, the Horst
Wessel Song, shows its poverty of thought and expression.

At the functions at Nuremberg, his speeches were mediocre
in content and poor in delivery. He would frequently
lose the thread of his discourse, pause perceptibly, and then
work himself up into a passable imitation of his elders of the
movement, with the same flamboyant gestures and breaking
voice, the only difference being that theirs was a natural out-
pouring while his was a careful but rather clumsy copy of
their model, more practised than spontaneous.

Von Schirach has been pampered with posts of great responsibility since his seventeenth year. He has never had
time to think, has never had his actions questioned, and has
been saved from criticism by his friendship with Hitler.
Apparently nobody can check him. He creates political
difficulties by his open attacks on the Christian religion.
His onslaughts three years ago on the youth organizations
of the various churches are still in memory as cases of brutal
suppression of opinions other than his own ; and his summary
expulsion of Erich Stange, the leader of the Evangelical
Youth Movement, after signing the agreement of December
19th, 1933, was a crude piece of victimization.

Von Schirach has pursued but one goal—the unification
of all the youth of Germany in his own organization, irrespective of the efficiency of that organization, or his ability
to provide enough leaders, or his blows to whatever beliefs
the boys may previously have had. To all criticisms, he
replied in effect with the title of one of his best-known writings,

To the Führer ! In his public speeches, he even took to the device of referring to himself in the third person as ' von Schirach ', so remote had he become.

But his power continued to grow, and more and more impressionable children listened to his commands : ' Join no organizations but Hitler's and be ready to die for Hitler.' ' Forward ! Forward ! The banner leads us to eternity.' So he goes on ; and the tragedy is that he is shaping the mentality of the next generation of Germans. But he takes no heed of the future, and the psychological problems of childhood and adolescence mean nothing to him. The song of the banner is enough, provided that 6,000,000 young Germans are all stamped into the same mould and emerge as unquestioning automata, physically fit and mentally sponges for the official Hitler hero-worship. The goal and the methods are simple, and all complexities are ignored. ' Command and we follow . . . the standard is more than death '—that is all. Whatever may be said of him, Baldur von Schirach is a great educational simplist.

The fight for the mind of youth starts in the cradle. The baby's earliest fairy tales must be in accordance with Nazi ideas. The *Führer* is ' the man sent from Heaven ', who triumphed over some evil people called the Allies and who started a long fight to kill the bad ogre—the Bolshevik— who is for ever trying to eat up honest little German children.

At the age of ten, each little boy gets a brown shirt with the pfennigs he has saved, or, if he is too poor, his comrades often subscribe for him. Henceforth he belongs to the ' Young Folk '. The little girl will join the ' Union of German Maidens ', and is supposed to be dressed in a uniform of white blouse and blue skirt, but, for some reason or other, the girls have to go without the uniforms more often than the boys. Little boy and girl alike are pledged to sacrifice everything for the *Führer* and are taught that he is everything and themselves nothing. After four years of this, the boy of fourteen joins the Hitler Youth, the outward symbol of his promotion being the change to brown trousers and the presentation of a red swastika arm-band as worn by adult members of the Brownshirt organization. Henceforth he is a Storm Trooper in miniature, and Hitler has arranged that the boy will have the same unit-numbers as his father.

When grown up, the boy goes to a camp for six months, compulsory labour service, for the most part working, stripped to the waist, in the fields. This is followed by two years' service in the army as a conscript, but, by the time the army gets hold of him, he is saturated with Nazi ideology, a fact which caused much friction in the early days of Hitler's power. After leaving the army, our young man may become a member of the Brown or Blackshirts, first on the active list and later with the reserves.

The Party attributes great importance to the training of future leaders. In the Labour Service camps, an eye is always kept on boys who stand out, and every effort is made to allow them to adopt leadership as a profession. Even the youngsters in the Youth camps are weeded out, and the picked ones sent for monthly courses at the various training schools. The very spirit of Hitlerism is inspired leadership of the duller masses, and it is realized that leadership can only be acquired by a long training, both theoretical and practical. Hitler himself experienced sufficient difficulties in this regard in the early days of his movement not to realize its importance now that his main task is to perpetuate his régime.

There are great training establishments—at Vogelsgang amidst the idyllic hills of the Eifel, at Sonthofen in Southern Allgäu, and at Crossinsee at the other end of Germany in Pomerania. The curriculum is very involved. First of all the boy's body is looked after ; then he receives a training in political science and in the ethics of National Socialism ; and lastly he is taught the business side of administration. At every stage the emphasis is on the development of his character, and he emerges from his years of training as a splendid animal, thinking only of Hitlerism and possessing the technical equipment for furthering the cause. If leadership is a matter of correlated body and mind, of unquestioning obedience, of devotion to one aim to the exclusion of everything else, and of efficiency in the *minutiæ* of administration, then the Nazis have solved the problem of obtaining it. Whether such a training breeds rigidity and intolerance is another question, and those who look on leadership as something far more subtle than a mixture between physical jerks and a kind of actuarial training will not feel disposed to accept the methods of Vogelsgang and Crossinsee. For a movement with the mentality and methods of Hitlerism, however, the training is admirable, for the leader of the future will be a clean-living zealot, wedded to the cause, decisive in action, and thinking and acting only along prescribed lines. The products of the course are certainly marvellous specimens of their type and undoubtedly a great improvement on their forebears who were washed up in the turbulent days of street fighting. It is impossible not to admire their physique, their unquestioning faith in an ideal, their submergence of any hint of self-seeking, and their general demeanour. Wonderful instruments, these, if only their leaders would confine their use to worthy aims ; but the spell is broken when one sees a group of such youngsters eagerly drinking in the absurdities of *Der Stürmer*, and finding nothing wrong with them. After all, they have not arrived at their present stage by experimenting with many philosophies, and weighing them and discarding the unsuitable ; rather are they so many human receptacles which have had only one argument poured into them. They have been intellectually fed as a French farmer fattens his geese for *foie gras* ; but the Hitlerite would say that, if barley alone produces good *foie gras*, why let the goose dabble round in all manner of foods ? Why let it find that certain weeds are poisonous when its guardians may keep it from that painful experience ? Anyway, Hitler is not aiming at perfect intellectual detachment in his officers ; he wants faith, obedience, zeal, and the unceasing hatred of certain doctrines, and his training methods produce those very qualities which, he would say, constitute physical and mental fitness for the struggles that confront the Third Reich.

It would be foolish to underestimate the enthusiasm of young Germany for their *Führer*. All other interests are disappearing, and it would be misleading to think that the religious bodies which are so vocal abroad are holding their own with the children. Again and again in Germany, even in Catholic Bavaria and the Black Forest, I found cases of children whose Roman Catholic parents tried to keep them in the few struggling Church societies that still exist for children. In every case the children wanted to join the *Hitler Jugend*. The brown shirt or drab blouse of Hitler won every time ; the children wanted to follow the drums and the fifes of their playfellows' bands and, as they saw it, be normal. To be outside Hitler's organization was the worst form of punishment. Hitler has captured the children heart and soul, and it is one of the oldest adages of dictatorship that he who has control of the elementary schools for five years is established in power for ever.

It is the queerest form of fanaticism. I have seen groups of boys in their teens gaping almost with idolatry at one of their fellows who had been singled out for a salute from Baldur von Schirach ; and I soon learnt not to answer the children's stock query : ' Have you seen the *Führer* ? ' by answering ' Yes, and I have spoken with him.' The resultant worship was too distressing.

Their attitude of mind is absolutely uncritical. They do not see in Hitler a statesman with good and bad points ; to them he is more than a demigod. Times out of number they answered my queries why they believed or did so-and-so by the reply : ' Because the *Führer* wills it ! ' There was no use going behind such a mandate ; questioning was worse than heresy. The children of Germany believe that right and wrong are as distinct as black and white. Germany is always right, the rest of the world always wrong, and as for the Russians, they are literally devils from hell. It was this utter lack of any objective or critical attitude on the part of youth, even with university students, that made me fear most for the future of Germany. They are nothing but vessels for State propaganda, and the copious draught allows no time for thought, even if they had not lost the habit.

The Youth Movement, considered as a movement, is essentially German. The German has always craved organization. Where the boys with us would consider an open-air life as natural, they have to organize it ; where we take sport as part of our normal existence, they sedulously arrange and rationalize it. With them youth must have a purpose. The natural instincts of adolescence to revolt are not enough ; life must be earnest. They quote the words of von Eichendorff, written well over a century ago : ' For our youth there is no ease of carefree play, no blithe immunity ; the quest of life engages it early. We come to birth in the midst of struggle and, in the midst of struggle, vanquished or victorious, we decline.'

Granting such a concept of the role of youth, we have to admit that the Germans are its foremost exponents. As one recent writer says : ' The Youth Movement is so essentially German that we would be justified in typifying the Germans as the people with a youth movement, or, to go still further, the people which has always had a youth movement and which will always have one.'

But there is one great difference with the Hitlerite youth movements. Every previous movement marked a revolt against authority ; the youths of ten years ago who became front-line fighters in the service of Hitler were also rebels ; but the youth of to-day are taught unquestioning obedience to authority. To rebel is unthinkable, to argue for themselves equally so. They must submit to a mental uniformity which by its nature is degrading. Hitler is not shrewd enough to allow them to break into mental revolt in their teens and then come back, by their own volition, to the tenets of National Socialism as a result of their own convictions. This is indeed far from the spirit of the early Youth leaders—far from Schiller and Hegel and Novalis—far from the ebullient youth of the period before '48—and abysmally far from the *Wandervögel* of the pre-war years with their instinctive revolt against Kaiserdom and their equally instinctive rallying to the Fatherland when it was in danger. The Hitler Youth Movement may be bigger than any of its predecessors ; it may have the blessing of the State ; but the sacred breath of liberty and of intellectual striving has gone from it. It resembles a giant with glandular trouble. The outward husk is imposing, but beneath is only mental aridness. If only one of the boys I saw in the most impressive Hitler camps would have questioned the propagandist lectures to which they were listening, if only one of them had asked a penetrating question, I would have felt more hope for the future of Germany.

Chapter Two

THE LABOUR SERVICE : THE FIGHT FOR THE YOUNG MEN

The Labour Service seems to me one of the most desirable of the Nazi experiments, at least under German conditions. Long before Hitler came to power, when he was evolving the shadow organizations of his ultimate State, he appointed Konstantin Hierl to work out a system whereby the youth of the nation, irrespective of social class, could be put through the mill of compulsory labour service. Hierl was a professional soldier with over thirty years service, and had obtained a reputation first as Director of the War Academy in Munich and later at the War Ministry. During the Spartacist troubles, he had raised the 'Hierl Detachment' and driven the Socialists out of Augsburg, so that his Nationalist sympathies were beyond doubt. In short, he was just the man to build up a nation-wide labour service along military lines, and this was the task Hitler allotted him when he became an organizing leader (*Organisationsleiter*) at Party Headquarters in Munich eight years ago.

About that time there was much discussion of voluntary labour service as a method of alleviating unemployment, and the Brüning Government passed a law in July 1931, allowing such camps. Political rivalries entered, however, and the Nazis proceeded to organize their own camps. Hierl called a meeting of leaders in the Kurmark region and, in the first weeks of 1932, mustered the first camp at Hammerstein in the Grenzmark. A few months later, the state of Anhalt—in this as in so many other ways a nursery of Nazi ideas—made such service State-wide.

Next year, fifty-eight-year-old Colonel Hierl became Secretary of State for Labour Service. He had a plan and a theory. 'The Hierl Plan', as worked out in his book, *Sinn und Gestaltung der Arbeitsdienstplicht*, went far beyond unemployment. It was to be a cardinal feature in building up the New Germany. It was far less economic than social. The idea behind it all was that manual labour provided the best means of breaking down social barriers and moulding the character of the young. Every young man would find himself in the regenerating process of hard physical work ; he would realise the comradeship of his fellows ; he would learn discipline ; he would come into contact with the German soil for which he was to be trained to die Boys from all parts of Germany and from all social classes were to be flung into camps, where their bodies were to be made fit by hard labour and their minds were to be moulded along the desired national lines. Incidentally they would relieve the congestion on the labour markets and accomplish works that could not otherwise be brought about. 'Labour service shall be the proud privilege of German youth and shall be service to the whole *Volk*', cried Hierl. In brief, his theory was far more concerned with the physical and mental wellbeing of the youth of the country than with economic gain or loss. That is where it differed from earlier experiments, and that is where the *Arbeitsdienst* of Germany remains unique.

The voluntary camps worked well, but Hierl was eagerly awaiting the day when labour service would be universal and compulsory. That day came on June 26th, 1935, when the Reich Labour Service Law was promulgated. It provided that every German man should serve for six months in a labour service camp at some time between his eighteenth and twenty-sixth birthdays. The authorities would have preferred a clear-cut scheme whereby every boy should serve for six months in a camp and then, immediately on achieving his twentieth year, go on to a military camp and serve his period as a conscript. But this was impossible because facilities did not exist and any such limitation would have kept out ardent Nazis who were a few years older— just the kind of men who were to provide the camps with leaders.

At present, 200,000 men serve in such camps for six months. Usually men who are called up for the summer term of duty go on to the Army at the end of their service, and those who serve in winter, persons like farmers and waiters, can pursue their ordinary avocations in summer. A camp-leader once told me that, in the villages, boys who were thought to be opposed to Hitlerite ideas usually found themselves put down for the winter term in labour service camps, because the work is naturally less pleasant in winter than in summer.

The camps are organized on thoroughly military lines. Discipline is rigid; the boys wear uniforms like soldiers; the only difference is that they carry spades instead of rifles and work in the fields. Three aims are sought—physical exercise, intensive drill, and training of the mind; and each day is divided between the three, although, as the Nazi literature on the subject points out, the training in National Socialism principles comes first and 'permeates the service from early morning until bed time'. That is why the army is said to have opposed the scheme from the first—because the boys are too well-trained in the Nazi way before the Army gets hold of them.

Everything goes according to routine. At each of the thirteen hundred camps in Germany, every boy will be doing the same thing at a given time. Individualism has no place in the scheme. Take a typical summer's day in a camp I saw near Potsdam. Reveille comes at five o'clock. After ten minutes of exercises, an hour is allowed for dressing and putting the bunks in order. Then comes a mass parade and the ceremonial raising of the swastika flag, with its emblems of a spade and two ears of corn. This is followed by an allocation of the tasks for the day, and the men swing off in platoons to march to the fields where they are working, or, if the distance is too great, go by bicycles. They work from half-past six till a quarter-past two, with half an hour's break for an early morning meal at ten o'clock. In all, counting the meal-time and the march from and to the camp, they work for eight hours in summer and seven in winter.

But at three o'clock, after they have eaten their dinner, the novel features of camp-life appear. If it is summer-

time, each man must take an hour's rest on his bed after
dinner, but in winter, the ordinary duties go on.   After a
short political talk, they go out for athletics or drill and return,
a little after five o'clock, for lectures on the New Germany
or on international affairs.   When I visited the camps, these
talks were usually highly tendentious accounts of events in
Abyssinia or the decline of democracy.   The boys then
go out to a roll-call ceremony and the lowering of the flag.
This brings them to a little after seven, when they have half
an hour for supper.   After this, they have an organized eve-
ing, of singing or discussions on Nazi literature, or a *Feiera-
bendgestaltung*.   The evenings are usually rather jolly, because,
as one supervisor told me quite seriously, ' they drink nothing
intoxicating, and are only allowed beer '.   Thus it will be seen
that it is a strictly regimental life from five o'clock in the morning until the ' lights out ' signal at ten in the evening.   It
is impossible, for instance, for a boy to perform his physical
tasks and keep his mental processes to himself.   The whole
time, there is deliberate leading of his mind in certain directions.   He is given a hearty and healthy life, with a premium
on good-fellowship and physical well-being, but mental
freedom is taken from him.   He must think as the masses
do, his mind must move along the orderly channels worked
out at Hierl's headquarters in the Potsdam Park.   For the
mass of average boys, the life seems a happy one, but for the
wayward minority, Hierl prescribes regimentation.   The
stress is on the group and on turning out identical specimens,
and that is why I think the future of Germany depends far
more on one rebel boy in a camp than on the 130 normal
' hearties '.   The Nazi creed, however, is ' *Volk* before Self ',
and they believe that the *Volk* finds its best expression when
the Self is completely subordinated.

The service is organized down to the last button of the last
man.   There are thirty ' Service-districts ', corresponding
to the political districts of the Reich.   Each of these is divided
in anything up to ten groups, each group has six to ten *Abtei-
lungen*, each of which occupies a camp.   In the whole of
Germany there are 1,260 camps.   Each camp is a duplicate
of the other.   The barracks are standard and built round a

square. One side is given over to administration and meet-ing-rooms, each of the other three has a self-sufficient community. Every camp has exactly 152 men, of whom seventeen are executive officials. Each of the three *Züge* or wings houses forty-five men, who in turn are sub-divided into three troops of fifteen. Everybody is plastered with badges of rank, for the Service has a military hierarchy with no less than fifteen distinct grades. In a word, in time of emergency, the *Arbeitsdienst* could immediately put 200,000 drilled and well-organized infantrymen into the field.

The system of training is equally intricate. Hitler realized from the outset that one of Germany's problems was to provide leaders for the various branches of his movement, and the labour service, in addition to being what he calls a school for the entire nation, is an admirable training-ground for leaders of all kinds. The boys who have graduated through the various Nazi youth organizations now take on the wider responsibilities of adult leadership, and in many ways the training institutions of the labour service—the troop-leaders' school, the *Feldmeistersschule*, the *Berziksschule*, and the *Reichsschule*—are determining the nature of the Nazi State of the future.

After his labour service and military training, the future leader signs on for ten years and receives a specialized training in the psychology of leadership and in the technical engineering aspects of the work. At any given moment, there are at least 25,000 leaders working in the camps, and, in addition to these who have chosen the labour service for their lifework, far greater numbers, after the discipline received during their service, have been absorbed in other departments of the Nazi State where a premium is placed on intelligent and obedient leadership.

Although it is forever being asserted that the main aim of the labour service is to train the mind and bodies of Young Germany, the economic aspects are not lost sight of. Here we have a body of 200,000 lusty young men, who receive twenty-five pfennigs a day as pocket-money, and whose keep never costs more than eighty-two pfennigs a day. That is to say, it is a disciplined labour supply for a little over a mark a day, a supply that can be sent anywhere and put to any kind of work.

So far the service has been used mainly to reclaim lands that can be used in the fight to make Germany self-sufficient in her foodstuffs. It is in keeping with the Nazi cult of *Blut und Erde* to bring the adolescents into close contact with mother earth, and wrest waste-lands away from destruction. There is something satisfying to them in triumphing over Nature. There were marshes to drain, swamps and moorlands to clear, erosions to be stopped, canals and irrigation channels to be built, land to be reclaimed from the sea, and public amenities to be created. Eight million hectares can be won back to cultivation, cry the leaders, four provinces the size of Saxony can be gained to the Reich without any war save with Nature.

It is impossible to estimate just what has been achieved. Hitler inaugurated ' the Fight against Water ' with great éclat in 1934, and announced at the Party Congress of 1935 that the first fifty peasants had already been settled on reclaimed marshes. The greatest concentration of camps was in Oldenburg and Westphalia, but the most far-reaching plans were in the south-west, in the area between the Rhine and the Danube. It is still too early to assess the economic results as a whole ; all that one can do is to say that the workers are building up potential wealth for the nation.

It has been asserted that the Labour Service Army constitutes slave-labour which competes with private enterprise. The authorities deny this and point out that none of their activities affect the labour market. Land is being reclaimed that would not otherwise have been touched ; forests are being cleaned up and tasks that would otherwise be too expensive (such as the tapping of pine trees to secure the resin that will ultimately make Germany independent of foreign supplies of turpentine) are being carried out ; and the sea is being pushed back. It is hotly denied that the labour service youths are being employed in road-making, which absorbs so many of the ordinary unemployed, except for scenic roads in the forests. One must add that, from one's own experience in Bavaria and in the Black Forest, a very liberal interpretation is given to the word ' scenic ' in this connexion.

It is also claimed that the system often means the use of labour at State cost to improve the lands of individual far-mers ; but, in answer to this, Hierl maintains that the system is proof against abuse. No schemes of reclamation are undertaken if they improve the land of one farmer alone. Usually, in a district in which there is waste land or where erosion is eating into the fields, the community appoints a committee which gets in touch with the nearest *Arbeitsdienst* office. All claims are most carefully considered on their merits before a decision is reached, and it does seem as if illicit individual gain has been effectively ruled out.

The whole experiment is a fascinating one for foreigners. One of the most typical sights in Germany is to come upon platoons of labour service men swinging along country tracks with shovels carried like rifles at the slope, or to see masses of browned boys working lustily in the fields and stripped to the waist in all weather. In the remotest woods one sees a red flag with a black spade worked in its midst and, as one approaches, a brown-clad sentry smartly springs to attention and brings his aluminiumed spade to the present, and somehow it does not seem absurd to be saluted with a spade.

Chapter Three

THE LABOUR FRONT : THE FIGHT FOR
THE WORKERS

I.—*The Industrial Sections*

The Labour Front was one of the first institutions set up in
Hitlerite Germany, because the trade unions were the centres
of organized opposition to the new regimé.   At ten o'clock
on the morning of May 2nd, 1933, trade unions were completely abolished throughout Germany, and their funds
were expropriated, together with the whole of their buildings
and records.   Within four days, Dr. Ley had taken over the
last of the 169 workers' organizations, and he said naïvely :
' It was just as if the leaders of the trade unions had waited
for them to be taken over, and breathed a sigh of relief when
they were finally relieved of their burden.'
     The theory was that a partisan body, organized on a class
basis, could have no place in the new nation where the whole
stress was on the community and none at all on the individual
or on any sectional interest.   ' National Socialism has abolished
class warfare ', cried Hitler.   Dr. Ley was rather more
honest in admitting that ' the taking-over was done to secure
our political power ', because the unions were so many anti-
Fascist nests.
     Realizing that problems of labour and industry required
some special treatment, Hitler gradually built up an *Arbeits-
front*, the German Labour Front.   As it exists to-day, it was
constituted by the *Law for the Organization of National Labour*
dated January 20th, 1934.   Briefly it takes over the tasks
performed by the old trade unions and adds to them
matters concerning industry.   Membership is open to ' all
German working people ', and it is most important to note

that this includes employers as well as employees. The German theory is that all alike are workers, some giving capital, some managerial functions, and some physical labour. Goodwill is the basis, because, as Dr. Ley said in one of his ebullient moments, the German worker was never a Marxist and the German employer was never a money-grubbing hyena.

Theoretically there is no compulsion to enforce membership of the Labour Front, but in practice no worker or employer can stand outside it.   An intense propaganda has been conducted to show that 'employers and employees alike are all working people in the Third Reich', and the result is that, to-day, the Labour Front has 26,000,000 members as compared with the 5,000,000 members the unions had when they were taken over. It must be added, however, that the latter figure is that given by the Nazis after the dwindling of the unions prior to their seizure.   When it is remembered that the population of Germany is only 66,000,000 and that women are discouraged from entering the employment market, it will be obvious that practically all working Germans belong to this new super-union.

But the Labour Front is not a Government department. It has no connection with the State, but is an entirely separate organization growing out of the old trade unions.   It is in no sense a branch of the Ministry of Labour, which continues to function as before.   As described to me by one of its directors, it is a spontaneous body formed to look after the interests of working men, whether employers or employed.

In practice, of course, there is close collaboration between the Labour Front, on the one hand, and the Ministries of Labour and Economics on the other.   With an unconscious humour, one of the directors explained the situation thus—that 'the new Labour Front gives the old Ministries the brains they hitherto lacked'.   What he meant was that the Labour Front gives advice on all industrial matters, and in particular, proposes new industrial laws.   Given this prompting the other two Ministries formulate the laws and put them into operation.

The Labour Front itself ranks at present as a body of the

National Socialist Party. Its leader is Hitler himself, its executive director is Dr. Robert Ley, who was previously leader of industrial matters for the Nazi Party. The central office is divided into twelve departments, and Germany is divided into thirteen districts for purposes of its administration. There is also a division according to crafts (the *Reichsbetriebsgemeinschaft*), with eighteen sections (such as chemicals, metals, paper, textiles, etc.), covering the whole scope of industry. As with so many Nazi administrations, there is a great amount of duplication and excessive organization, but it is claimed that the overlapping is being gradually eliminated.

As far as practical administration is concerned, the three main departments of the Labour Front are the Department of Matters, the Department of Persons, and the Administrative Offices. The first of these is the key-post. It is sub-divided into an educational department for the professions ; a social office dealing with such matters as wages, working conditions, and especially the initiation of new laws ; an office for self-government, a new department which is defined as an attempt to educate employers and employees in habits of co-operation ; and finally a personal office, to investigate individual complaints, and what are called ' offences against the social honour of members of the Labour Front '.

The practical working of the Labour Front is something quite novel in industrial history. Its nearest approach is the system of workers' councils in Russian factories, although the Germans would scout any such idea.

In each factory is a factory council, called ' a confidential council ', consisting of workers and presided over by the employer. Any suggestions for improvements of working conditions and any complaints about conditions are placed before the ' confidential council ', and attempts are made to settle them within the factory. If this proves impossible, a formal round-table meeting is held, at which employer and workers each put their respective views. At such meetings the employer must be ready to produce the most minute details of his costs and profits. If neither side will give way, there is a further appeal to a State official called ' the Trustee of Labour '. There is one such official for every district in Germany. After reviewing the evidence, he gives a verdict, either insisting that the employer shall pay more wages or ordering the workers to continue as before, as the case may be.

There are also elaborate provisions for round-table conferences between certain districts, certain industries, and even for the whole of Germany. In case of a large-scale quarrel, the parties meet round tables in the elaborate rooms of the Social Office of the Labour Front in Berlin. The whole system is based on discussion and co-operation, with a mandatory verdict. The idea is to ' get in before the expense and bitterness of strikes '.

Coupled with this is a peculiar institution for the ' social honour ' of workmen. This is to raise the prestige and self-esteem of the workers. The State has instituted ' courts of social honour ' to try any person who attempts to lower the dignity of labour. Such courts are not concerned with disputes about wages and hours, but with the honour of the worker. If a man feels unworthily treated in his factory, he applies for a court of honour, and the employer is summoned before a tribunal consisting of a professional judge, a representative of the workers, and a representative of the employers. No figures as to the number of such trials in the local industries are as yet available, but the Central Office told me that in the two years of existence of the Reich or Central Courts of Honour (dealing with the more important cases), only thirty cases have been tried.

It is obvious that such a system depends for its successful operation on the resources of a totalitarian State. Its basic assumptions are that trade unions are prohibited organizations and that strikes are out of the question, because the penalties for striking are those for ' State sabotage ', in other words, for treason. Equally important conditions are that membership is virtually compulsory and that all awards must be accepted without question.

Granting these basic postulates, the system seems to suit the conditions. The emphasis is on a new collaboration between capital and labour ; and it must be stressed that the element of constraint is present just as much for employers as for employees. All pre-existing associations of employers were abolished along with the trade unions, on the ground that they, too, represented particular interests.

The position of the employers is an interesting one. The Law for the Organization of Labour makes them leaders, but they are taught that responsibilities go with this privilege, and they are severely punished if they transgress the principles of co-operation on which the Labour Front is organized. If a strike is impossible in the New Germany, so too is a lock-out, and the punishment in either case is just as drastic.

Moreover, the 'confidential councils' have very definite powers, because the complaints come from men who know actual factory conditions, and they know that they can appeal to wider authorities, if their employer-chairman tries to thwart their legitimate demands. The power of making him produce his accounts is freely employed, so that it is impossible for him to make the profits he formerly did under the old uncontrolled system.

Probably the most valuable results of the new Labour Front are through the suggestion of supplementary laws to the Ministry of Economics or the Ministry of Labour. There is a direct channel of access from the factory-bench to the Ministry in Berlin, and it is claimed that factory laws are now made by workmen and not by Civil Servants.

The Nazi authorities hold that the new institution is popular with the workers, but there is no way of verifying this statement. They say that the monthly contribution of the average workman is now only 1·60 marks (assuming his salary to be 120 marks a month), and that the employers contribute according to the size of their business. Inquiries about the distressed industrial regions in Silesia and Westphalia elicited the response that there is no difference in the number of members here than in the rest of Germany, and that 'the more distress, the more satisfaction with the new habits of compromise'. Questions along these lines were not kindly received whenever I went to the Labour Front headquarters.

A very significant statement by the central office is that

' practically all working people belong to the Front, except Jews, whose membership is legally forbidden '. This needs no comment.

Briefly, the position seems to be that the Nazis are emphasizing industrial co-operation by employers and employed, within the narrow limits left after the abolition of the trade unions and employers' associations. As officially defined, the idea is ' to raise the national income by the co-operation of all, with everybody benefiting '. But, interesting as the experiment is, it remains essentially dependent on the sanctions of a totalitarian State.

In so far as other countries are concerned, the main interest will be in the possibility of adapting the ideas of ' the Social Office ' of the Labour Front, so that the practical men in the factories may make their suggestions known to the Ministry of Labour by a regularly organized channel. By means of the Labour Front, Germany had interposed a new body— one might say, a buffer between the Ministries and the working classes ; and she claims that the very presence of this body bridges the gap that hitherto caused so much friction through ignorance and misunderstanding. In other words she claims that she has gone one stage in advance of the trade unions and employers' organizations that exist in other countries, and, without overthrowing capitalism, has produced a new balance in industry.

Beyond everything in the German world is the dictatorship of the State, so that even measures which are nominally voluntary (such as membership of the Labour Front) have ultimate coercion behind them, and everybody knows this. On the other hand there is undoubtedly a better industrial spirit in Germany, and the mass of workers believe that the Labour Front not only gives them a scope (which they had not expected in a totalitarian system) but that they are working for the power of the Fatherland. Patriotism has thus been evoked as the last ally of the Labour Front.

II.—*Organized Travel Movements*

From the human point of view, one of the most interesting experiments in Germany has been the attempt to supplement wages by providing facilities for travel or enjoyment. A most popular section of the Labour Front is the department known as 'Strength through Joy' (*Kraft durch Freude*). This was set up at the end of 1933, and only the lower paid workmen can take advantage of its facilities. The limit is a variable one. A typist cannot enter the organization if she earns more than 150 marks a month, whereas a worker with four children is still eligible even if he earns as much as 500 marks.

The idea is to get the workman away from his everyday surroundings. Any workman who wishes to travel gets into touch with the works member of the 'confidential council' (set up by the Labour Front) and thus with the district office of the movement. He receives a card which is stamped with his weekly contribution and, when he has saved enough money, he goes on one of the trips. In the first year of operations, 3,000,000 workers took such trips, and this year the number is expected to exceed 6,000,000. When the hotels were filled, the trippers went on hired boats. To-day six vessels go to Madeira or Norway, and the Labour Front is building boats of its own. Last summer 150,000 workers took sea trips, a week's cruise to Norway costing less than thirty marks.

In addition, eighty recreation homes have been built, and at present the Government is constructing a huge spa on the island of Rügen to accommodate 20,000 people. Seaports are being organized along the entire northern coast, and there is barely a region of Germany that is not being opened up by some form of this tourist activity. The motorist in Germany encounters the huge buses with the *K.d.F.* symbol in the most inaccessible spots and frequently finds towns overrun by them, until his zest for the organization almost changes into a feeling of exasperation.

The amazing feature is that, apart from administrative personnel, the scheme is claimed to be self-supporting, because hotel proprietors and railway owners[1] are satisfied with smaller profits in order to get the extra business. The central authorities in Berlin told me that this applied to building ships of their own, but I fail to see how huge liners can be made to pay at a daily rate of six and a half marks per person.

Nevertheless, *Kraft durch Freude* appears to be an excellent device for providing holidays for people who would not otherwise get them. Its varying success in different districts provides a kind of social barometer. At headquarters in Berlin, regional graphs (which cover whole walls) enable the authorities to see at a glance how many people from each town are taking holidays, where they are going, how many more or less are going than at this time last year. They are multi-coloured marvels of statistical ingenuity and, if accurate, afford excellent data about the prosperity and loyalty of each region in Germany. I investigated the applications from Silesia and the distressed Rhineland area and was amazed to find no essential difference from elsewhere.

Another department of the organization arranges theatre facilities for the same class of people. A census of the great Siemens factories taken when the Nazis came to power showed that three-quarters of the people never went to theatres. The Government therefore arranged with theatrical managers that blocks of seats should be made available to workers at special rates. Workmen who received good reports thereupon take part in a ballot for these seats, so that for seventy-five pfennigs, a man may find himself in the front row of the stalls or up in the gallery.

The position here is rather complicated, because the Propaganda Ministry frequently intervenes, giving grants in special cases and sometimes taking over whole theatres. Some propagandist plays may be opened to the public for nothing, while, at other times, the Ministry takes over an ordinary commercial theatre when some play or picture with an historical moral is being presented. There may be a direct

[1] Railways have now been taken over by the State.

grant for a given play, or merely indirect aid through a reduction of taxes ; and, to complicate matters, such grants may come either from the Labour Front or from the Propaganda Ministry. The upshot of it all is that a worker may go to selected plays for seventy-five pfennigs, to operas for ninety pfennigs, and to ordinary plays in outside theatres for half the ordinary rates. Officially no compulsion is exerted on owners of theatres, only ' persuasion '. The Labour Front argue that the owners welcome their intrusion because empty seats are filled and plays booked in advance ; but it is obvious how such a system must work in the direction of making the theatre a subsidiary propagandist body for the Party.

Films, other than moralizing historical presentations, are outside this scheme in the towns. But, in the country districts, film shows and concert parties circulate in parts where otherwise they would not pay. There is a definite move to educate the musical taste of the people, in the direction of chamber music, for instance. Orchestras are sent round to factories, and, for a few pence, workers can hear conductors like Feuchtwangler.

Already 25,000,000 people a year benefit from these facilities, and, once again, it is claimed that the State pays nothing, although obviously the subventions from the Propaganda Ministry and the losses in taxes must be counted on the debit side. If one puts aside the propagandist element, one must admit that this movement is definitely providing facilities that would not otherwise exist, although it is at first a little strange to pay many marks for a seat in a theatre and find a neighbour who has paid only a few pfennigs. The system reaches its height in the *People's Theatre* in Berlin, the former circus in which Max Reinhardt staged his most flamboyant spectacles. The great circular building has now become a People's Theatre, at which two-thirds of the seats are reserved for workers. Last year the productions varied from *Peer Gynt* and *The Merry Wives of Windsor* to operettas of Strauss and Lincke. It must be added, however, that a popular revue, *Let's have a Good Time*, had by far the longest run.

A further department of the ' Strength through Joy ' movement is that which provides facilities for cheap sport. This arouses more attention in Germany than it would in a British country, and my mentors could not understand my lack of interest in this phase of their activities, a phase of which they were particularly proud. The idea that sport was not a matter for the Government found no support with them ; and I had to listen to accounts of the intricate organization for popularizing sport amongst the German masses. The Labour Front provided funds for endowing this department, and a huge pyramid of committees was set up from factory to the whole Reich. It was all taken very seriously. Lectures are a regular part of the programme, and the aim is to improve the bodies of the Germans, and in no sense to create new records. It was in the academically serious atmosphere of this department that I felt myself most a foreigner in Germany.

No arrangements are made for football and handball, on the ground that these are already too popular, but a workman can obtain an evening's sport by paying twenty pfennigs, or, if he wants instruction in swimming, ten pfennigs more. The accompanying lectures even in central Germany, go as far afield as sailing and ski-ing. From a little over half a million in the first year, the number of people using these facilities has swollen to 6,000,000 a year. This was stressed as one of the greatest achievements of the new régime, and my arguments that British sport needed no such State aid were received with kindly sympathy as still another instance of how we were losing the race. Even my aide from the Foreign Office, a man who had taken a degree in an English University, thought my attitude to Government-organized sport—so palpably one of the most cherished achievements of the Third Reich—a little flippant. For the women, there is a special department called ' Jolly Gymnastics and Games '. It should be added that only ' citizens ' may share in this comradeship of sportsmen ; in other words, Jews and part-Aryans are excluded.

And so, runs a piece of propaganda, ' the contentment of the day's work vibrates into the leisure hours in which fresh strength is gained for the next working day ', and, at the same time, one's pride of nationality and heritage is increased. At first I was inclined to interpret ' Strength through Joy ' as a spectacular embellishment of government, but, after further investigation, I realized that it was one of the most striking forms of social service I had yet seen and, at the same time, a most efficient method of propaganda. The Germans rank it with the Labour Service camps as a great instrument of national regeneration and one of their most original contributions to social history. It is an officially organized campaign for *Health, Joy, and Homeland*, and, as such, is a cult peculiarly Teutonic.   Nevertheless, propaganda apart, it is a most attractive organization. Beethoven for sixpence, Bavaria for eighteenpence and Norway for six shillings a day, the sea for the mountaineer and the mountains for the sailor—its prospects are most alluring, and I regretted my inability to accept Dr. Ley's invitation to go on a cruise to the Norwegian fjords—eight days for twenty-two marks— if I insisted on paying for myself.

Chapter Four

WOMEN AND POPULATION : THE FIGHT
FOR THE RACE

Nazi leaders make no secret of their belief that women's duty is primarily domestic. The cult of 'the three K's'—*Kinder, Kirche, Küche* (Children, Church, Kitchen) is definitely in the ascendency. Hitler has frequently endorsed it,[1] while Goebbels has said that 'women's particular field is the care of the coming generation,' and Frick who is in charge of the health organization for mothers, is always extolling the virtues of family life.

Hitler's speech to the women who had assembled for the Nuremberg Congress under the vivacious Frau Scholtz Klink, was particularly natural and ingenuous. As he said himself, he was not being seriously reported and so could speak freely. 'You ask me what I have done for the women of Germany,' he said. 'Well, my answer is this—that in my new army I have provided you the finest fathers of children in the whole world ; that is what I have done for the women of Germany.' Politics !—he admitted that they were excluded, but it did not matter because they proved strong meat even for men, and were a dirty game at the best. 'What does it mean to enter the Reichstag ?' he went on. 'It was only a bag of rotten apples, and under me, it no longer

---

[1] Hitler is said (probably falsely) to be the author of the following rhymed couplets, addressed to women :

> 'Take hold of kettle, broom and pan,
> Then you'll surely get a man !'

and
> 'Shop and office leave alone,
> *Your* true lifework lies at home.'

counts, anyway.' What really mattered were such things as husbands, children, the ' Mother and Child ' movement, winter relief, hospitals for mothers, a sound population with eugenic principles, and the bringing up of children ready to sacrifice everything for the New Germany. ' You must produce more young children who will be as good soldiers for Germany as their fathers '. That was the subject of his pleading, as he went on in a heavily playful and somewhat patronizing manner.[1]

To his audience he had denied the benefits of higher education and careers ; instead he wanted to make them good cooks and prolific mothers, yet they cheered him to the echo, these specially chosen representatives of the Girls' Movements from all over Germany. They saw nothing restricted in the limited future their *Führer* offered them ; if he had ordered them then and there to marry privates of the line, they would have done so blindly.

Hitler has experimented with a Women's Labour Service, on the model of the conscript Labour Army for men. At present it is on a voluntary basis, except for girls who are entering universities or marrying ' political leaders '. They have to serve for six months. The first such camp was opened at Schurmbach in 1935, and others followed. The girls live in houses, not barracks, and spend most of the day working for farmers' wives, learning to milk cows and make cheese and the like.

Their routine is a rigorous one. Arising at five-thirty, they have exercises and singing until seven o'clock. After breakfast they have to work from half-past seven until three o'clock, either in the settlement or on a neighbouring farm, with half an hour for lunch. Then they have an hour's compulsory rest and classes until half-past six. The evening is always devoted to singing or lectures, and they have to go to bed at half-past nine.

A high official in the Labour Service Corps who took me over one of these Girls' Hostels outside Berlin was rather

---

[1] At the Congress two years before, he had specifically said : 'Whereas man makes his supreme sacrifice on the field of battle, woman fights her supreme battle for the nation in childbirth.'

sceptical about the whole project, despite the rumours that labour service was to be made compulsory for girls as well as men. The problem of leadership was proving a very difficult one, he said, because Hitler had ordered that leaders had to be women who were not appreciably older than their charges, and it was proving very difficult to find enough of the right kind of women. Moreover, in my guide's opinion, the problem of women's service would only be solved by allowing each girl another to look after her !

This patronizing attitude was typical of the outlook of German men towards the women. I heard no voice raised in favour of the participation of women in public life, except from a Scandinavian investigator who said that ' a country which ignores the potentialities of half its people (all the women) is mad '. Again and again officials of the Labour Army said deprecatingly : ' Of course you can't expect a women's camp to have the discipline and seriousness of a men's camp '. Women are clearly relegated to marriage and the home in practice as in theory in Germany to-day. Last year, Rudolf Hess, speaking on this topic, said that Germany did not interfere with other nations' ideals of womanhood, and therefore foreigners should not criticize Germany's ideas. Germany, he said, wanted women to be mothers, and the Party was opposed to them entering the professions or becoming ' mannified ' caricatures. The ideal German woman is one ' whom we can succeed in loving ', and who will add to the race. A special privilege is given to Leni Riefenstahl, the former film star, who is now allowed to earn a million marks a year as virtual dictator of the German film industry. For the others, there are *Kinder, Kirche, und Küche.*

Hitler particularly wishes to increase the population of Germany. This was embodied in Point 21 of his original Programme. It is an essential part of his racial theory that only the biologically desirable physical specimens should bear children. ' There shall be no race-pollution ', he said. Since the end of 1933, a Sterilization Law has been in operation. Under it ' Hereditary Health Courts ' are set up, with courts of appeal and a Supreme Court to give final verdicts.

Individuals afflicted with various hereditary complaints were to be sterilized (although why St. Vitus's Dance, alcoholism, and blindness come under this category is not clear) ; and the courts have operated, even in the case of foreigners.

Positive aid to desirable parents was considered still more important. There is a special section of the new Penal Code dealing with the family. A husband may not give away his property by will to anybody except his wife and children. Everything is done to protect the race. Industrialists are punished if they overwork expectant mothers. Abortion is an offence, campaigns for birth-control are forbidden, and anybody who sneers at motherhood in word or writing is liable to heavy penalties. In this fashion a cabinet of men who for the most part have no children seeks to protect the family system.

A system of marriage-loans has been introduced, both to assist marriages and to take young women off the labour market. Each approved couple obtains a loan of a thousand marks, not in cash but in certificates with which they can buy furniture. Such certificates must be cashed with the small artisans. As one of the scheme's aims is to encourage small industry, they cannot be taken to the big stores. The loan is repaid in a curious fashion. The debtor is released from a quarter of his obligations with every child he has ; so that if he has four children he has to pay nothing. Twins count as two. When I inquired at a ministry what happened if there were no children,[1] the official rang up the officer in charge of this scheme and he replied : ' When couples have passed our medical test, there always *are* children ! ' The scheme has been so successful that the total appropriation set aside for the purpose was soon exhausted, and additional grants had to be made from the budget. Up to the end of 1936, 700,000 people took advantage of it and were lent 420,000,000 marks. The congestion on the labour market was relieved because preference was given to girls who had been working. Civil Servants are spoiled still further, for they receive a bonus for every baby as well. Income tax is also reduced by 15 per cent for each child.

[1] Actually the loans are amortized at 1 per cent per month in such cases.

In addition Hitler has organized a national health service, based on the assumption that the State's first duty is to look after the healthy sections of the community, not the weaklings. An organization was set up in the Ministry of the Interior in July 1934, under an official who occupied the three posts of Ministerial Director of the National Health Department, leader of the Reich Committee for Health Service, and chairman of the State Medical Academy in Berlin. All health services were centralized, and the Department was given surprisingly wide powers. It looked after the health of children and workers ; it controlled the training of doctors and midwives and dentists and chemists ; it had charge of genealogical research ; it made investigations into measures that would increase the population ; and it had a variety of duties ranging from water supplies to serology, from means of securing fertility to disposal of corpses. There is a regular organization of public health offices for every district in Germany. They control everything, from keeping insects out of open-air baths to seeing that farmers keep their cows clean.

One of the most important problems dealt with by the health offices is 'racial and hereditary culture', especially advice on marriage. At the moment, offices to give such advice are being established throughout the country ; and ultimately a certificate from such an office will be an essential pre-requisite for any marriage. This was foreshadowed by the law of October 1935. Despite a lack of *Lebensraum*, Germany is doing everything to fill the cradles. There is even a special paper, *der Völkische Wille*, the organ of the 'Reich Association of the Rich-in-children Families'.

Unfortunately the statistical improvement has not been great. Hitler aimed at an increase of 45 per cent over the low birth-rate of 1933, but all the propaganda could not raise it beyond 23 per cent. At this rate Germany's population will reach 68,000,000 in 1945, after which a steady decline is forecast, to 47,000,000 at the close of the present century.

On the other hand, the physical standard of the race is undoubtedly improving. The Nazis are raising a generation of blond physical beauties. Of the conscripts called up for service last year, three men out of four were classed as physically fit, and only one in every thirty was described as unfit for service of any kind. These are the men born during the war, who were said to have been affected for life by the privations of the war and the blockade.

Provisions are made for sport and physical training from the kindergarten onwards. Every university has its institute of physical education, and the undergraduate must attain a certain standard of physical efficiency before he can take his degree. Since they spend six months in the Labour Service Corps before they come to the university and are compelled to take part in the open-air exercises of the Storm Troops during their course, it is obvious that their health is well looked after.

It is little wonder, then, that the Germans carried off the great majority of the prizes in the last Olympic Games. The whole nation is given over to intensive physical training at the moment. It is normal for young factory workers to spend their evenings in the gymnasia provided by the *Kraft durch Freude*, and arrangements are made by which youth leaders attend short-course camps all over Germany and then return to their own districts to act as instructors. ' All for the Race ' is the slogan one sees plastered on thousands of walls in German villages.

Chapter Five

PUBLIC WORKS AND THE GREAT ROADS : THE FIGHT FOR EMPLOYMENT AND PROGRESS

I.—Public Works

An essential part of Hitler's programme of recovery was the stimulation of public works. This was nothing new in itself. The Weimar Republic had spent much of its loan-money on public buildings and housing schemes ; and Brüning had evolved a ' works-creation programme ' financed by short-term loans. Hitler now extended this device and made it his main weapon in the fight against unemployment. In addition to his motor roads (to which I shall refer later), he compelled the unemployed to join labour gangs to clear slums, to carry out his schemes of town-planning and to erect blocks of cheap flats for artisans. At every stage he evinced a personal interest in such architectural work, and everywhere in Germany one sees signs of the great building revival. The Third Reich is indeed the paradise of the engineer and architect, and Germany has evolved a delightful neo-classical style of architecture, which combines simplicity with symmetry and reaches its ultimate expression in such buildings as the new Air Ministry in Berlin or the House of German Art in Munich.

Hitler was even more interested in the smaller hamlets than in the large towns. He has made models of ' farm groups ' which are designed so as to eliminate the loneliness of country life and to bring city amenities to the peasants. He is building 100,000 ' semi-rural ' houses every year for artisans. ' The Beauty of Labour ' department of the Labour Front works in the same direction. It claims that the application of planning can transform the most desolate factory region, and much has been achieved through the co-operation of its technicians with workers and employers.

II.—*The Motor Roads*

Much propaganda has been made out of the gigantic system of motor roads or *Autobahnen* in Germany ; and undoubtedly they are one of the most amazing of the many sights paraded before visitors to Nazi Germany.

On a late autumn day in September 1933, Hitler himself turned the first sod of the new roads at a spot just outside Frankfurt-am-Main. He had announced his plan at the first National Labour Day on the previous May 1st, and had passed an enabling law on June 27th. At that moment almost a third of the ' working ' population were unemployed. Most of these were not only on the dole ; from the Nazi point of view, they were becoming a menace to the new Government because their enforced idleness was turning them towards subversive political activities. It was to bring these men back to the employment market and to replace their psychology of disillusionment and despair by one of hope that Hitler set to work with pen and protractors on the map of Germany. No plan could have appealed to him more than turning hundreds of thousands of Germans on to the task of changing the face of the land. He also wanted to bring north and south into closer relationship and bridge the old localism that was cutting across his schemes for a united Germany. Some say, too, that he wanted to draw Germany together in one great strategic unit.

He created a new department called the Reich Motor-Road Group and placed it under the command of Dr. Fritz Todt, a forty-two-year-old engineer from the Black Forest and one of the earliest members of the Party. Working in close contact with Hitler, Todt drew up a scheme of almost five thousand miles of roads. The roads were to be the same everywhere, whether running easily along the northern plains or cutting through the most difficult passes of the Bavarian Alps. They were to consist of two parallel tracks, each twenty-five feet wide, and with sixteen feet of lawn or shrubberies between them. Traffic was to proceed in one direction only along each road, and it was estimated that there could be four lines of cars on each. Nowhere were there to be level-crossings. Where ordinary roads already existed, bridges or viaducts or tunnels were to be built. Cars entering or leaving the main roads have to glide off or on at certain points. Cross-traffic is thus impossible. Normally the concrete roads were to cut through pine-forests and plainlands, as nearly as possible in straight lines.

Naturally such roads are very costly, but Hitler planned to surmount this difficulty by using cheap labour and inducing suppliers of raw materials to cut their profits to a minimum. Such things can be done under a totalitarian Government. The financing of the roads is typical of the general jugglery going on in Germany's public accounts. The bill is expected to exceed a hundred and eighty million pounds; but Hitler is dealing with this sum in the same way that he is coping with all the other breath-taking expenditure in Germany. He is issuing short-term Treasury bonds and periodically renewing them; that is, he is simply expanding credit time and time again. The State is allocating £33,000,000 a year to the roads; but nobody is perturbed by their cost. Officials in Dr. Todt's Ministry in Berlin told me that half the cost of the roads has been saved in other directions, because half a million men have come off the dole and are either making roads or making concrete. This figure seems optimistic, because only 120,000 men are actually employed on the roads, and the auxiliary work of manufacturing cannot absorb many more than this, at the outside. The State claims that it is saving 120,000,000 marks a year in unemployment relief and is receiving 80,000,000 more marks in taxation on the raw materials being produced for the roads. By these ingenious calculations, the Roads Ministry argues that a third of the sum allotted to road-making would have been spent on relief payments and so does not count, and another quarter goes back to the Treasury in the form of taxes. The net cost to the State, then, is a little over a third of the amount nominally allocated every year—that is, about twelve million pounds a year. This analysis is interesting but far from convincing. The one obvious fact is that the roads have already provided 52,000,000 days' employment.

The labour position is also fascinating. It has often been stated abroad that the conscripts of the Labour Service are forced to work on the new motor roads, but this is not the case. A few of the conscripts are working on scenic roads in undeveloped parts of the southern mountains ; but the *Autobahnen* are built by ordinary manual labour from the cities. I saw many camps of the road-workers, both in north and south Germany. They live in wooden, barrack-like buildings and have their food provided by a mess. In many ways their life is semi-military. They make only a small contribution for their food and clothing, and their diet, while plain to the point of frugality, seemed to me no worse than that which I had sampled in military camps and training schools elsewhere in Germany. When the scheme first started, nobody paid any attention to the conditions under which the road-workers lived ; and they were so bad that Hitler, shocked with what he saw, set up a special department of the Labour Front to provide decent camps. As a result, architects devised uniform types of buildings which combined comfort with mobility. I should say that life is hard for a road-worker in Germany, but then the standard of living is low in their industrial cities. The best paid amongst them receive forty marks a week, but the average seems to be about sixpence an hour for an eight-hour day. Rates vary all over Germany, and in many cases the meagre wages are eked out by contributions from the charitable organizations in the towns from which the workers come. Usually a man working on the roads received less than he would have done in a factory at home. As far as I could make out, road-making was about as compulsory for the older unemployed as labour service was for the youth of Germany, although officially there is no element of compulsion.

Experts abroad tend to think that the propaganda element has been overdone, and that, after all, 600 miles of road in three years (with all the organization of a despotism behind the work) is not such a stupendous record, even if one takes into account the fact that each road is double.[1] Marvellous as these roads are, there is some truth in this criticism.

Travel on the new roads is rather peculiar. With no fear of cross-traffic and with a perfect concrete surface, there is no speed limit. While being officially conducted over these roads, I have taken notes when driven at eighty or ninety miles an hour. Dr. Todt himself has bought a supercharged car and Hitler has stated that his example of travelling at a hundred miles an hour will gradually become the norm. ' To survive in these years of trial ', said one senior official, ' German life must be speeded up to a hundred miles an hour '.   Railway bus services operate along the motor roads to a schedule of sixty miles an hour and heavy traffic is already moving from Berlin up to Stettin or Hamburg and out to Cologne at almost this rate—economists have already worked out by just what percentage this new mobility will reduce the cost of German manufactures ! They have also calculated to what extent the extra wear-and-tear on engines will give an impetus to the automobile industries.

This also applies from a military point of view. Officials in their expansive moments readily agreed that the network of roads had a military significance.   ' We are not building roads just for aeroplanes to look at ', one man said. ' Of course they can rush military supplies and troops to the frontiers in time of need. In fact ', he went on, ' you can learn a lot about German foreign policy by simply looking at the map and seeing which roads have been completed first.'   The reasons why the roads from the northern ports were completed at an early stage are obvious ; it is equally obvious why the roads have been built from the industrial parts of the Rhineland ; it is easy to see why the earliest roads should have been built around Essen and Mannheim ; and easier still to see why they ring the frontier around Czecho-slovakia and Austria. They point arrow-wise towards Salzburg in the south, and out from Dresden and Chemnitz, and from Frankfurt-on-Oder and Beuthen towards the heart of Poland. Two roads lead into Holland, two into

[1] The first completed strip, that from Frankfurt to Darmstadt, was opened on May 19th, 1935.

Belgium, two into Austria, and two into Poland, and the remainder link up the factory districts with the ports. The Germans say that this is only to bring fresh fish from the North Sea to southern Germany and to take Bavarian dairy produce to the industrial cities ; and perhaps they are right. If they are, strategic considerations have an uncanny habit of following economic necessities in Germany.

All in all, these straight white roads are very typical of Nazi Germany. They are needlessly grandiose but most impressive. Efficiently made and more than efficiently managed, they somehow seem to reduce the individual to insignificance. When one dashes along them, the pines become a solid mass of verdure, and the dazzling concrete mesmerizes one, until one comes to cease thinking and to realize that one is only an automaton in a machine age. They are boring, mechanical, and rather inhuman ; and after a time, one feels like making a stand for individualism by zigzagging hither and thither instead of keeping in place on the straight white lines ; but doubtless the special police squadrons and the breakdown gangs that clear picnickers and broken-down cars away in a few minutes would soon stop this. ' An *Autobahn* must always be kept clear '— this code has become as exaggerated as the attitude towards the Royal Mails in the early days of the post office. The roads are marvellous but uncanny, efficient but deadly monotonous ; and, above all, on their present scale, extremely needless. A case might be made out for single-track roads in such a national system ; but, under present German conditions, double roads are the sheerest form of extravagance, unless their *raison d'être* is to move military supplies. Even so, with 600 miles finished, there remain 3,800 miles to complete.

Chapter Six

THE DRIVE FOR A COMMON MENTALITY :
HOW A NATION IS HYPNOTIZED

I.—*Culture*

It was part of the Nazi creed that no aspect of life could stand outside the totalitarian State. Instead of the democratic licence that had hitherto prevailed in literature, art, and the drama, there had to be organized development. As soon as the régime was established, therefore, the Government proceeded to institute a series of trusts that would cover the whole cultural field.

In October 1933, a Reich Chamber of Culture was set up, under the ubiquitous Dr. Goebbels. This consisted of seven Chambers, each dealing with some aspect of cultural life (Literature, Press, Broadcasting, Theatre, Music, Art, Films). Each of these has a president and an executive board, and includes professional organizations from the whole of Germany. The presidents come together from time to time and meet as the Reich Advisory Board of Culture. Although the organization is now completed, Dr. Goebbels recently admitted that the task had been very difficult, and that his first two years' labour were slower than they otherwise would have been, because of ' the self-willed nature peculiar to people of intellect and artistic temperament '. Oddly enough, according to Goebbels, the men of culture proved amazingly conservative. An official account said : ' The will to something new almost invariably met with inherent opposition which the Minister ascribes as much to latent

obstinacy as to the initial recoil from the inrush of revolutionary ideas to which people of intellect are naturally more
susceptible' [*sic !*].   It was therefore counted as a concession
when, in November 1935, Goebbels set up a Reich Senate of
Culture composed of competent intellectuals.

The functions of these cultural bodies are said to be, firstly,
the provision of uniform and spirited leadership ; secondly,
the sifting of the worthwhile from the mediocre ; and thirdly,
setting forth juridical standards.   I am not certain what the
last means, but it is obvious that the scheme places all control
of cultural life in the hands of Dr. Goebbels, ' as *spiritus rector* '
runs one account.   The real aim is to develop culture along
National Socialist lines.   The Statute instituting the Chamber
of Culture specifically stated that ' it is the business of the
State to combat injurious influences and encourage those
that are valuable, actuated by a sense of responsibility for
the wellbeing of the National Community '.   In another
place, it states that ' all creative forces in all spheres must
be assembled under Reich leadership with a view to the
uniform moulding of the will '.   Beyond this, it goes on,
creative effort is to be individual and unrestricted.

It is only necessary to supplement this astounding view
of culture by stating that membership of one of the Chambers
is compulsory for every intellectual or artist, and that expulsion
due to ' cultural misbehaviour ' means starvation.

The executive president of the Chamber of Culture is
Hans Hinkel, one of the oldest members of the Party.   After
a few months of fighting in the war, he enlisted in the Ober-
land Free Corps after the Armistice and was so active in
sabotage in the Rhineland that the French sentenced him to
eight years' imprisonment.   He then became a reporter
on the first National Socialist newspaper to be established
in North Germany and later on Hitler's *Völkischer Beobachter*.
After the Revolution, this thirty-two-year-old reporter
became director of cultural organizations in Prussia and
later head of the Theatre Union.   To-day he enforces the
cultural ideas of Goebbels throughout Germany, and no
more need be said than that his actions are a reflection of his
training.

The Chamber of Culture is now four years old and, in so far as its goal was the subordination of cultural life to Nazi ideals, it has been completely successful. In each of its seven sections there has been a purge of undesirables and a unification of outlook. The creation of art was not part of the Chamber's functions. As Goebbels has repeatedly said : ' The uniform moulding of the will ' was more important.

Turning to each of the divisions of culture we may see how Hinkel's ' moulding ' worked out. Literature was placed under Hans Blunck, a retired civil servant. His theory is that contemporary literature goes back to the period of Romanticism, but a Romanticism purged of the egotism and the undue subjectivity of liberalism. He holds that the writers of Nazi Germany now represent a synthesis between two groups. On the one hand were ' the writers of the people '[1] who reacted from individualism to an emphasis on the responsibility of the individual to his community. They were led by the moralizing historical novelist, Edwin Kolbenheyer, and it was only the connecting link of a common nationalism that drew them into the fold of the second group, the adolescents of the Nazi Youth Movement who clamoured for revolt and romantic nationalism. They were the writers of the *Fronde*, and their viewpoint was that of the eternal opposition, save that they were destined at an early age to become the official spokesmen of the New Germany. According to Blunck, their strength lay in the application of their talent to such political topics as treaty-revision ; they trans-muted politics by applying ' the eternal German romanticism '. Scepticism and negation were swept aside, and in their place was a new creative will. As Blunck naïvely concludes when writing of the men in charge of German literature at the moment, ' every one of them has produced a life's work, which at this late stage is appearing before the public for recognition and appreciation for the first time '.

The literary output of these ' secret poets ', as Blunck calls them, these rulers of Germany whose transformation from fighting opposition to official beatitude occurred with surprising uniformity on January 30th, 1933, is not of high

[1] *das volkshafte Schrifttum.*

quality. Hitler, Rosenberg, and von Schirach are Germany's best sellers. *Mein Kampf* certainly does not sell for its literary merits, while the turgid outpourings of Rosenberg have only to be compared with a Swift or a Bolingbroke to be revealed in all their weakness. von Schirach is described by Germans as a great lyrist, but to the outsider his verses are but the jingles of an undeveloped adolescent. These men are supposed to be links with the *Burschenschaft* of 1848 or the great national revival against Napoleon ; but their writings lack fire and expression.

There is a marked paucity of literary output in Nazi Germany. Political tracts and heavy histories and works on military science sell well. While pornographic literature has disappeared (one of the salutary results of the new régime), the censorship on all remaining books is as harsh as in the first days of Hitlerism. A striking feature is the vogue for translations of foreign novels, although this is probably only an expression of the German lack of creation.

On the other hand, Goebbels is probably right when he says that he anticipates a greater productivity once the transition period is over. The exalted mysticism and the fervid patriotism of the new régime lend themselves to a peculiar mixture of expressionism and realism, a combination of idealism and actuality—everything that the German means when he speaks of *der neue Zeitgeist*. The individualist must shackle his belief to this standard or be for ever silent, and it must be remembered that the German system of education produces a type of mind that will find its form of revolt, not in opposition to the governing régime, but in romantic expressions of self-sacrificing patriotism that outrival those of his teachers. The adolescent will be more divinely mad than his mentors, and will allow himself the indulgence of a mystical exaltation that takes the form of a delight in sacrifice and immolation. By abnegating his individualism, he is finding the strongest expression for that individualism, and is thus unconsciously revenging himself on his instructors who teach the all-embracing virtues of uniformity. But whether this will produce the variety essential to literature is another question. Hans Blunck cannot have it both ways.

He contends that the strength of the present official writers (who now 'are revealing an almost immeasurable wealth of talent in all domains of creative art') was due to their campaigns against authority in their youth, their *Sturm und Drang* period ; but, if this be so, what can provide the *Fronde* of the coming generation ? Germany is relying on romanticism, on 'the deep passion to be allowed once more to accept the Mother as holy and the Child as a miracle' ; but it remains to be shown whether romanticism can flourish as an inspiration to young writers when it is officially directed and its various stages controlled by a Reich Literary Chamber which must report in turn to a Reich Chamber of Culture and to a Minister of Propaganda.

Hitlerism was associated with intellectual intolerance from the outset, although they called it the elimination of decadent thought. One of Dr. Goebbels's most spectacular efforts was in organizing the street riots in the winter of 1930 that resulted in the withdrawal of the film *All Quiet on the Western Front* from all Berlin theatres. The French pacifist film *The Wooden Cross* met a similar fate when the Nazis came to power. The youth of Germany were to be taught that war was fine, ennobling, romantic, chivalrous ; and truth was to be cast aside. Germany is one of the two countries in Europe to-day in which youth does not revolt against the idea of war.

One of the most disgusting episodes of the régime was Goebbels's famous bonfire of 'undesirable' literature. This product of seven universities even enlisted the aid of immature university students to pick books from their libraries and add fuel to his bonfire in the Opera-platz in Berlin. He even had the audacity to quote from a Renaissance scholar who welcomed the breaking of the bonds of medieval darkness in these words : 'O Century ! O Science ! What a joy to be alive !' To this accompaniment, the works of Remarque, Freud, Schnitzler, Marx, Gide, Zola, Proust, Helen Keller, Einstein, Ludwig, the two Manns, Wells, and even Jack London and Upton Sinclair were burnt, together with tens of thousands of other books.

Copies of all these offerings to the flames were kept in

Berlin and Munich. At Party Headquarters I was taken through room after room of confiscated literature. Since most of it is easily accessible in any good British library, I evinced no desire to work on it; but I was nevertheless informed that the records were all available to me except the confiscated literature. The custodian was a very intelligent man, a trained research worker. I asked: 'How could I write of National Socialism without considering the case of both sides?' In answer, he conducted me to another library which contained every sympathetic account ever written of Hitler, down to cuttings from local newspapers in small Australian towns, of which I, an Australian, had never heard. 'Here is the truth', said the librarian, 'and, in depicting the truth, one has no need of filth and lies.' In that building, although I raised the issue with many officials, not one would admit that it was necessary to cover all sources, friendly or inimical, in writing modern history. They are so convinced of the success of their propaganda that the propaganda has become truth to them, as unassailable as Holy Writ. To my riposte that most of the forbidden books were in the British Museum, they answered that such negligence accounts for the decadence of Britain and that a clean broom like Hitler is needed. They were genuinely sorry for a government which permitted free discussion of social and political problems; and many of them refused to believe that a Conservative Ministry allowed the open sale of Communist literature. Asked whether the restrictions on literature were mere phases of the transitional period, they all replied to the effect that the restrictions would become needless once the whole nation was educated up to Hitlerism. To lift them was unthinkable: one man said that, if they did that, they would be like a doctor who offers noxious drugs to unbalanced patients. My argument that a drug-taker, cured of his vice and fully convinced of the benefits of health, could face a whole drug-cabinet without giving way, was passed over in silence. Rigid control of the mind is so much an engrained principle of National Socialism that it was almost heresy to question it. Intellectual detachment is treason to them (had not Göring once said in public: 'I am

not concerned with both sides. I see only those who are
for National Socialism and those who are against it, and I
know how to deal with the latter ! ').

II.—The Press

The president of the Press Chamber is one of the ' old
fighters ' of Hitlerism—that Max Amann whom I have
previously mentioned as the first manager of the Party and
one of the rebels of 1923. He was a Catholic born in Bavaria,
and his first task was to act as Goebbels's assistant in the Press
campaigns against the Republic. He has been a permanent
official of the Party since its inception and publisher of its
leading newspapers. Without his business ability the *Völkischer Beobachter* and *Der S.A. Mann* could not have survived
their early days ; so that it was natural for Hitler to give him
charge of the Press organization as soon as it was instituted.
Another of his claims was that his anti-Semitism was even
more marked than that of Julius Streicher.

Amann turned with relish to his job of dictating to the
Press and moulding the older journals to the needs of Hitlerism.
The new German Press Law provided him with a code of
morals and the powers of a dictator, assuming that he did not
quarrel with Goebbels. Thereafter, only persons who were
Aryans and whose wives were Aryans could become journalists. Every journalist had to be registered on a professional
list, entries on which the Minister could veto at will. If a
man is struck off the list for misconduct, he can no longer
exercise his profession ; and misconduct includes such vague
offences as weakening the strength of Germany externally
or internally, or ' confusing selfish interests with the common
interest ', or offending the honour and dignity of any German.
Any offender is tried before a professional court whose
members are nominated by the Minister of Propaganda.

Even this Act was insufficient. Since it served to cause
a bitter struggle with the Press, Goebbels amended it in
April 1935 by an even more stringent law which compelled
all newspaper publishers to register the names of shareholders,

to declare the number of shares held by each, and to afford proof that all shareholders possessed Aryan ancestry as far back as 1800, a test that is even more sweeping than that imposed on Government servants. To dispel doubts, summary power was given Herr Amann to dismiss any editors or reporters without reason being assigned. Finally, no professional or class organization was to be allowed to publish any newspaper.

Such Acts obviously place all power in the hands of the persons administering them, and in practice the Press Laws have been used to secure the complete subordination of the entire German newspaper world to the Ministry of Propaganda. Fifteen thousand German journalists became an organized corps of official propagandists, and every German newspaper became a replica of the other. This is one of the saddest features of the new régime—to see a body once pulsating with vigorous life reduced to a state of chronic anæmia and bereft of all vitality. The Press Law is in no sense a dead letter. The censorship under it is a daily one, its control extends down to the tiniest *minutiæ* in the smallest provincial newspapers. The honoured term *Schriftleiter*, formerly the glory of every recognized journalist, is now an emblem of servitude.

The initial 'clean-up' was naturally the most drastic. It may be said to have ended by April 1934, by which time a thousand newspapers had been suppressed by the authorities and a further 350 had ceased publication voluntarily. Old-established moderate papers were swept away with Socialist and Communist sheets. Even the *Vossische Zeitung*—'*Aunty Voss*,' the very type of respectable middle-class journalism—ended its life of 230 years, although, in its swan song, it expressed the hope that the existing restrictions would only mark a period of transition, and that the German Press would ultimately regain its healthy variety. Other newspapers had to submit to purges of their staff and, sometimes, as in the case of the *Berliner Tageblatt*, were forced to come under entirely new ownership.

Even within the circle of Party publications there was a steady drive for uniformity. Thus, the old *Deutsche Zeitung* and the *Ostpreussische Zeitung*, though official organs of the Government's agricultural policy, were offered up as sacrifices to 'Press unity' and had to cease publication. Dr. Ley's own profitable side-line, *Der Deutsche*, also had to give way to Goebbels's own *Angriff*. Not even the head of the Labour Front could keep his own newspaper as the organ of that Labour Front.

In this way—further examples are needless—the face of German journalism completely changed. A deadening uniformity settled over the Press—what Dr. Goebbels extolled as 'most praiseworthy discipline and solidarity'. On occasion, as after the night of June 30th, he contrasted the decency of the German Press with 'the most evil kind of revolver-journalism' practised abroad, and denounced the professional lie-manufacturers who were poisoning world opinion.

He maintains that his restrictions have nothing to do with liberty of opinion. The Press is free, so long as it does not concern itself with disruptive influences. He even invited criticism, while adding that 'criticism for the sake of criticism is an impossibility'. The editor of one of the most widely circulated weeklies, the popular *Grüne Post*, took such statements at their face value, and protested against the monotonous presentation of news under the new conditions, appealing to Goebbels as 'a friend of wit and irony'. The answer was suppression and imprisonment.

So obvious was the opposition, however, that Goebbels modified the requirements of the Ministry and, after the middle of 1934, it was again possible for newspapers to exercise a limited choice in the presentation of their material. They did not have to publish only official reports of speeches, and they were allowed to make their own arrangements for reporting public ceremonies. It remains true, however, that, while German newspapers are not (as they were in the worst period) duplicates with merely different names, 'official copy' still has to be printed according to order, and real criticism is out of the question. One moment of ebullience means ruin for an editor, a single error of judgement will entail his downfall, so that it is better to take no chances and produce only a dully monotonous sheet. More and more, the editors are blindly following Hitler's own paper, the *Völkischer Beobachter*, and realizing that the day will come when no place will remain for non-Party publications. Many of the Party leaders live on the proceeds of the newspapers they own, and it is against human nature that, in a totalitarian State, they should not take measures to ensure the dissemination of what they regard as the truth, especially when it means more dividends to themselves.

The worst aspect of this position is that it carries into peace-time that censorship and control which we only associate with the exigencies of a period of war. The internal aspects are not our concern, for it means nothing to us if the Nazi leaders are as immune from criticism as our wartime leaders, and it is equally no concern of ours what steps Germany takes to build up a uniform mentality at home. But the problem becomes very different when the system means that the mass of Germans have absolutely no idea of what is happening in the outside world, except through the official Nazi channel. Events in Russia and Spain are known to them only through the eyes of the German Government, and I doubt if there was ever so great an opportunity for an interested government to mislead a whole people.

There were many examples last year of the working of this system. Most Germans believe, for instance, that Russia constitutes an immediate military menace to their borders ; that the Popular Front in France is a kind of anarchy ; that French devaluation was a sign of French weakness as contrasted with the impregnable position of the mark ; that Czechoslovakia allowed Russia to build aerodromes on the German frontier ; that the issue in Spain was from the outset only a question of order versus Communism ; that Hitler's Saturday afternoon coups were accepted abroad as signs of Germany's overwhelming strength ; and that scheming foreign nations tried deliberately to encircle the Reich. They believed these things, because they were dinned in so often in their Press. If foreign nations protested, the protests found no mention in the German Press. The German public were forced to accept as facts the mixture of incomplete statements and unwarranted premises handed out to them by Goebbels and Amann ; in fact, the position is the more dangerous if their warping of news in certain directions is the product of genuine belief rather than material policy. If this is so, it is the case of the warped few warping the entire nation.

I view this control of the Press, together with the control of the minds of the young, as the most important factor in German life. It is interesting, therefore, to see how Dr. Goebbels justifies his regimentation of the Press. He starts from the assumption that the so-called ' liberty of the Press is one of the great abuses of democracy ', and that criticism should exist only to strengthen the nation as a whole. His whole structure is based on this reading of the past and the acceptance of this function of the Press. The Revolution of January 1933, he says, meant a fundamental upheaval in every part of German life, and it was only natural that the Press, too, should undergo drastic changes. There had to be a process of adaptation—*Gleichschaltung*. In this process editors who ' failed to understand the new epoch ' had to go, and their ' superfluous papers ' with them. This pruning, however, ' should in no way be ascribed to Governmental interference ', holds the official statement. It is due entirely to the change in the German reader himself, who has reached a new political and cultural level and will no longer tolerate the petty malodorous copy of the ' general advertiser ' type of journal. The sectional papers of parties and vested interests have gone—the foul growths ' that sprang up like mushrooms after a warm summer rain ', and that meant that ' anybody who wanted to form a more or less unbiased opinion about the real state of affairs was forced to read several newspapers a day '. In their place are papers, scorned abroad as ' a Press in uniform ', which give leadership and guidance in accordance with the spirit of the times. The number of newspapers appearing and their circulation do not matter in the slightest ; the only justification for their existence is ' the service which is to be rendered by them to the nation '. And so all papers which possessed the right to live and were of value continue to exist, and the disappearance of the unworthy organs will serve to increase the circulation of these that have stood the test.

That is the official point of view. It depends entirely on the assumption (laid down in *Mein Kampf*) that the function of the Press is to strengthen the Government, and that it is no abuse of Governmental functions to force all opposition journals out of existence. As Dr. Goebbels says, his system leads to a decent, noble, and dignified treatment of events, and ' the German people turns away with disgust and abhorrence from the kind of lie-manufacturer I have described, and answers their hysterical and pathological outbursts of fury and hatred with a loud and audible *Pfui Teufel* '. On another occasion he said that the best editor is the best propagandist, the man who realizes the propaganda value of news ' even without special instructions '. This being so, one can only add that he has been most successful in putting his ideas into practice. His control continues in every direction. Quite recently a journalist on the *Börsen-Zeitung* was jailed for life for showing foreigners the type of instructions received by editors from the Ministry of Propaganda, the plea being that it was against State interests to tell outsiders how strictly the German Press is controlled. He even attempts to control the foreign Press. Since he came to power, he has expelled from Germany sixteen members of the Foreign Press Association, the majority of them for criticisms which would evoke no notice in most countries.

The matter comes back again and again to fundamentals. If one believes in a totalitarian State, then one must accept Press control and admire Goebbels's efficient methods ; but, on the other hand, if one takes a stand for individualism and liberty of opinion and refuses to be fed with ideas by the government of the day, then the position of the Press in Germany can only be deplored.

Amongst his other functions, Dr. Goebbels is lord of Germany's broadcasting. While all transmitting stations are owned by the Post Office, Goebbels supplies their programmes and controls all staff appointments through the R.R.G.—the *Reichsrundfunkgesellschaft*. His actions reach far afield. At one moment he is dictating the programmes that come to Australia on the short wave more clearly than those from any other country ; at another, he is giving orders to jam transmissions from Russia and Czechoslovakia ; or again, he may be tightening up the control of the thousands of *Funkwarte* (radio officers) who must see to it that the ordinary German citizens listen to the programmes they should hear and refrain from listening to the treasonable transmissions of Otto Strasser or the Russians.

Germany to-day has over six million wireless listeners—more than Great Britain. This is due partly to the cheap set produced by Herr Hitler's orders, partly to the people's dissatisfaction with the newspapers, and not a little to the wish to pick up illicit information from foreign stations, despite the risk. In addition to these individual sets, there exist many thousands of communal receivers, which bray out on every town square and in every street when Hitler orders ' a national reception ' on some subject of first-rate importance. Not a school, not a factory, not a house escapes such a *Gemeinschaftsempfang* ; and woe betide any careless or ill-intentioned citizen who is found away from a wireless set during broadcasts of this kind. Hitler has perfected this kind of noisy appeal, and his organization is so effective that it can be said, without fear of contradiction, that the great majority of the people hear such broadcasts, whether they wish to or not.

Goebbels's monopoly is naturally exploited solely for National Socialist ends. He finds it easier to ensure complete obedience in the case of twenty-six Government-owned broadcasting stations than with thousands of news-papers ; and he has faith in the superiority of the spoken over the written word, especially if the words be repeated often enough. Moreover, he realizes that the air has no frontiers, and his stations at Munich pour tendentious in-formation into Austria, that at Königsberg into Lithuania, and that at Dresden into the Germanic regions of Czechoslovakia. In fact, he would be perfectly happy if only his engineers were capable of devising sets that could receive German broad-casts alone. Then he would indeed be ' lord of the air ' ; as it is, the large number of prosecutions for listening to foreign stations show the limitations on his power and testify either to human curiosity or foolishness, according to one's point of view. Outside news certainly penetrates to Germany in this way ; that was what made Goebbels's orders to the Press not to mention the British dynastic crisis last November so naïve.

As against this, however, it cannot be doubted that most Germans fall ready victims to the official broadcasts, especially on matters of foreign policy ; and one cannot but admire the excellence of the technique and propaganda of the German *Rundfunk*. It is very hard, even for a foreigner, to resist its messages, so convincingly are they delivered, because fervid partisanship permits an emotional intensity out of the question in a system where objective impartiality is sought. Goebbels has realized the terrific possibilities of broadcasting as applied to political propaganda, especially in a country where Party and State are interchangeable terms ; and he is at present reaping the reward of his pioneering in this direction. We may call it the subordination of truth to propaganda ; he describes it as employing a mighty weapon in the interests of the nation.

III.—*Education*

The Nazis have laid a heavy hand on education. They know that the text-books of to-day are shaping the political realities of the decades to come, and accordingly have made every part of education—curiously enough, even mathematics—a training ground in Nazi ideology. As soon as the child enters an elementary school (*Grundschule*) at the age of six, his days are given over to the idealizing of the Nazis. He counts up Storm Troopers, he sews crude figures of Black Guards, he is told fairy stories of the Nazi knights who saved the civilized maiden from the bad Russian gnomes, he makes flags and swastikas. After four years of this, he emerges to the *Volkschule* or *Mittelschule*, thinking of Hitler and his cabinet in the way that we regard Christ and His disciples. Their schoolwork is secondary to their activities in the youth organizations, especially when they reach the secondary school stage.

The whole of their education is tendentious. One of the earliest reforms of National Socialism was Dr. Frick's ban on the older form of education that failed to preach morals. Frick upbraided the teachers for having fallen behind in the national regeneration and warned them that they had to atone for their past faults by intense propaganda for the Nazis in the future. His warning particularly applied to the teaching of history. History was not a matter of objective fact, he told them, but a machine for inculcating German patriotism. All great men of the past were connected with Germany in some way or other, said Frick; all life-giving streams of civilization were due to the penetration of German blood or influence, all German history has been a struggle against encircling enemies, and never more than since brutal Imperialists forced her into a war of self-defence in 1914 and diabolically ground her to the dust. All world-history since the war has meaning only as bearing on the rise of Adolf Hitler; no other fact in the world counts as much as the new-found regeneration of the nation and the rise of the *Führer*.

This was the pattern to which the facts had to conform. When they could not be made to do so, they omitted whole slabs of them. 'How can you do this?' I asked a noted German historian, and he replied, 'My children must eat'; and, in several other cases, the reply was that the means justified the end. The German nation was being benefited by the false teaching, and, after all, said one historian, what difference was there between propaganda in peace-time and propaganda in wartime, especially nowadays when actual military operations were probably the least important part of war? There is probably nothing more revolting in Germany, not even in the stories of physical atrocities, than the degradation of professional historians.

Rust and Hinkel are the administrative leaders of German education to-day. Bernard Rust was, for over twenty years, a schoolteacher in Hanover, but his experiences as a battalion commander in the war made him chafe at the restrictions

to which he was submitted.   He sought relief by interfering
in provincial politics.   At last his extremely pugilistic nationalism lost him his job.   A schoolmaster cannot very well
conduct a vendetta against the parliament of his province.
At this time Rust was approaching his fiftieth year, and he
was saved from starvation only because the Nazis elected
him to the Reichstag and made him leader of the Hanoverian
group of the Party.   His promotion was rapid.   He became
first Commissioner and then Minister of Education in Prussia,
and later, in the whole Reich, distinguishing himself at each
stage by his efforts to subordinate education to Hitlerite
doctrines.   He claimed that even scientific subjects could be
used as media for instruction in National Socialism.   His
doctrines naturally reflected his personal experiences, and
he approached his task with a bitter feeling against the
professional leaders of education in Germany, against those
who merely did their jobs without interfering in politics.
Rust is a sallow little man with habitually clenched teeth.
For ever spoiling for a fight, he is never happy unless knocking
down obstacles.   Subtlety means nothing to him ; he prefers
to use his head as a battering ram.

At present, then, education is a weapon in the fight for a
Nazi *Weltanschauung*.   Preference is given at all stages to
Nazis.   Most of the scholarships are reserved for children
who have been members of some Party organization.   With
a few exceptions, non-Aryans are excluded, and plans are
being made for the segregation of such children in special
schools of their own.   For nine out of ten such unfortunates,
education necessarily ends at the high-school stage.   The
professions are closed to them.

Yet there is another side to the educational question in
Germany.   The Nazis have introduced order and efficiency
in administration.   Previously the educational system was
cluttered up by too many administrative organizations.
Much dead wood existed, and the ruthless pruning of Dr.
Rust did much good.   Moreover, it would be erroneous to
assume that the earlier system was free from political elements.
Many German teachers had adopted a defeatist attitude and
this penetrated their whole teaching.   In some of the larger

cities, the children of the poorer districts were being taught
Bolshevik ideas ; and, throughout Germany, much evidence
existed to support Rosenberg's attacks on *Kultur-Bolschevis-
mus.* This applied particularly to art, music, literary criticism,
and history, and was quite as destructive as the super-
patriotism of the Nazis—in some ways more so. Despite the
good points of the German system under the Republic,
it had lost much of its objectivity. Even where it was not
openly subversive it suffered from faults of emphasis, such
as the discarding of many non-practical subjects as mere
frills. It would thus be a great mistake to assume that the
Nazis took over an educational system as detached from
politics, say, as the British system. Of course, this does not
excuse the new Nazi tendentiousness ; but it explains why,
quite apart from their concept of politicalized education,
they were so concerned about the ' purification ' of teaching.
I have seen curricula from working-class schools of Berlin
and Hamburg that are grotesque travesties on education ;
yet these had received the blessing of the Republican authorities. As recent German writers have pointed out, it was
not the Nazis who started the idea of making education a
field for *Kulturwaffen*—a clash between rival systems of
Kultur : the Communists set the ball rolling, the Hitlerites
merely kicked the goal.

Chapter Seven

THE PRESENT PLACE OF THE JEWS

The stupidity of the first boycott of Jews on April 1st, 1933, and the degrading anti-Semitic measures of the Hitlerite Government, have made the name of National Socialism despised throughout the world. Probably no other phase of Hitlerism has received such universal condemnation.

This makes it all the more necessary to see if Hitler has any case against the Jews. It is useless to deny that a grave Jewish problem existed in Germany. Outsiders say that Germany is not the only country in which one person in every hundred is a Jew ; but such statistics fail to take into account the peculiar position attained by the Jews in the disturbed post-war years.

The Hitlerite case is as follows. Germany was in the unfortunate geographical position of being the first stage in the perennial westward push of the Jews—the *Ostjuden*. They started from the Polish marches to move towards New York and, unless forced on, tended to stop in Berlin and Hamburg. Almost half of the Jews in Prussia congregated in Berlin, where they proceeded to obtain an unduly large share of good professional positions. They showed no disposition to work on the land or at hard manual jobs. Whereas a third of the Prussians were farmers, not one Jew in fifty was to be found on the land, according to the vocational census taken eight years before the Nazis came to power. Practically two-thirds of them went to trade or commerce. But it was not this fact, so much as their undue hold on the professions, that hurt the Germans. In Berlin, for example, 50·2 per cent of the lawyers were Jews, and it was a truism that the barristers' room in any Berlin State Court was a Jewish club. In medicine 48 per cent of the doctors were Jews, and it was said that their influence was greater than this, owing to their systematic seizure of the principal posts, especially in the hospitals. More than two-thirds of the school and welfare doctors in Berlin were Jews ; so, too, were half the teachers in the medical faculty in the University of Berlin. While the Jews claimed that this predominance was due to their natural ability, the Aryans attributed it mostly to illicit Jewish combinations and influence.

It was not only the arithmetical side that perturbed Germany. Far more serious, in their eyes, was the Jewish grip on culture and their influence on the mind and morals of the community. Germany believes that the Jews always flourish in times of national distress. The average German thinks that such events as the Russian revolution and the November revolution in Berlin are happy hunting-grounds for the Lenins and Litvinovs, the Rosa Luxemburgs and the Karl Liebknechts. A race without roots, they say, always delights in assailing the roots of other people more favourably situated. Sometimes they did this openly (the Germans think that Magnus Hirschfeld's *Institute for Sexual Science* and his writings about homosexuality and the *third sex* were examples of this direct attack) ; sometimes indirectly through their control of publishing and theatres (twenty-three of the twenty-nine theatre managers in Berlin were Jews). The largest and most important newspapers in Berlin belonged to the Ullstein group, a Jewish stronghold. The *Morgenpost*, with its cir-culation of over a million, was Jewish ; the powerful *Vossische Zeitung* was Jewish ; the *Berliner Illustrierte Zeitung*, which went into almost two million homes, was Jewish ; the famous *Berliner Tageblatt* was for the most part edited by Jews and derived its news mainly from Jewish correspondents abroad (nobody who knew it in its heyday, however, could possibly deny that Alfred Kerr made a fine paper of it !). So marked was Jewish power over the Press that the German nation was once described as ' a people with severed vocal chords '.

The Jews had also made great inroads on the educational system, although statistics mean little unless we proceed on the German assumption—which will find little sympathy abroad—that every Jew in office is necessarily an evil force.

In some universities, however, such as Breslau and Göttingen, it was a drawback not to be a Jew. In 1914, taking the whole country, 30 per cent of the professors were Jews. On a numerical basis they should have been 1 per cent. They were particularly strong in the medical and philosophical faculties.

The next part of the German indictment of the Jews concerned their political activities ; and here we leave the field of fact for vague propaganda. It is true that the first revolutionary government had ten Jewish members, while in Prussia Jews were appointed to five ministries and to the leadership of the Press Bureau, the Food Ministry, and the Education Department. The Nazi headquarters claim that ' 80 per cent of all the most important administrative posts in the Reich and in the provinces and communities were in the hands of the Jews until the death of Rathenau '. This statement is certainly not proven, although it is clear that the Jews held far more than one-hundredth of the high offices !

Probably the Jewish menace in politics has been exaggerated. Hitler claims that Jewish groups financed the political movements of the Left but produces singularly few facts in proof of his contention. The Nazis particularly objected to the political activities of the Jewish vice-president of the Berlin City Police.

Of late, however, the noisiest argument against the Jews is their connection with Communism. Hitler never refers to Communism without describing it as ' Jewish Bolshevism ', and his most popular claim is that he saved Germany from Communist domination—in other words, from Jewish hegemony. This is another of the myths on which National Socialism has reared itself, and it has been reiterated so often that even many foreigners have come to believe it. The actual evidence is entirely unconvincing ; and ' the Jewish-Communist revolution ' remains on the same plane of unreality as the ' plot of June 30th '. Moreover, it has been overlooked that the story of a nation on the point of toppling into the arms of Jewish-Communism is absolutely incompatible with the other Nazi story of Hitlerism as a great upsurge of the whole people.

These were the main arguments in the German case against

Jewry. On analysis it waters down to very little except racial prejudice. But it fitted in with the traditional stock-in-trade of any politician bankrupt in constructive ideas. Hitler bawled *Juda verrecke !*—'Down with the Jews !'—from the beginning of his political career. Indeed, anti-Semitism was the only clear idea he had when he founded the Party. He capitalized the lowest features of a traditional racial hatred, and thus gave his movement a certain emphasis on destructiveness from the beginning.

Starting from the undoubted facts that a Jewish minority had secured an over-large measure of professional success, and that in some cases the preferment was due to racial influence, Hitler reached the position that 'there can be no good Jew'. He proceeded to condemn 600,000 human beings wholesale, irrespective of the individual's own characteristics. If his discriminatory acts had any justification whatever, he neutralized this by a mass racial persecution. The answer to the Jewish problem was not brutality and blind punishment of women and children, but a removal of the conditions that were said to give the Jews unfair advantages.

But the Nazis would not restrict the problem to its economic setting. They even jettisoned the cultural approach as being too narrow ; and ended by a wholesale attack on the Jewish race as a race. The fact that a man is a Jew renders him unfit to be a member of any civilized society—one Jewish child can contaminate a whole school ; one drop of Jewish blood taints the whole life-stream, and so on. Streicher even had a theory that, if a woman once had a Jewish child, her blood would be so affected that all of her later children would also be Jews !

Hitler was not content with redressing the real or fancied wrongs Germany had suffered at the hands of the Jews. He had to go on and extirpate the Jews root and branch, and this necessity became the more pressing once he developed the racial aspects of his philosophy. The doctrine of *Blood and Soil* necessitated an increasingly virulent form of anti-Semitism, for it meant that he could never mitigate his attack on Jewry without cutting at the roots of his whole philosophy. That was the *impasse* into which the anti-Jewish violence of Goebbels, Rosenberg, Ley, and Darré led him.

The attacks on Jews began as soon as Hitler came to power. The so-called 'atrocity campaign' in foreign newspapers against Hitlerism led to the official boycott of April 1st, organized by Julius Streicher. Jew-baiting continued sporadically until the beginning of 1935, when it assumed a much more virulent form. Streicher had been publishing a weekly paper called *Der Stürmer*, which printed the most loathsome kind of propaganda against Jewry. Streicher realized that a mixture of pornography and low racial diatribe could be made to pay, and Nazi organizations saw to it that his paper reached all party bodies and even the schools.

After months of unrestrained brutality, events came to a head at the Nuremberg Congress of 1935. Two laws were passed by the Reichstag on September 15th—'the Nuremberg Laws'—which definitely relegated the Jews to a position of serfdom in Germany. They are very short laws, one consisting of seven terse clauses, the other of three. The first states that 'only a national of German or kindred blood' can be a citizen. The other—*the Law for the Protection of German Blood and German Honour*—forbade marriages between Jews and Aryans and nullified marriages contracted (even abroad) in defiance of this law ; it forbade extra-marital relationships between Jews and Aryans ; it stopped any Jew from employing female domestic servants under forty-five years of age (since reduced to thirty-five) ; it forbade Jews to hoist national flags ; and it provided penalties of penal servitude for breaches of its terms. The Party's legal leader described these acts as 'the first German charter of liberties for centuries' and said that 'on them will depend in the future the definition of such terms as morality, order, decency, and public morals. They are the basis of liberty, the kernel of modern German justice'.

The Nuremberg Laws definitely established a class of helots in Nazi Germany ; and no words can aptly describe the conduct of the trials of persons accused of 'race defilement'. The prostitution of a legal system in the service of an insane racial prejudice is not a subject on which to linger.

At present, the German Jew has no civil rights. He is not a citizen ; he cannot vote or attend any political meeting ; he has no liberty of speech and cannot defend himself in print ; he cannot become a civil servant or a judge ; he cannot be a writer or a publisher or a journalist ; he cannot speak over the radio ; he cannot become a screen actor or an actor before Aryan audiences ; he cannot teach in any educational institution ; he cannot enter the service of the railway, the Reichsbank, and many other banks ; he cannot exhibit paintings or give concerts ; he cannot work in any public hospital ; he cannot enter the Labour Front or any of the professional organizations, although membership of many callings is restricted to members of these groups ; he cannot even sell books or antiques. If he is starving he can receive no aid from the *Winterhilfe* organization, and if he dies in battle his name will be on no war memorial (for has he not seen the erasing of the names of his forebears from such memorials by order of Goebbels and Frick ?). In addition to these, there are many other restrictions applying in certain localities. The upshot of them all is that the Jew is deprived of all opportunity for advancement and is lucky if he contrives to scrape a bare living unmolested by Black Guards or *Gestapo*. It is a campaign of annihilation—a pogrom of the crudest form, supported by every State instrument.

Many areas in Germany are now ' freed ' from Jews entirely. Julius Streicher, for his zeal, was made *Gauleiter* of the Franconian region, which included Frankfurt-am-Main and other thickly peopled Jewish centres. His ' purge ' has been a drastic one, and yet no worse than that in parts of East Prussia or Baden or Hesse. More than half a million Jews still live in Germany. The wealthiest among them can turn their money into goods (at heavy losses) and export these from the country ; and Jews who can get a living in other countries can sometimes escape : but the stark fact is that most of them must remain in Germany. Not unnaturally they drift to the cities, because there they are not as obvious subjects for persecution as in small villages ; but nowhere in Germany is their lot tolerable.

The traveller in Germany is impressed by the general consensus of opinion that such persecution is a good thing. I had expected many people to argue that it was an unwelcome necessity, forced on them by propaganda or by the pressure of events, but this was not the case. They gloried in the persecution, they were proud of their achievements, and looked forward to the day when not a single Jew would survive in the Reich. As one deputy said : ' Only through the radical extermination of the evil and alien part of our German blood can the future of our people be made eternally secure.' I met nobody in Germany who adopted an apologetic attitude—nobody who saw anything wrong in the attack on individuals irrespective of their personal worth. Everybody accepted the idea of race penalization as such.

The campaign goes on everywhere. Here shops would be closed ; there notices forbidding people to buy would be posted on shops still open. In a marvellous bathing establishment outside Rothenberg was a sign ' No Jews can bathe here '. On the roadside outside most country villages were signs ' No Jews allowed in this village ' or ' Jews forbidden '. In some they ran the whole gamut from ' Jews are not welcome here ' to the minatory ' Death to Jews here '. Outside one lovely medieval village in Franconia the sign read ' No Jews or wandering animals allowed in these precincts ', but this grouping may have been unintentional.

One of the more unpleasant sights at the Nuremberg Rally was the mushroom growth of street stalls selling anti-Semitic literature. Even the back of the Party-structures in the city square was leased for such purposes. Wartime propaganda was nothing like it. Some of the cartoons were physically revolting ; it was the sheer portrayal of filth (rather than the degradation of mentality that would stoop to such horrors) that upset one. A collection of cuttings from *Der Stürmer* or the *Judenkenner* has to be seen to be believed, and one has to go through the list and choose the most innocuous in order to find one that can be reproduced in a book for an English-speaking public. Yet Streicher, the producer of these monstrous cartoons, is still governor of Franconia, and time and again was singled out for special honours during that Party week. Most of the shop windows were emptied of their ordinary goods and displayed two huge portraits side by side, Hitler and Streicher ; and, at the gatherings, Streicher sat in the place of honour. Hitler is an untrammelled dictator. If he lifts his finger he can close down all the papers in Germany, yet he allows Streicher to continue his paper and go from bad to worse.

One of the most painful sights I saw in Germany was at a boys' camp in a Franconian forest. Young Titans, they were living an idyllic existence. After a display of staggeringly efficient physical exercises they were dismissed and crowded to the *Stürmer*-stall to get the last issue of Streicher's paper. Young boys gazed at the cartoons in rapt admiration ; and, when I asked the Black Guard officer with me whether he did not see anything funny in the grotesqueries of *Der Stürmer*, he replied : ' It is not funny. They must be taught the truth about the Jews. It is part of their spiritual upbringing.' I turned away from these sturdy adolescents and their ' new religion.' They were still rapt. Here was something to fight for. There is nothing quite so saddening as such a perversion of youthful idealism and enthusiasm.[1]

A few weeks later I was being shown round a famous collection of Party relics in Munich. The curator was a mild old man, a student of the old German academic class. After showing me everything, he led, almost with bated breath, to his *pièce de résistance*. He produced a small sculptured wooden gibbet from which was suspended a brutally realistic figure of a dangling Jew. This piece of humourless sadism, he said, decorated the table at which Hitler founded the Party, seventeen years ago. Asked if it were not funny, I replied that it was very, very tragic. Sobered for a moment, he replied, and this showed how far apart are the average

[1] As I was walking towards the gate of the camp I overheard an enthusiastic English peer say to my Black Guard officer : ' Gad, sir, this is a marvellous camp. It is just like the Boy Scouts, only better. Do you think you would let my son come here for a few months to get the spirit of it ? ' I looked back at the growing groups round the newspapers and then at a cartoon in my hand showing a Jew disembowelling a beautiful young German girl.

German and British mental processes : 'That is true. It is tragic—tragic to think what a hold Jewry had on Germany before the *Führer* came.' The horror of the gross little gibbet and all that it signified completely passed him by. To him it was natural and desirable for, after all, had not Hitler written in *Mein Kampf* that the true enemy of the world to-day is the Jew and that National Socialism 'must hold up for universal fury the wicked enemy of humanity as the true cause of all miseries' ?

Worst of all, worse even than the individual suffering of to-day amongst the Jews, is the creation of a national mentality bred on such hate as that which the German feels for the Jew. 'The other nations are not yet awake,' a university professor said to me, 'and the time will come when the world will be grateful to us for upholding civilization against the Jews.' I showed him my Australian passport with the name of a Jewish governor-general on the front cover, Isaac Isaacs, and told him of that other Jewish commander-in-chief, Monash, who first broke through the Hindenburg Line ; and his only retort was that such a degradation of a fine community only proved the truth of his contention !

The most tragic thought of all is that Germany is behind Hitler in his campaign against *Rassenschande* or race-defilement. I spoke about it to peasants and great industrialists, army officers, and factory labourers ; and all approved of it, although a few regretted the tone of *Der Stürmer*.[1] When a nation can willingly concur in a pogrom against half a million Jews —when it sees nothing tragic in the starving of little children and the holding of them up to execration in kindergartens— when it sees nothing funny in the official decree of the town of Königsdorf that 'cows purchased either directly or indirectly from Jews are not allowed to be served by the communal bull', then it reaches the point where its institutions are utterly incomprehensible to us.

In *Mein Kampf* Hitler writes that 'the black-haired Jew-

[1] That there is some opposition, however, is evident from the numerous attacks in Party papers on 'Jew-lackeys', that is Aryans who disapprove of brutality towards Jews.

boy lurks for hours, his face set in a satanic leer, waiting for the blissfully ignorant girl whom he defiles with his blood '. The pogroms since he came into power, and the Nuremberg Laws, are simply the expression of this earlier statement. It is not enough for them to make Ahasuerus take up his staff again and wander. He must be bent and broken, and his grandchildren with him. That is the measure of the New Germany's degradation.

Chapter Eight

SWASTIKA VERSUS CROSS

Dr. Goebbels, in issuing his code of behaviour to the Press, asserted that the German nation was never interested in the Church conflict and that only malevolent foreigners could be concerned with the domestic quarrels of the German people in these matters. This instruction was so well carried out that even during the most acute phase of the trouble it was impossible to follow events in the German Press, or even to realize that any problem existed at all.

Goebbels claims that the quarrel is only a question of organization, but this will not do. The issue is far more important than mere organization. It deals with the fundamentals of spiritual liberty. No section of the community can stand out against the laws of the State, say the Nazis ; no secular authority can interfere with liberty of conscience, retort the pastors and the priests. The laws of National Socialism, on the one side, stand clearly opposed to the dictates of the spirit, on the other. If there is a conflict between the law of God and the law of man, both Churches say, the latter must give way. It is the age-old struggle between laws temporal and laws spiritual, a struggle in which neither side can surrender without sacrificing its principles.

Almost from the first, National Socialism found itself at variance with the Churches. It is true that Article 24 of the Party programme said that ' the Party is built on the base of a positive Christianity ', but the whole trend of Nazi philosophy and practice entailed a conflict with the Churches. A totalitarian State could brook no other loyalties within its borders, and it became part and parcel of the Nazi programme, not only to allow no other organizations, but to smash them. The difference of opinion broadened into a struggle over the questions of rival youth organizations and the education of the young. It soon became impossible for a man to become a good Nazi and a good Catholic at the same time, because the whole tendency of teaching in the camps and within such formations as the Black Guards was against the Churches. The rift widened as the *Blood and Soil* philosophy was pushed to the foreground and, when Hitler formally endorsed a *Weltanschauung* at the 1935 Party Congress, a final conflict was inevitable, because *Weltanschauung*, if it meant anything, entailed a fight for a Nature religion (or at the very least, a local Germanic religion) based on *Blood and Soil*; and this position could never be reconciled with the theory of Catholicism or Lutheranism. Hitlerian mysticism is poles apart from the spirit of the older religions. The only way of preventing a conflict was by keeping the rival forces from coming into contact, but Hitler ruled out such a policy from the outset and deliberately chose to measure the force of his movement against organized Lutheranism and Catholicism. Not content with having Jewry on his hands, he raised an issue of conscience which millions of Germans could not take lightly.

A student of history would have hesitated before raising the forces of religion against him, but Hitler felt that he had evolved a force greater than that of any religion. It is not necessary to conclude that he endorses the more extreme views of Rosenberg and the paganists, but, on the other hand, he has dissociated his movement from the religions from the very beginning, and the fact remains that he alone could have prevented the anti-Christian activities of his lieutenants. He could easily have stopped the paganist propaganda, just as he could have eradicated any other unwelcome propaganda ; he could have come down on the near-pagan utterances of his Youth Leader, Baldur von Schirach ; he could have stopped Himmler from dosing the Black Guards with anti-Christian doctrines ; and he could have prevented the ostentatious resignation from Church membership of such leaders as Himmler, Colonel Hierl (leader of the Labour Service), Dr. Frick, and Rust (his Minister of Education), all of them occupying positions directly concerned with the minds of young people. He did none of these things, for two reasons. Primarily, as the years went by, he came to interpret National Socialism as no longer a mere political or national movement, but as an all-embracing philosophy of life ; and secondly, his whole mental training—Chamberlain and Eckart as rarefied into Rosenberg and Darré—led him to look on Lutheranism and Catholicism partly as political forces and partly as intolerant ideologies which would not witness the upsurge of National Socialism without trying to make a stand for the mind and soul of their adherents.

The passage of the years lent bitterness to the conflict of ideas, and the struggle between the Nazi Church and the older bodies became just as acrid as any of the religious wars of past centuries. The extreme Faith Movement said explicitly. ' The Cross must fall if Germany is to live '—the national *Hakenkreuz* is more important than any Cross of Christian legend, any symbol associated with Jewry and a false internationalism. Neither Rome nor Wittenberg were to reign over the minds of Germans, but Berchtesgaden alone.

' We wish for no other God than Germany,' Hitler has said, and von Schirach, in his more moderate moments, cries to the Hitler Youth : ' I am neither a Catholic nor a Protestant : I am a National Socialist.' The goal was expressed in its clearest form when the *Nationalsozialistische Monatshefte* reproduced in huge letters that occupied a whole page, a saying of Ernst Arndt : ' To be a People—that is the religion of our time.'

Apart from actual repressive measures, Hitler's main weapon has been the German Faith Movement, formed in June 1932, seven months before he became Chancellor. Its leader was Joachim Hossenfelder, a young man who, like so many other Nazis, had not been content with the fighting on the Western Front, but had joined the Free Corps, who continued the struggle in the Polish borderlands. Race was more important than humanity, held this modern crusader, and, before he was superseded eighteen months later for his political manœuvrings, he had built up a Church whose theology subordinated Christianity to National Socialism.

The idea was not new, because Franz Seldte had already organized a similar body in the service of the Steel Helmets, but Hitler's accession to power gave the Faith Movement an unequalled opportunity. It was organized on the familiar model of the Brownshirts, with an elaborate structure of regions and districts, down to the tiniest local unit.

It was not easy to warp theology into the framework of *Blood and Folk*, but the turning-point came with the rise of Pastor Ludwig Müller, a fifty-year-old army chaplain who had gained Hitler's confidence. 'Müller of Königsberg' had worked for Hitler in East Prussia for many years, and it was his view that theology should be allowed to drop into the background and that the Faith Movement should be made a political force to buttress Hitlerism. He became Bishop of Prussia in August 1933, and, six weeks later, a few days before he was to be elected Bishop of the whole Reich, Hitler gave an address over all broadcasting stations saying that the Churches had to take a stand in the folkic and political revolution and that the people should vote for Müller's section in the forthcoming Church elections, because it alone viewed religion as part of the revolution. He specifically stated that the State had no desire to negotiate with twenty or thirty Evangelical Churches, but wanted a single Reich Church under a single Reich bishop. Under these direct instructions, supplemented by the local efforts of Brownshirts, and by dubious electoral devices, the Protestants of Germany voted for Hitler and Müller. Four days later Müller marched through the door on which Martin Luther had posted his theses and stood in Luther's own pulpit to read out his programme for the Lutheran Church to act as the handservant of National Socialism.

His talk was of Christian soldiers, of crusaders in a new age. Indeed, this typifies the man. Hitler's first bishop has the mentality of a soldier. He apes military forms and mannerisms. He loves military brusqueness. His reports are like dispatches from a general to a commander-in-chief, and he sees himself as a wartime officer accepting his commander's orders unquestioningly and using any means to put them into operation. This is the man who, since September 27th, 1933, has been in charge of Hitler's efforts to weld his people into a single National Socialist Church. It was he who replaced the old democratic system of Church rule by a new authoritative control; it was he who ordered that services should open and close with the Nazi salute; it was he who introduced the Horst Wessel admonition— 'Banners up, close the ranks, free the streets for the Brown battalions'—into Lutheran ritual; it was he who dealt with his opponents as if they had been traitors on a battlefield. Whenever he was in a tight corner he would turn to patriotism. He would appear in the pulpit wearing his two Iron Crosses on his cassock and borrow trumpeters from the cavalry regiments to play fanfares during the service. He would recite his own war experiences and work up the atmosphere of a recruiting meeting.

But his efforts did not succeed. It was announced that he was to be inducted into his new office on December 3rd; actually a year elapsed; and that delay was the measure of the opposition to him within the Protestant churches of Germany.

Actually the Evangelical Churches saw their liberty of conscience threatened, and when they were specifically ordered by Müller to make of their most sacred days an opportunity for 'imbuing members of the congregations with a sense of patriotic duty', and when they were told in episcopal proclamations that Hitler was ' a gift from the hand of God', they took a stand, in the face of all manner of pressure. They refused to sanction ' attacks on the Cross' by proselytizing it in political propaganda and expressed their undying belief in Holy Writ, even those parts of it denounced by the Nazis as Jewish preaching.

Their leader was Dr. Martin Niemöller, the Lutheran vicar of Berlin-Dahlem, another of the extraordinary persons in the German scene. He has been a pastor for only thirteen years. Originally he was a naval officer, commanding a submarine in the later years of the war, and bearing a rifle against the Spartacists. Then he became a farmer, only to be ruined by inflation, and later, while he was studying for the Church, a railway worker, a clerk, and a harvester. Not a man of any mental subtlety, he appears to have undergone no great development since his time as a naval officer, and, like Müller, relies primarily on direct force and stubbornness, probably derived from his service days.

The dissident pastor first attracted notice as a key-member of the Youth Movement of the Reformation which was formed to combat the German Christians whom Müller led. Although he had been a member of the Nazi Party for several years, Niemöller opposed the election of Dr. Müller as Reich Bishop and flatly refused to carry out his orders to have uniform services throughout the land. Müller, he held, could not treat the pastors as if they were recruits on a parade-ground, and he formed a Pastors' Emergency Federation as a fighting nucleus within the Youth Movement of the Reformation. Coining the phrase 'We must obey God rather than man', he rallied those who wanted to stand out against the attempts to make the Church a mere voice for Nazi propaganda.

He has been frequently suspended from office, and even arrested and placed under the surveillance of the Prussian political police. It is admitted even by his friends that he does not know how to temper his zeal with any tact, but if he had not answered the brutally direct attacks of Hitlerism by equally brutal and direct methods, the Lutheran Church would have collapsed. It needed the heavy, resounding blow of a man like Niemöller, for a subtle paper warfare would have made no impression on the Nazi authorities. For a time Niemöller had about a quarter of the pastors in his organization, but it was difficult to keep an organized front, because the powers of Bishop Müller were all-embracing and were supported by the State and, after all, the pastors—usually a very poorly paid set of people—had to live. At the very least, a pastor from Berlin might find himself sent overnight to some starving flock in Lower Silesia, and very few of them could stand up to the weapon Hitler conferred on Müller early in 1934—the authority to retire a pastor at will. The use of this knock-down power really confined the struggle to young pastors who were not hampered by family ties, and even then, a pastor could do little if he had no wages, no pulpit, and no flock. A decree even forbade them from using printed material or writing to the Press to further their cause.

The result was that many were forced into submission, and by the middle of 1934, Bishop Müller, after invoking all the authority of the Minister of the Interior and the political police in his support, was able to report that twenty-two of the twenty-eight regional Churches had submitted to his policy of centralization. Opponents were being weeded out still further by a rigid application of the Aryan clause. Where this did not suffice offending clergy were openly deposed. Great street demonstrations followed the deposition of the Bishops of Württemberg and Bavaria in the autumn of 1934, but, notwithstanding these, commissars from Berlin forcibly took over the offices of the Bavarian Church. Less than one Bavarian pastor in twenty favoured the Reich Church and the outcry was so great that Hitler had to release the two bishops from protective custody.

Another weapon was now brought into play. Dr. Frick, as Minister of the Interior, threatened to take away the State's financial support of an institution which only served to promote disunity within the State. Hitherto clergy had been paid very much as Civil Servants were, but if the Government stopped collecting the special church tax, they could not possibly continue to live as pastors. The very mention of the proposal split the Confessional clergy of the opposition into two groups, and Frick pressed home his advantage.

But the gap was so obvious and the pastors were gaining so much support in the country districts that, in September 1935, Hitler gave dictatorial powers to Hans Kerrl, the Reich Minister for Church Affairs. *A Law for the Safeguarding of the German Evangelical Church* was signed by Hitler at Munich on September 24th. It consisted of a foreword and a single clause. The foreword stated that it was the will of Evangelical churchgoers that the regional Churches should be amalgamated into a single German Church ; the clause bluntly provided that Kerrl should issue ordinances with binding legal force in order to restore orderly conditions within the Church. Kerrl was instructed to appoint a Central Church Committee for the whole Reich, its task being to control the Evangelicals and, if need be, to dismiss any Church officials. The powers which Bishop Müller had tried to exercise were thus given to State authorities by direct enactment, the State's view being that it had to mediate between two rival sets of theologians.

Although Pastor Niemöller replied to this by a strongly worded pamphlet which was confiscated, the appointment of Kerrl's committee eased the situation. Kerrl himself is a moderate and is deeply concerned with religion. Unfortunately, in the early part of 1936, the good effects of the amnesty he proclaimed were lessened by the raids of secret police in certain localities, and it became a byword with the Confessional clergy that Kerrl's edicts were valid only to the point at which they aroused the opposition of those Party zealots who frowned on religion and favoured the growing pagan movement. Nevertheless, Kerrl succeeded in releasing many pastors from the ban imposed on them, and it appeared as if the clergy were past their worst sufferings.

On the other hand, the rise of paganism could no longer be ignored, and under this heading came the numerous activities of the Party, which, while not directly paganistic, inclined the youth of the country in an anti-Christian direction. The doughty old Ludendorff was still boasting of his heathen *Tannenberg League* and trying to convert the country from his Munich bookshop, but far more important were the activities of von Schirach and Rosenberg. Von Schirach was imbuing the Hitler Youth with an undue admiration for the old pagan tribesmen, and Dr. Ley was converting his May Day festivals into Nature rites, and publicly gibing at ' the fools who speak of the earth as a vale of tears, of eternal sin and guilt, and of contrite hearts ', just to make his meaning clear. The Eastertide of 1936 had been kept by many Germans as a pagan festival, the bookshops were displaying pagan literature. The blue banner of the German Faith Movement appeared in the country, proudly flaunting its golden sun-wheel ; a pagan rally was held at Burg Hunxe in the Rhineland ; and everywhere the boys appeared to be more concerned with their open-air dedication—the *Jugend-weihe*—than with religious confirmation. The Song of the Goths was their creed, ' Up the Viking banner, up the blue sun-flag' their hymn. A pagan newspaper, the *Reichswart*, was flourishing ; and even the *Schwarzes Corps*, the official journal of the Black Guards, while laughing at some of the excesses of the pagans, urged fair play for them.

The organization of the pagans was called the German Faith Movement, for what reason it is not clear. Its prophet was Wilhelm Hauer, a theological professor at Tübingen, who preached the idea of an Aryan German faith. ' My movement,' he said, ' is the logical perfection of the Party.' In his book, *Deutsche Gottschau*, he argued that the real Deity was the spirit of the race and that ' national history is more than a sequence of facts : it is a *Werden*, a becoming, an evolution ; it is the Spirit of the Race always in suspense, always in movement, a progress of Being, a revelation'. Hauer owed much to his studies of Buddhism in Asia, and his academic status allowed him to spread his doctrine through the universities. The facile Count Ernst zu Reventlow popularized his ideas, and the movement spread until the end of April 1936, when the two leaders were displaced. Much mystery surrounds this episode, but it is surmised that Hauer was coming to rival Rosenberg. Under the guise of carrying Rosenberg's ideas farther and explaining them, Hauer was throwing his undoubted erudition and his analytical skill into too clear a relief with the rather muddled expositions of Rosenberg. This is probably the explanation, especially because those quarters of the Party which do not look kindly upon Rosenberg raised voices in favour of the pagans.

On the whole, it may be said that the neo-pagan movement has no real strength in Germany, although it must be repeated that many State festivals are given a primarily pagan inter-pretation and that it is an easy step from the anti-clerical policy of certain influential Nazis to a positive paganism. Youth taught to revel in physical fitness is susceptible to such teachings, and it is amongst them that the spirit of paganism is developing. What is originally a healthy reverence for the national traditions may easily become an anti-Christian religion.

The growing importance of the movement roused both the Evangelical and the Catholic Churches to protest. The pagan celebrations of *Ostermond* in place of the Christian Easter were too serious to be overlooked. The Confessional groups, stung into unity by the new challenge, addressed a letter to Hitler in May and put to him a ' clear question '— whether ' the attempt to de-Christianize the German people is to become the official policy of the Government through the further participation of responsible statesmen or even by the fact that they merely look on and allow it to happen '. Quotations from Goebbels, Ley, and Rosenberg were cited, and the concern of the writers was expressed against ' the honours often done to Hitler in a way that is due to God only ', a fact which was true, but rather tactless to mention. The occasion was also taken to point out that Kerrl's Ministry had been used to keep the Church in administrative and financial dependence on the State and to rob the clergy of any freedom of teaching. To the glorification of Aryan man, the pastors retorted by saying that God's Word showed the sinfulness of all men ; and to the Nazi decrees that made anti-Semitism a duty, they riposted by the Christian commandment of brotherly love. They closed by protesting against the more practical grievances, especially the activities of the secret police, who had arrested 700 pastors and maintained a constant espionage on the remainder.

It is true that some of the more accommodating members of the Confessional Church, including several bishops, had already broken away. Nevertheless, the memorandum represented the views of the great majority. No official reply was received from Hitler, and the authors were placed in a somewhat difficult position by a leakage of the memorandum into the foreign Press. The pastors then felt that honesty impelled them to make a public statement of their views, and, at the end of August, a manifesto was read in thousands of Evangelical churches, calling on Protestants to defend Christianity against the folkic and totalitarian claims of the Nazi Party. The fervour with which the embattled

Evangelicals sang *Ein' feste Burg ist unser Gott* was just as intense as that with which the Nazis sang their *Die Fahne hoch*.

The united front thus presented led Hitler to reconsider his position, and the year closed without further attempts to dragoon the Evangelicals into submission. The State Church could produce no theologians who could stand up to the devastating onslaughts of Asmussen, Dibelius, and Karl Barth, and no preachers who attracted the crowds as did Jakobi and the ever-energetic Niemöller. Finally the new stress on the army and the Four Year Plan led the Nazi casuists to wonder whether the continuance of the quarrel with the Evangelicals was worth while. None of them felt strongly about the issues from a religious point of view, and they were disposed to postpone the political issues involved to a later and more auspicious date. The truth was that National Socialism had met with a decided reverse, and the passage of the months merely emphasized that defeat.

The latest position is that the State Church Committee itself has issued appeals against the anti-Christian propaganda and has been supported by the Evangelical leaders. On New Year's Day of this year, the pastors once more made a plea for religious freedom and a protest against the unchristian tendencies of the Youth Movements, and assured Hitler in return that they would stand behind him in the fight against Communism. The Evangelicals show no disposition to recede from their position and have taken a definite stand against the steps of Rust to interfere with the freedom of theological training. Rust issued a decree that no student associated with Evangelical movements could be allowed to enter a university, a measure which the Evangelicals viewed as a reaffirmation of the Nazis' hostility to religion. The extraordinary feature of these recent episodes is that the State committees of moderates have shown a marked tendency to fall into line with the Evangelicals whom they were appointed to control. It is frankly admitted at the moment that, whatever Kerrl's private feelings may be, he is powerless to impose his will on the Party, and the Churches have no illusions about the real feelings of the Nazi authorities, however much of a lull there may be because of other exigencies. The basic conflict of ideas between *Blut und Erde* and the Christian ethic is too impassible for it to be otherwise ; and the conversion of Dr. Zöllner and his church committee is more a danger signal than a gain for the Evangelicals, because it shows how hopeless even moderates find the antagonistic attitude of Party authorities. The Reich Committee consequently resigned early this year.

The latest stage was reached in February 1937, when Hitler announced that, in view of the disunion, a General Synod should be elected to draw up a new constitution for the Evangelical Church. The importance of such a move—whether it is a prelude to a complete absorption of the Church by the State, or whether it marks a compromise on Hitler's part—depends on the method of election to the synod. If the ' packed ' elections of 1933 are to be repeated, Germany must face a long period of Church warfare.

While this long fight for the Evangelical Church was being waged, Hitlerism was also confronted by a struggle with the Roman Catholic Church. Here the issue was different. The form and beliefs of the Catholic Church were fixed, and any modification of ideas or organization to fit in with the ethics of National Socialism was ruled out from the beginning. The Evangelicals, a purely German organization and largely dependent on the State, could conceivably amend their beliefs and alter their financial and administrative structure ; but the Catholics could not do so. They could never submit to State control, never change their point of view. They had no difficulties of dogma or conflicts of leadership. Nor could they ever acquiesce in any National Socialist doctrines that claimed control of the souls of Catholics : the idea of an all-embracing *Weltanschauung* could never be reconciled with Catholicism. Thus Hitler could make no attempt to dragoon the Catholics into submission by altering the financial or administrative bases of their Church. His only alternatives were to allow the Church to go on untrammelled, or to win over young Catholics by persuasion, or to resort to individual terrorism.

Perceiving these difficulties, Hitler sent von Papen to arrange a Concordat with the Papacy. Signed on July 3rd, 1933, this document was a compromise. The Pope promised that priests would abstain from all political activities, whilst Hitler undertook not to interfere in German Catholic life. Actually it solved little, because trouble immediately arose over the training of the young and the freedom of the Catholic Press. The Archbishop of Munich, Cardinal Faulhaber, led the Catholics in their fight. When the Nazis began to develop their racial theories, he launched a series of attacks on them and protested vigorously when priests were arrested. 'Not blood but faith is the foundation of religion,' he said. In short, a new *Kulturkampf* was being waged between Church and State, and feeling amongst the extreme Nazis became very acute against the clerics, who were known as 'the blacks' or 'the black moles'. Göring even accused the Catholics of stealing Nazi ritual for their services !

The Nazis insisted that all children should become members of their youth organizations and, especially in Catholic Bavaria, tried to close the Church schools (although these had been guaranteed by the Concordat). Towards the end of 1936 the Catholic bishops offered Hitler co-operation in his fight against Bolshevism if he respected their privileges. Nevertheless, the assault on the Catholics has continued, especially in Bavaria.

The issue can be solved only by the complete withdrawal of the Hitlerites from their present stand, and they are unlikely to do this when so many of their leaders are anti-Christian and so long as they accept Rosenberg's doctrines, for, of them all, Rosenberg is the most fanatically opposed to the Catholic Church.

The Nazis say that *the Cross must fall if Germany is to live*; the older Churches retort *Germany cannot live without the Cross*. Hitler has allowed himself to be manœuvred into a position in which it is difficult for him to compromise. Even from the crudest secular point of view his policy has

been impolitic, to say the least. He appears to have encouraged a deliberate conflict between his ideology and that
of the Churches, whereas an astute statesman would have
avoided such an issue at all costs. The present dictum of
the Nazis runs thus : ' To serve Hitler is to serve Germany ;
to serve Germany is to serve God.' No Church can accept
such impious reasoning.

Chapter Nine

LAW AS A POLITICAL INSTRUMENT

The Nazi theory is that law is merely a weapon in the political struggle. Kerrl, the Civil Servant who became Minister of Justice in Prussia, asserted in the first days of the revolution that law should lose its obsession with 'dead objectivity', which was a deplorable legacy from the former age of liberalism. Hitler endorsed this view. He made known his conception of law in his stadium speech early in March 1933. He definitely stated that 'the motives and aims of offenders are to be taken into account as much as possible' —in other words, that the same crime would be a different offence if committed by a well-meaning Nazi on the one hand and by a Socialist on the other. Although such a conception cuts right athwart the older idea of law, it still prevails in the Third Reich.

One of Hitler's first acts was to institute special courts for political offences—courts where the offence did not have to be legally proved and from which there could be no appeal. The provisions were even retrospective. Henceforth a man could be hanged for a crime which carried only a light penalty at the time it was committed. This clause was invoked to punish those unfortunates who had fought the Nazis in the early days of street fighting. They were hunted down and punished years later for offences for which Nazis were receiving the highest honours in the State. The misuse of the forms of law for this wiping-out of old grievances is one of the most sinister, although by no means one of the best-known, aspects of Nazi rule. A general amnesty was given to Nazis for all offences they had committed during the struggle for the 'National Regeneration', and one of Hitler's first acts was to free the five Silesian Brownshirts who had butchered a working man of Potempa in front of his wife and children. He even treated these men with marks of official esteem, while he hounded down honest men whose only fault was that they had opposed him when he was in opposition. Punishment they might have expected, but certainly not the prostitution of the courts of law to bring it about. Hitler's conception of law, as primarily a political weapon, has set the clock of the jurists back to the eighteenth century, back to the days of irresponsible despots and *lettres de cachet.*

Another peculiar institution of the Nazis is the 'People's Court', set up in April 1934 to deal with treason cases. These cases had previously gone to the Supreme Court, but the delays were such that the public had forgotten the crime long before the punishment was announced. The Nazis claim that the People's Court is not an emergency institution, hastily devised to meet a crisis, but a permanent Court governed by the ordinary criminal statutes. This may be so, but the fact is that in practice the Court is a political body. The Bench is made up of a Senate of five members, two lawyers and three laymen, the latter 'chosen from those professions most likely to be acquainted with the significance of the crimes, that is either military, police, or party officials'. The accused may choose his own counsel, if the choice is not 'inadvisable in the general interests of the State'. The death penalty may be imposed in cases of treason or conspiracy or 'in other cases under particularly incriminating circumstances'. One piece of literature from Nazi headquarters insists, however, that usually the sentences are from one to three years' imprisonment, 'the former for lighter and the latter for major delicts emanating low-down, dishonourable tendencies' [*sic*]. Used in conjunction with the new Penal Code, which makes intention the all-important factor, the People's Court may justly be described as a negation of impartial law. This is especially the case since the end of 1933 when the Party was identified with the State, and an offence against the Party became *ipso facto* an offence against the State.

It might not be so bad if they did not boast about it. I

have just received a piece of Nazi propaganda entitled 'National Ethics as the Source of Law'. This boasts that 'the distinction between law and morality is done away with'. It is a heritage of the bad old days when the State jurisprudence was the only source of law, and when only deeds which were punishable by the letter of the law could be penalized. Then follows the amazing statement that the National Socialist conception of the law goes back to the old German idea and 'makes the public conviction of what is right and wrong the foundation for its jurisprudence', and it is obvious that, since the public has declared for the Party, the sole function of law is to enforce Party ideas. The new Penal Code, then, discards the 'formal' conception, according to which only a breach of the law is punishable : instead the code is based on the 'material' conception, according to which any action that injures the interests of the community is punishable. As the Nazis naïvely add, this considerably enwidens the scope of the code.

To make subordination to Party interests doubly certain, it is provided that not every breach of the law is punishable. Henceforth breaches of the Penal Code may pass unchastised, if based on self-defence or 'state of distress'. The official explanation says explicitly : 'Self-defence against illegal attack is in future to be limited by the demands of common sense.' An attacked person may pass the limitations of self-defence if he is frightened, dismayed, or surprised. Still more far-reaching are the provisions relating to 'state of distress'. These have to be read to be believed. As officially defined, 'action in distress or emergency means the prevention of a serious damage to oneself and others through illegal measures', with common sense acting as the decisive factor. Any action is permissible if it averts a common danger.

Apparently, then, the main function of a judge will be to determine what is 'common sense' and what is prejudicial to the interests of the Nazi community. The older objective conception of law has gone by the board. 'The National Socialist Code is intended to be the living outward expression of the national ethic which has its roots in the character of the people.' In other words, justice is entirely political, and judges are servants of the Party in the same way that Brownshirts or Black Guards are. Law is personal, emotional, political—the law of the cave man. After the enactment of this code, the Courts would be nothing more nor less than agencies repressing all interests opposed to Hitlerism. The changes cut right athwart the legal development of centuries. At a blow, all of the hardly won gains have been lost. The German legal system to-day is but the servant of the administration ; and, to an impartial mind, her legal degradation is more pronounced than that of the most corrupt amongst the smaller South American republics. A servant of the Party can escape the penalties of any misdemeanour by pleading ' common sense ' ; an opponent of the Party has, in effect, no legal rights. Göring has seen to it that ' the scandal of the Reichstag fire trial can never be repeated '. In any future State trial, the accused would be condemned beforehand by the very fact of their accusation by responsible members of the executive. I repeat, the legal position of Germany is so absurd that it would not be believed, did we not have the irrefutable evidence of the new Penal Code itself. In comparison with this, all other sectional wrongs become insignificant, because this code affects every living German. It ties 66,000,000 people into subservience to the political party which happens to be in power for the moment —a state of affairs that seems inconceivable in a civilized community in the twentieth century.

In the autumn of 1933, Hitler called together a Criminal Law Commission, presided over by the Minister of Justice, Dr. Gürtner, in order to rewrite the sixty years' old Penal Code in accordance with the philosophy of National Socialism. The Commission reported at the end of 1936. It starts with the assumption that the good of the community comes before the good of the individual, an assumption which, in practice, means a writing down of individual liberty in favour of the Folkic State. The Nazis say directly : ' The Penal Code is an expression of the moral standard of the nation ' ; and, since that moral standard is National Socialism, the code must be primarily concerned with the preservation of National Socialism. The old code merely punished offenders, but the new one becomes ' an offensive weapon, by means of which the German nation as a whole is to be protected from public enemies '. It is as much concerned with the avoidance of crime as with its punishment ; and this means that the punishment is not for the crime but for the criminal intentions of the perpetrator. If his intentions are good, he goes free : if they are bad, he is severely punished, even if the crime is not actually committed. Intention is sufficient. The Germans say that this is getting away from the weak ' sociological ' conception of law in the last sixty years to the honest code of the ancient Germanic peoples—to the retributive theory.

Under the old code, individuals could threaten the interests of the community, because some law was inadequately worded or another had a gap not intended by its author but speedily found out by ' Jewish-Socialist ' lawyers. The new code makes this impossible, because the spirit rather than the letter of the law is to be considered. The code is to be administered in accordance with the morality of the nation (that is, National Socialist morality) to maintain national interests. It is no wonder that Hess took as his text for an address to the Congress of Jurists the old statement of von Treitschke : ' The practice of law is a political activity.'

As applied to the individual, the code means more drastic punishment. The Nazis reject the modern theory that the criminal's *milieu* was responsible for his crimes (how could they do otherwise without admitting flaws in the Nazi community ?). A criminal, then, is not a man forced by his surroundings into crime but a degenerate who sins against his community. The Nazis, therefore, look on punishment as more important than reform ; they are going back, they say, to the healthy outlook that pertained before the middle of the nineteenth century. The punishment must be real and immediate ; it must be a deterrent to others. Thus, many provisions of the new code change long terms of imprisonment under easy conditions to shorter terms with more drastic treatment (with these ideas, it seems rather short-sighted of Hitler to close the room in Nuremberg

Castle which has the torturing *Iron Woman* to those who attend his Party Congresses).

Another corollary of this position is that there need not be uniform punishments for any crime. The retribution must vary with the intentions of the criminals ; it also varies with the position of the offender. If crime is primarily a breach of faith towards the community, higher-placed officials must have heavier penalties. Nobody—high or low—need be punished for a breach of the law if he can prove good intentions or non-culpable ' negligence'. Nobody can be punished unless he was conscious that he was breaking the law. In other words, Nazis can beat up their enemies and plead any of several justifications under the new code ; while a non-Nazi can be condemned to any punishment, because of his bad intentions towards the community. The new code is, in effect, infinitely flexible, alike in favour of Nazis and against their foes. The old legal safeguards have been removed, and the ' morality' of one party substituted for the abstract legal conceptions that took centuries to evolve. The older law, says Hess, was abstract and academic, ' floating in the clouds and with no ground under its feet'. Real law, he goes on, must be in harmony with the spirit of a State at any given moment ; it must be an active fighting servant of the community. He might have added that its duty includes snuffing out enemies of the régime and even reading their minds to lay evil thought. The old judges, said Hess, allowed form to triumph over substance : the new ones must forget their narrowly juristic rules and be primarily comrades (*Volksgenossen*) in the communal band. Dr. Frank, the Reich Law Leader, goes even further. Last year he told the Congress of Jurists that every judge must ask himself, before giving judgement : ' How would the *Führer* judge in my place ? '

The code also embodies novel punishments. The most severe is capital punishment by decapitation—an honest old German punishment, says Göring. Hard labour is to be genuinely hard. The drift towards easier conditions in jail is to cease, as being nothing more than ' a one-sided educational tendency ', which forgets that a jail sentence means punishment. For many crimes, proscription (that is, the loss of civil rights and of German nationality, and the forfeiture of all property) is laid down. It has been frequently enforced, especially against refugees who have left Germany. Perhaps the most novel provisions relate to the fine. In future fines are to be made proportionate to the assets of the accused. The idea is to equalize punishment of the rich and poor. A fine is to consist of the forfeit of so many days' average earnings. The criminal is to suffer a like privation in every case. In certain instances all private assets may be confiscated, irrespective of their amount.

Many clauses deal with ' Protection of Honour '. Serious punishments are meted out to those who insult the German nation, or Hitler in any of his capacities, or the army, or any respectable character in past German history, or (specific-ally) Hindenburg, Horst Wessel (the Berlin boy of doubtful antecedents whom Goebbels made into a national hero), or Leo Schlageter (the murderer shot by the French for wrecking trains in the Ruhr). Punishments are provided for anybody who insults another individual or family, and who pries into the past to secure disreputable facts, whether true or not—a perfect law for the protection of political parvenus. There is no time limit for the punishment of such crimes, although, after a certain period (' the length of which is to be calculated according to the intensity of the criminal intention expressed in the crime ') prosecution may be at the discretion of the Public Prosecutor.

An official explanation of the new code insists that its key-note is Loyalty—loyalty to the nation and the State, loyalty to the governing authorities, ' loyalty to the political party which is the vein of the State ', loyalty to the family and the race, and loyalty to the national strength in all its forms, whether political, economic, or military. ' The National Socialist Movement is considered in the penal laws to be the quintessence of the nation and the representative of its political will ' ; and punishments may be incurred for offences committed against it by any German, whether he is a member of the Party or not, and whether he resides in Germany or not.

The Nazis are becoming keener every year on their theory that law is the expression of the will of the nation. They have even joined issue with the Fascists on the matter. Italy, they say, adheres to the Roman idea that the State is the centre of everything : Germany substitutes the nation as a whole. The Nazis see themselves as ' guardians of the public law ', the law of the people ; they organize exhibitions to prove that this is the only justifiable conception of law, right back to the time of the ancient Egyptians. Last November the corner-stone of a vast *Haus des Deutschen Rechts* was laid in Munich, to perpetuate the new idea of law as a ·living, malleable expression of a nation's current morality. In Dr. Frank's words, the Nazis have closed the unhappy gap that hitherto existed between justice and the people. Spirit has triumphed over form, common sense over arid academic theories, and healthy evolution over a paralysed static conception. Law is living and vital : it changes with the community, and is justified only in so far as it gives expression to the spirit of the community and its rulers.

The German sees in this ' a higher law of life ', but the foreigner, not yet liberated to the plane of National Socialism, sees only the moulding of law into an instrument to serve the ends of one political party. Goebbels said, at the Jurists' Congress last year, that ' we have restricted individual liberties only where they clash with the needs of the people '. If he had substituted ' the Party ' for ' the people ' (although the two terms are synonyms to him) he would have spoken the truth. *Volksrecht* is the goal, and the Hitlerites are the only expression of the *Volk*—nothing could be simpler.

Hereafter, justice in Germany is to be moralized, although any non-Nazi judge, if he has a family to think of, must cast off all of his moral principles or starve. ' Abstract law ' remains only as a butt for the wit of a Hess ; in its place is a variable system in which ' the intensity of criminal intention ' is the determining factor. Apparently this would necessitate a battery of psychoanalyists or mind-readers at every case, were it not for the fact that, as Dr. Frank once said, a criminal may be detected just as easily as a germ can. It is no wonder that an eminent British authority recently stated that the rule of law, as we know it, has disappeared from Germany—not only in practice (a loss which might be put down to immediate political necessities) but in theory, which is far more important. But the German is not concerned with this. He wants, and has obtained, a perfect instrument for the enforcement of a given political and racial theory. That theory, for the moment, happens to be National Socialism, and law is but its maidservant. 'The law and the will of Hitler are one ', said Göring.

PART V
HITLERISM AND THE WORLD

Chapter One

GENERAL FOREIGN POLICY

I.—*Conflict of Policies in the Wilhelmstrasse*

Hitler's general foreign policy is based on a few general assumptions—that every fetter of the Treaty of Versailles must be struck off, that Germany must expand from her present cramped frontiers, that ' the lost Germans ' constitute a sacred cause for which to fight, and that the Germans are a people of destiny in a decadent world. To these are added a belief in striking resounding blows and a conviction that everything goes to the man who has the greatest force at his command and threatens to use it. ' Necessity knows no law,' Bethmann-Hollweg once said ; Hitler believes entirely in this point of view. It follows from this that the validity of treaties is not final and unquestioned ; considerations of place and time may alter everything. Any agreements that have become unpleasant may be repudiated by unilateral action when the time is ripe ; and, if the bluff is not called, the gain is a double one, for in addition to freedom from the repudiated obligations must be added the internal propaganda value of the victory.

A corollary is that, under the personal rule of a dictator, the older system of diplomacy goes by the board. The delicate interactions—and, indeed, the protections of traditional diplomacy—are swept aside by amateurs who cannot appreciate the importance of form or the safety offered by tortuous methods. Instead, the dictator will blunder through to an unduly simple conclusion of a complicated problem and announce it by a resounding blow.

There are many groups behind Hitler, each with different ideas about the future of Germany's foreign policy. Probably the most powerful comprises the sheer opportunists—those who believe that Germany must seek her own advantage in any international crisis. Followers of this school refuse to be committed to a long-range policy. They believe that a strong and unscrupulous power can always profit from ' the dynamic of events ' ; and they fear that adhesion to any fixed line of policy would only weaken the Reich. ' Profits from all and commitments to none '—that is their policy ; and they think that they can interfere in every difficult situation. Sometimes quarrelling Powers will be content to offer bribes to Germany to keep out ; sometimes Germany can bluff by bringing about a *fait accompli* and rely on the unwillingness of her adversaries to go to war to right a wrong ; sometimes she relies on the divisions between her opponents ; and, in the last resort, she can deliver what is in effect an ultimatum. This is the biggest card in the opportunists' pack—the implied threat to go to extremes. The Germans believe that if they become sufficiently strong to be feared they can secure gains which would be out of the question if they were to remain weak. It is a revival of the old policy that the readiness to use force will obviate any necessity of its use in practice.

Goebbels and Göring apparently lead the exponents of this policy, although the former leans strongly to a belief in a central European policy.

The next group behind the scenes comprises the various Imperialists and pan-Germanists. These all want expansion in some form or other. The Easterners, led by Alfred Rosenberg, want to revive Germany's traditional move to the east, through the maze of Baltic states and the inchoate mass of Poland. They are lured on by the fields of the Ukraine and the unknown wealth of Siberia, and they talk of ' the European-Asiatic axis '.

Against them the Southerners wish to dabble in the muddle of central European and Balkan politics. They rely on the crumbling of concerted resistance, once the Czech salient is shattered ; and they argue that the agricultural riches and the other raw materials of the Danubian countries would really allow Germany's policy of *Autarky* to function. Moreover, the vast populations there would provide markets to keep the wheels of the German factories spinning busily. There is no end to the goal of the Southerners. Once they start to move along the central axis of world affairs—the Berlin-Bagdad line—once they revive the old *Drang nach Osten*, the way to the infinite resources of the Orient is theirs, and that way lies world domination.

The final groups of advisers—the group of Joachim von Ribbentrop, Hitler's former ambassador-at-large and later Ambassador to the Court of St. James's—wants a policy of co-operation between the countries of western Europe. Anglo-German co-operation as a prelude to Anglo-German-French understanding is their avowed aim, and they turn their backs on the glamourous but destructive dreams of a wider Imperialism.

Nazi policy thus reduces itself to a clash between various schools of thought, with Hitler—always the supreme empiricist —torn from one to the other. He sees, in foreign affairs, only a vast reserve of opportunities to secure successes for his glorified stump-oratory at home. Nothing in his training has fitted him to understand the interwoven complexities of any important international question. He relies on instinct and on the political gains he can extract from his actions; and nothing could be more dangerous than this for the world at large. A demigod has neither the mentality nor the facilities to analyse a grave international issue; indeed, his very intrusion makes the outcome a great lottery. It is the unexpected, the incalculable, that proves so devastating in foreign affairs.

If his writings mean anything, Hitler himself is an 'Easterner'. In practice, however, he has gone no farther than repudiating clause after clause of the Versailles Treaty and achieving 'equality' for Germany. That done, he spoke frequently about 'the powers of disorder', until, at last, he divided the world into those powers which followed Russia, those which stepped into place behind Germany in opposing Russia, and the remainder who refused to be 'awakened'. Add to this endless generalizations about the desirability of peace and you have a picture of Hitler's foreign policy.

As with so many other parts of his policy, it started by being negative and destructive, and has never grown beyond this stage.

II.—*The Actual Events*

THE THUNDERBOLTS

October 14th, 1933.—Germany leaves the League of Nations and Disarmament Conference.

March 16th, 1935.—Germany introduces universal conscription and announces an army of thirty-six divisions (repudiation of Part V of the Treaty of Versailles).

March 7th, 1936.—Germany reoccupies the Rhineland (repudiation of Articles 42–43 of the Treaty).

November 30th, 1936.—Germany seizes control of the rivers.

January 30th, 1937.—Germany withdraws signatures from the Treaty of Versailles and declares the Treaty ended.

Germany's foreign policy springs from her belief that the Allies broke their promises to disarm after the war and that they wish to encircle Germany while making hypocritical gestures for peace. To them, the League of Nations was based on an erroneous idealism ; it neglected the fundamental racial *Volk* for a non-existent universalism. Indeed it was probably a mask to cover the militaristic policy of the victors. As Goebbels pithily said in June 1936 ; ' The League is good but air-squadrons and army-corps are still better.'

Germany thus believed that force alone counted in international affairs—force coupled with diplomatic agreements between dependable allies. Her opponents seemed to be proving this. Hitler came to power on January 30th, 1933 ; on February 16th the new agreements of the Little Entente were signed at Geneva, bringing Czecho-slovakia, Jugoslavia, and Rumania together as a strong entity in foreign affairs— and incidentally blocking Germany's expansion towards central and southern Europe.

The proceedings of the Disarmament Conference and the

League of Nations in the next few months convinced Hitler that he was right ; and it is said that he was influenced by his personal adviser, von Ribbentrop, to stake everything on building up Germany's strength outside the world-concert of nations and, if possible, come to some kind of an understanding with England.

He therefore left the League of Nations (October 14th, 1933) and proceeded to rearm. A hint of his ultimate foreign policy was soon given. In January 1934 he signed a non-aggression pact with Poland, guaranteeing peace between the two countries for ten years ; and he made it known that he wanted a series of such pacts with his neighbours (Russia and Lithuania[1] always excluded). But he failed. France had been too long in the field, and Germany could effect no breach in the network of treaties and alliances with which France had hemmed in the Reich.

In desperation, Hitler turned to the dangerous waters of Austrian politics, and, throughout the first half of 1934, kept Europe in a constant state of tension. This piratical diversion met with failure once more, and one may say that Nazi foreign policy reached its nadir in the days immediately after the assassination of Dollfuss in July 1934.

During this time, and especially after he sensed the feeling of hostility abroad to his general policy, Hitler had been arousing the country to feel its subordination under the inequal treaties that had ended the war. 'We cannot get what we want abroad because we are weak,' he said in effect, ' but we could get it if we were sufficiently strong.' This protest soon found expression in a gradual repudiation of the disarmament clauses, first in fact and later in name.

Germany certainly had much cause for complaint (although she overlooked the basic fact that she had lost the war). No proud nation could endure the yoke of the treaties for ever, and the French claim that they constituted a Bible of international affairs, unchanging and unquestionable, could not be accepted, especially in such a time of unnaturally rapid evolution as the post-war years. Germany felt, too, that the rest of the Allies were still against her, either through ignorance

[1] For the reasons, see Chapter V, Section II.

or sloth or caution. How far England was from realizing the changed conditions, for example, may be seen from the fact that the Macdonald Peace Plan of March 1933 even wanted to keep Germany deprived of all military planes.

Nevertheless, the position crystallized during the year 1934. Germany had left the League and had made certain proposals for the realization of her military equality. She wanted ' defensive ' armaments, a short-service army of 300,000 men, and pacts of non-aggression ; she would even accept a ten years' control of her armaments if such an arrangement were made reciprocal. France, countering these proposals, would accept only 200,000 German soldiers and would not allow any ' defensive ' weapons until the Reichswehr had been transformed into a short-term army. Her whole emphasis was on a ' probationary period ', during which the new Germany would have to prove her goodwill. Not unnaturally Hitler refused to have anything to do with such proposals. He wanted equal rights then and there and would not give up his right to any weapons which his opponents intended to keep.

One must admit that the thinly veiled hypocrisy of the French arguments at this period did much to produce the German exasperation which has led to the present friction in Europe. The one obvious fact was that a reawakened Germany wanted equality in fact as in name : she was determined to rearm, whatever the opposition might be : whereas the French still thought in the mentality of Versailles and endangered the structure of European peace by their worship of ' security ' and their refusal to compromise. How any sensible statesmen could ever have thought that the Germany of 1934 would not rearm is almost beyond comprehension.

In 1934 Germany wanted aeroplanes and tanks and artillery. She wanted to throw away the dummy wooden barrels and the imitation weapons forced on her by Versailles. Quite rightly, she said that the very sight of them was an affront to a free nation. She was prepared to come to an agreement about the size of her army and the conditions of service ; she was ready to limit her expenditure on certain arms if the other nations did the same (even, she said, to destroying her last machine-gun) : but every instinct of national dignity compelled her to rearm then and there.

The breakdown of these interchanges meant that Germany accelerated the pace of her surreptitious rearmament, until Hitler's open denunciation of Part V of the Treaty of Versailles on March 16th, 1935. Hereafter there was no limit on the size of armaments, and Germany reintroduced military conscription. The whole nation plunged into an ecstasy of arms—men made arms and played with arms ; workers obtained employment to make arms and capitalists drew profits from arms ; youths were conscripted to use the arms and children were taught the divine attributes of arms. In a word, the Third Reich became a Nation in Arms and revelled in the worship of Moloch. The strong wine of militarism tingled through her unaccustomed veins and she indulged in acts that a clearer head would have rejected. And the drunkenness spread abroad until every factory on Tyne or Danube or Rhone was working day and night, piling up arms and munitions. And the people of Europe became prosperous by forging the weapons for their own destruction—all because a tubby little man in an ill-fitting brown tunic cried hoarsely : 'We are not to be treated as shoe-shiners ! '

The declaration of March 16th, 1935, was followed by a few breathless days of protest, but Germany sensed Britain's half-heartedness and ignored both the Notes of protest and the League's resolution condemning treaty-breaking.

Yet the outcome was not all gain for her. Hitler's aggressiveness hastened the negotiations between his rivals and definitely brought into the European arena the Colossus which he had wished to force back into Asia. France and Czechoslovakia, feeling themselves threatened by Germany's new foreign policy, signed pacts with Russia (May 2nd and 16th, 1935), providing that each of the signatories would come to the aid of the other in the event of unprovoked aggression. This meant that Germany was at last encircled ; at least, if she contemplated any act of aggression.

Hitler's only offset to this check was the Naval Agreement with Great Britain (June 18th, 1935). Clearly he had lost in the exchanges. A common front was henceforth raised against Germany, and the passage of every month drew its members more closely together. Moreover, although Germany had boldly launched her project of a new army on March 16th, many years would be needed to bring it to completion, whereas her enemies had long since perfected their military machines.

Hitler therefore became slightly more conciliatory when he addressed the Reichstag on May 21st and welcomed the diversion of attention to the Mediterranean. The next year was Mussolini's strutting period.

All eyes were on Abyssinia—and the whole episode provided a marvellous hunting-ground for Hitler. In the first place, the Stresa Front between France, Italy, and Great Britain was shattered ; in the second, Austria was placed in a difficult position and lost much of the support she had hitherto enjoyed abroad, a fact that must be of advantage to German schemes in the long run ; and in the third place, Italian resentment at sanctions naturally drew attention to the wrongs of the ' Have-not ' Powers. For the moment the clash of Germany and Italy over the Austrian bone was forgotten, and the two countries came together in a common hostility to the ' Haves ' and a common hatred of Bolshevism. The way was being cleared for the present division of Europe into the Powers of Order and the Powers of Disorder.

But that is not all. Not only was Italy removed from the Stresa Front ; the other two partners were openly at logger-heads. France's objections to sanctions had aroused keen hostility in England, and the Germans saw that they could profit from this divergence of views.

Accordingly, the world awoke on the morning of Saturday, March 7th, 1936, to receive the news that German troops had crossed the bridgeheads and reoccupied the Rhineland —an act they would certainly have been a *casus belli* at any other time. As recently as the previous May 25th Hitler had openly and formally promised to respect the clauses of the Treaty relating to the Rhineland ; but, in his scheme of morality, changes due to the ' dynamic of events ' were sufficient justification for breaking his word.

He therefore told the Reichstag that he was tearing up Sections 42-43 of Versailles and the Treaty of Locarno that day, and that new elections would be held on March 29th. All this he had done in the name of peace—' to bring about understanding among European peoples, especially among our western peoples and neighbours '. After a campaign which outdid any of the previous douches of patriotism to which Hitler had subjected the nation, 98·81 per cent of the people voted for him. It would have been miraculous if they had not done so on such an issue.

Hitler thus felt able to play a strong hand in the subsequent diplomatic game. The reoccupation of the Rhineland was followed by a few days of fear. How immediate Germany's plight was in those crucial days will probably never be known. A high official in Germany told me that France had in effect applied an oil-sanction, and that, if the German Army had received the order to march, it would have been paralysed almost at once. Inconceivable as such a lack of preparation may appear, it becomes credible when one thinks of the general opportunism of German policy. Hitler never expected his bluff to be called—never dreamt that he might have to follow up his Reichstag speech by a mobilization order. As a result the directors of German policy experienced many nasty hours that week-end.

But the dangers passed, although France was not easily appeased ; and once more the farcical aftermath of March 16, 1935, was repeated. Once more there were Notes and protests to the League of Nations, but once more German bluff succeeded, because Britain did not feel sufficiently strongly on the matter to take definite steps. It seemed as if a repetition had come to condone the habit of treaty-breaking, as blow on blow was dealt those Powers which tried to keep the word they had pledged.

German diplomatic opinion believed that the imposition of sanctions against Italy was a mere experiment, ' to see if they could be employed against us later on '. It is amazing how frequently this view was expressed to me by officials

and industrialists in Germany last year. My statement that
sanctions were disinterestedly imposed in that particular
case was nowhere believed. The German view was that we
were trying out a new weapon in international affairs, and
that the weapon failed.

A conviction that this was so spurred Hitler on to move
to the Rhineland. If France opposed sanctions against
Italy, she could not make Britain invoke them against
Germany, and, anyway, sanctions were a failure. Hitler
took the chance that the nations would not go to war ' to
keep Germany out of her own territory ', and events proved
him right.

Similar arguments led him to seize control of the German
rivers on November 14th, 1936. Although peaceful negotiations towards the same end were progressing satisfactorily,
Hitler chose the spectacular method of unilateral denunciation.
There was not the slightest need to do so in this case ; and
the incident merely proved that Hitler not only adopted
treaty-breaking when it was forced upon him by the pressure
of events, but even used it voluntarily as the weapon he
preferred in international dealings. Knowing that the
countries which had swallowed the camel of conscription
and the Rhineland would not boggle at the gnat of the rivers,
he went on—but the world was just bored. Hitler had not
learned the meaning of anticlimax.

In the meantime, attempts had been made to secure a general
European settlement and avert, even at that late moment,
a race that was hurtling the world towards war. Germany
submitted a Peace Plan, based on non-aggression pacts (for
twenty-five years) with her neighbours, such a settlement to
be guaranteed by Britain and Italy. As a bait for Britain,
she offered an Air Pact for western Europe. She offered
to return to the League of Nations if the League were dissociated from the Covenant, if colonial equality was discussed,
and if her Peace Plan in general were accepted. As far as
weapons were concerned, she desired ' moral disarmament '
(whatever that may be) and the abolition of heavy guns and
heavy tanks (forms of defence in which she happened to be
very ill supplied). She also proposed international dis-

cussions on pressing economic problems. So much for western Europe ; for the east, she proposed a security pact, which differed from Hitler's previous suggestion of May 21st, 1935, in that it now included Lithuania, while still keeping out Russia.

These proposals, though undoubtedly an advance on the existing chaos, proved on analysis to be far too naïve to be accepted. There was much to justify the French contention that they gave a temporary peace in the west while allowing Hitler a free hand to shape his destiny in the east ; and everybody knew that a Germany, strengthened by the resources of eastern Europe, could turn at will on the isolated west.

The plan sounded well, and had its good points if the world could only have been convinced of Hitler's peaceful intentions. If he really desired peace, however, the French counter-plan was a far better guarantee. France proposed a series of mutual assistance pacts within the League (and it was obvious that such regional pacts were far more effective a safeguard than the many nebulous non-aggression pacts which had sprung up like mushrooms since the war). To strengthen the prospects of immediate peace, France suggested that there should be no demands for territorial changes for twenty-five years and that treaty-breakers should be met by sanctions, military if necessary. The French plan, it is true, went on from this to an untenable idea of a commission of control, with forces placed at its disposal by the various nations ; but it at least served to show the hollowness of the German plan.

Great Britain sought to clarify the situation by a questionnaire addressed to Germany, a much-discussed and much-abused document. Hitler was asked whether he would include Russia in a peace plan, what guarantees he would give that his word would be worth any more in the future than it had been in the past, and whether he would promise not to take aggressive steps in certain named danger zones. A German *Führer* anxious for permanent peace could have answered most of these questions in the affirmative ; but the months dragged by and Hitler made no reply at all. The delays made it clear that his Peace Plan was only a trap for the unwary : when the test came, he either could not or would not align himself with the powers of peace, however numerous his protestations.

The questionnaire is said to have been tactless—almost insulting ; but two facts override all others, even the niceties of diplomatic manners—first, that a satisfactory answer could have been given to some at least of the questions, and second, that no permanent *rapprochement* with Great Britain is possible unless and until Hitler endorses the general inter- pretation of international affairs for which the questionnaire stands. It is argued that considerations of political prestige prevented Hitler giving a satisfactory answer ; but if the peace of Europe is to be kept in jeopardy to maintain Hitler's internal power, the position is most unsatisfactory. It implies that, at some future date, Hitler may take steps abroad to maintain that power at home.

Since the Peace Plan, Germany has been mainly concerned with the erection of a ' Front of Order ' against Bolshevism— in other words, a division of Europe into two armed camps on differences in political doctrine, the twentieth-century form of the wars of religion, and the most marked retro- gression in the history of modern times.

Germany envisages an anti-Bolshevik *bloc* in which Italy, Spain, Japan, Austria, Hungary, and perhaps England will co-operate. Naturally such a conception has no place for the League of Nations or collective security ; these wider chimeras are to be replaced by pacts between anti-Bolshevik powers which are ready to muster their forces and fight immediately the ugly head of Bolshevism is raised. The world will be dominated by Fascist totalitarianism, ruthlessly employing sudden force wherever necessary. The faded olive-branch of Geneva will give place to the bayonets of the dictators, and ' civilization ' will force ' Bolshevism ' back into Asia, where it belongs.

The Germans of to-day have thus been taught to believe that every country must choose between ' the powers of order. and the powers of destruction '. Germany herself has accomplished her task. All classes have responded to the call ' Germany awake ! ' ; the newer and wider call is now

' Europe awake ! ' and the Spanish conflagration and the impending Bolshevization of France proves how urgent the choice is. Germany sees herself as the guardian of European civilization against the oncoming wave of destructive Bolshevism, but she cannot hold back the tide unaided. So runs the German case, in all its delusive simplicity.

Hitler's final statement of foreign policy was in his Reichstag speech on January 30th, 1937, when he was delivering an account of his four years of trusteeship. He completed his attack on the Treaty of Versailles by announcing the withdrawal of Germany's signature. ' I declare that Versailles, which deprived us of equality and degraded our people, has found its final settlement '. He rejected the thesis of Germany's war-guilt and magnanimously announced that ' the so-called period of surprises has now come to an end '.

Unfortunately he did not make it clear whether the new period would be one in which nations honoured their signatures. On the contrary, he reaffirmed impenitently the theory that ' the honour of a nation ' justified it in unilateral treaty-breaking whenever it felt itself strong enough to do so. To make the moral quite clear, he quoted recent examples. ' Universal compulsory military training and the reoccupation of the Rhineland could, unfortunately, not be arranged by amicable negotiations. The honour of a nation can never be vindicated by bargaining, but is an inherent quality that each nation must affirm for itself.' The words are quite clear : Hitler solemnly endorsed a doctrine of international anarchy in which the strongest power could fix its own code of morals. He refused to recognize any change in the international code since the war and, in the name of ' evolutionary common sense ', sneered at international co-operation and reverted to the law of the jungle. The amazing feature of the whole speech was the utter temerity of the assumption behind it that other nations would accept Germany's word in the future. It is inconceivable that any other Power should take her word as binding when she has treated her past engagements so lightly (not only those forced on her by Versailles, but others voluntarily entered into), especially since the brutally realist confessions of her *Führer* and *Reichs-*

kanzler in his last formal speech on international affairs. The milestones of Hitler's four years of power are broken treaties; and on each occasion Europe was deliberately menaced with the spectre of war. Hitler has run up the flag of stark amoral opportunism, and has not even had the grace to admit that conditions forced him to a policy of piracy. He approves any methods as long as what he considers ' the honour of a nation ' is satisfied. This is the code of Bismarck and von Treitschke—it is the reactionary product of a mentality that has been blind to all that has happened in the world since 1914.

Hitler has not even been successful. So far he has achieved only one diplomatic victory. The plebiscite of January 1935 returned the Saar to Germany. But that is all. None of the other ' lost lands ' have been won back. Indeed, the prospect of their reincorporation has never been worse, because Hitler's activities last year have drawn his enemies more closely together than ever before. The result is that to-day Germany stands encircled not because of the malice of her enemies, but solely because of the fears aroused by the ' so-called surprises ' and the general tenor of her policy. Russia, France, and Czechoslovakia are closer friends than ever ; Italy shows no sign of surrendering her freedom of action ; and Britain is feverishly rearming. If ever there was a country without friends, that country is Germany to-day. She may have regained her honour, but only at the cost of reawakening the gods of war and putting an end to the long series of diplomatic victories achieved in the later years of the Republic, victories moreover that aided the cause of world peace.

Chapter Two

THE SOVIET BOGY IN THEORY AND FACT

Germany thinks that she alone is awake to the menace of the Moscow Comintern. She views the Comintern as a disruptive force, constituting an immediate threat which is backed by the military might of Russia. She looks upon the distinction between the Comintern and Stalin's government as a specious fiction, for to her every foreign worker for the Comintern is an agent of Voroshiloff's army.

The trouble is that the Germans look back to the civil strife of the post-war years and so are unable to see the matter objectively. They have been told so often that, unless they make a stand here and now, unless they save Europe despite itself, they will see all the horrors of Spartakism and inflation back again. The result is that they believe the story *in toto*. Goebbels's new mass-propaganda has skilfully seized the weak point of their mental armour and thrusts again and again at the same spot. The syllogism is that the official view of the future must be true because every German knows from his own individual experience that what is said of the past is true. Because there was a civil war in Germany fifteen years ago, there must be a stand against Russia now—it is terribly confused reasoning, but, in arguing from the proven to the unproven, from the truth to the hypothetical, it convinces Hans and Peter and Paul. Moreover, it tickles their feeling of racial superiority to think they are the first, the only people in Europe to realize the menace : as always, they are in the van of the civilized ranks. So we have a crusade— what Wells has called ' an irrational moral rage '—growing upon itself ; and facts no longer count.

In truth, while a strong case may be made out

against the Comintern, there seems nothing to justify the German charge that Russia constitutes an immediate military menace to other countries.   Germany fails to draw the moral from Stalin's steps to exterminate the Trotskyites.   Since this section actually believed in world revolution, their extirpation (which took place just before the Nuremberg Congress, at which Hitler's anti-Russian campaign was launched) should have been interpreted as a gain for peace. But this would not have suited Germany's book, and in consequence the trials and the executions were viewed as showing only the internal disorganization of Russia, in contrast with the order of the totalitarian Reich.

A cardinal feature of the bitterness between Germany and Russia is that it is most convenient for both sets of dictators.   Dictators are always hard put to it to find material for emotional propaganda ; but the ranting about ' Jewish Bolshevism ' never palls in Germany, while the diatribes against Hitlerism serve a similar purpose in Russia.   A wag has said that Hitler and Stalin provide each other with atrocity stories about themselves—and this at least gives a proper emphasis to the situation.

It would be most misleading to take such propaganda at its face value.   Campaigns which would have led to inter-national incidents before 1914 are now accepted as normal tactics in the domestic life of dictatorships.

On the surface, the constant friction between Germany and Russia is the most disturbing element in European affairs. Anti-Communism was the third of Hitler's early ' hates ', coming closely behind his opposition to the Jews and the Treaty.   He chose to preach the myth that he had saved Germany in the nick of time from a Bolshevist revolution (though the last Bolshevik *putsch* had been in Munich and with the Spartakists many years before).

Opinion is divided as to the reality of the Bolshevik menace to Germany in 1933.   I do not think that any evidence exists to prove that a Bolshevist coup was contemplated in German politics, or that Germany would have ' gone Bol-shevik ' if she had not ' gone Hitler '.   Certainly there was nothing to prevent Hitler, once in power, from dropping these campaigns of hate and proceeding to a work of constructive consolidation.

It is difficult to see what justification exists for keeping up the tension between the two countries. The so-called 'proofs' adduced by Goebbels and Rosenberg at the Nuremberg Rally were pitiably weak. The speech of Goebbels, although hailed in the German Press as marking an epoch in modern history, is nothing more than a collection of unproven assertions, with no attempt at impartial evaluation of the various factors. Substituting hate for sense and malignancy for statesmanship, it definitely marked the nadir of Nazi political philosophy. Any first-year university student would have failed had he presented such material in an essay; but Goebbels translated it into twenty-four languages and dispatched it to the four corners of the globe.

The relations between the two countries were determined by Germany's initiative. She chose to launch the propagandist campaign and started the violent denunciation. One cannot point to any particular virulence in the Russian Press before Hitler came to power; and there is little doubt that Germany's relations with Russia would have been no more bitter than those of England had it not been for Hitler's unreasoning onslaughts.

There are two aspects to the friction; first, the doctrinal opposition to 'Jew-Marxism', and secondly, exasperation with Russia for holding the vast lands beyond the Ukraine when Germany needs them so badly for her bursting population and for the maintenance of her principle of *Autarky*.

Germany's eastern Imperialism is best stated in the terms of the Treaty of Brest-Litovsk imposed on Russia. Russia was to become practically a German gateway to the vast plains. Despite this treaty, Russia and Germany came together after the war and agreed to the Treaty of Rapallo in 1922. This established good economic and political relationships between the two countries; and in Chicherin's time Russia made every effort to continue along this basis. A neutrality treaty was signed on April 24th, 1926, and was extended in 1931, and later by Hitler himself.

This treaty also had economic implications and allowed a

great invasion of German technicians and workers for the Five Year Plan. Germany provided credits and poured in the necessary machinery ; and for a time the economic links between the two countries were very strong.

Difficulties arose when German manufacturers began to perceive that, by industrializing Russia, they were really destroying their own markets. Moreover, Russia embarked on a new foreign policy, based upon international manœuvres at the League of Nations. She also tried to build up a series of non-aggression pacts with all of her neighbours, in order to secure her frontiers while immersing herself in her Five Year Plan. Chicherin's limited idea of a close Russo-German co-operation was now jettisoned in favour of the wider game—especially now that Hitlerism was rising to power on the crest of a wave of anti-Bolshevist denunciation. Russia began to reach out to Paris and Prague.

Despite the hullabaloo, political relationships between the two countries remained—and still remain—satisfactory. It was Hitler himself who gave a third lease of life to the Neutrality Treaty on May 5th, 1933, and, in some of his early speeches, he said that the fight against Bolshevism could continue within Germany without prejudicing the good relations between Germany and Russia.

Unfortunately, the whole tenor of German policy was in a different direction. It became obvious that the guarantees Hitler offered always markedly excepted eastern Europe, and Russia became alarmed. As Hitlerism was approaching the end of its first year of power, Litvinov sought reciprocal guarantees. 'We have not the slightest intention of interfering with the sovereignty or the rights of Germany. We should like German policy to be in accordance with German declarations,' he said. But Germany did nothing in this connexion. She also rejected Russia's offer in 1934 that both countries should guarantee the territorial integrity of the small States along the Baltic seaboard. The proposals for an Eastern Pact met a like fate.

The increasing bitterness in Germany and Hitler's obstinate refusal to join any collective system led Russia to negotiate pacts of mutual assistance with France and Czechoslovakia in 1935. Stalin held that Hitler's refusal to consider any of the several peace plans for eastern Europe left Russia no other choice ; and it certainly appeared as if Germany had set her face against accepting the existing territorial settlement east of the Vistula.

The final stage came in September 1936, when Hitler issued a challenge to the whole world. Countries had either to enter the Fascist or the Bolshevik camp ; no compromise was possible, no third alternative remained. It was war—war to the death—with the survival of civilization as the prize.

During all these years the trading ties between the two countries had been maintained and even strengthened. The last two years have seen a striking expansion of Russo-German trade. In the early days of the first Five Year Plan, Germany sent so many goods to Russia that the balance was largely in her favour—so much so that Russia imposed severe restrictions on German goods. Trade continues, despite the growing obstacles, and Germany remains Russia's second-best customer. She gets from Russia much of the foreign exchange she needs so badly ; and she also draws many of her vital raw materials from across the Dnieper. That is one reason why the army officials in Germany regretted the growing bitterness ; they would have preferred to make certain of the chemicals and other supplies they wanted from Russia.

The army, it is rumoured, have great faith in the new Russian Army and think that a Russo-German understanding would build up a *bloc* that could effectively dominate the world. They esteem the Russians, while they are not certain of the Italians. Moreover, they fear a campaign in the vague marshlands of eastern Europe.

For all these reasons, it need not be assumed that the present hatred between the two countries is necessarily permanent. By using his control of propaganda, a dictator may easily change his policy, even in the most unlikely directions. For instance, Hitler could stress the economic and political relationships with Russia and could at any time tell Germany that the Russian Government no longer endorses the Bolshevik penetration of Germany. By stressing the positive facts of co-operation and by halting the destructive propaganda, he could even bring the two countries together, especially if he could construe the winning-over of Russia from the French and the Czechs as a diplomatic victory. History has seen far stranger reversals of policy than this ; and Hitler has still not decided irrevocably in favour of any single line in foreign politics. He may decide to stake everything on the penetration of central Europe, or on the encirclement of France, or even on colonial expansion ; and, as each of these would involve dropping his eastern Imperialism, it might suit his book to come to friendly terms with Russia. After all, he did renew the Berlin treaty and expand trade with Russia, and he feels a considerable pressure from those of his military advisers who value the Soviet resources. Confronted by such a dynamic situation, we should indeed be wrong to take the rantings of the last Nuremberg Rally as a final expression of policy, although one must add that, up to the moment, the anti-Bolshevik tirades in Germany have lost none of their force.

Chapter Three

THE LOST GERMANS

The Holy Place of Nazidom is the Feldherrnhalle, in the heart of Munich. There, looking down on the Ludwigstrasse, is a kind of classical temple built nearly a century ago to celebrate the great Bavarians. The building has now been converted into a Nazi shrine, because here the first Nazis gave their lives for their cause in the abortive rising of November 1923. Black Guard sentinels stand night and day, and every German must salute the sacred spot as he passes. On the wall behind the sentries is a great scroll bearing the words GOD MAKE US FREE, and on either side are five wreaths, with flowers renewed every day. Each wreath carries the colours of a lost province, and not a day passes without tens of thousands of Germans coming here and mourning for their losses. The ten names are as follows : Alsace-Lorraine ; the Palatinate ; Rhine-Ruhr-Saar-Eupen-Malmédy ; Schleswig-Holstein ; East Prussia, Memel, and Danzig ; Sudeten Deutschland ; South Tyrol and South Styria ; Posen ; Silesia ; and the colonies.

Here is the measure of Germany's grief ; here are the lands she views as torn from the living flesh of the Fatherland. Some of them, it will be noted, have never formed a part of the German Reich, lands like the Tyrol and the German parts of Czechoslovakia. Nevertheless, they are all grouped together, and the average German feels as strongly about them as he does about the lands wrenched away by the Treaty of Versailles. The Nazis have been very astute in giving such a prominent place to their territorial grievances ; it is quite clear that anybody visiting the Feldherrnhalle will feel resentment at the loss of the provinces named above, and will also feel that the National Socialists place the fight for their recovery on a par with the homage paid to their own dead. It is all very clever.

The first article in the Party programme deals with these lost lands. It runs : 'We demand the union of all Germans to form a Great Germany on the basis of the right of self-determination of nations.' This article has never been altered. Hitler has always preached the gospel of Pan-Germanism—the doctrine that every man of German race, whatever the political vicissitudes of the moment, must some day or other come back again to the German nation. He has fanatically opposed those parts of the peace treaties which base nationality on any other factor than race. To him, race and nationality are synonymous terms. Without such a conception the whole Nazi philosophy, the whole idea of the *Folkic* State, would fall to the ground. The very idea of a racial minority is anathema to him. A State must be a homogenous racial unit. Germany itself has no minorities (the Jews are not counted) ; and any other State that claims dominance over German minorities must cede them to their Germanic Fatherland.

The German has never wavered in this idea, although it is obvious that its practical execution is utterly out of the question without war. Hitler says, for example, that he has no conceivable cause for quarrel with France : his Party Headquarters place fresh flowers on ' the grave of Alsace-Lorraine ' every day at the Nazi shrine. How can the two be reconciled ? Not a congress goes by without his renewed confession of racial faith ; not a day passes without racial articles in his official Press. National Socialism without a racial basis is unthinkable ; National Socialism on a racial basis means war : the dilemma is fairly posed.

What are these racial enclaves that are tucked away on every part of Germany's frontier ? Some are lands taken by the Treaty, others are Germanic by race. On the west, Eupen and Malmédy went to Belgium after the war, with 49,561 Germans ; and France took Alsace and Lorraine. The racial position there defies analysis, but Germany claims that, of the 1,874,000 inhabitants there, three-quarters speak either German or the Alsatian dialect, which is a form of

German, and are thus fit subjects for an irredentist movement.
On the other extreme of Germany are the 681,000 Germans
in Posen (now Polish) ; 426,400 in the Polish Corridor ;
300,000 in that part of Upper Silesia which has gone to
Poland ; 318,300 in Danzig ; and 105,000 in Memel. Together
these eastern losses total over 1,800,000 Germans, all of whom
have been torn away from the Fatherland they belonged to
eighteen years ago, all of them brutally de-racialized and
deprived of their German heritage, all of them living martyrs
for no other reason than the accident of their birth. The
40,000 Germans in northern Schleswig (now Danish) are in
a like category.

The position in the south is rather more complicated.
Here there were no territorial adjustments after the war.
From Alsace to Silesia, the frontier was not altered at the
Peace Conferences : the changes affected the old Austro-
Hungarian Monarchy, not Germany. Nevertheless, Pan-
Germanism claims these provinces. The German minorities
in Czechoslovakia, Austria, and Italy have just as much a
place of honour at the Feldherrnhalle as their kinsmen taken
away from Germany by the Treaty. In Austria alone there
are 6,500,000 Germans, pure in race, traditions, and language,
and destined for an *Anschluss* with Germany. Germany
claims that at least two million of them are Nazis and that
most of the remainder would prefer absorption by Germany
to the loss of their independence to Italy. Along the German
frontier in Czechoslovakia are the Sudeten Germans, number-
ing 3,124,000 (although there is much intermixture with
the Czechs). In the Tyrolean provinces ceded to Italy
so that Italian guns could be mounted on the Brenner Pass
are 300,000 people of Germanic race, previously belonging to
Austria.

German propaganda says nothing about the 2,750,000
Swiss-Germans or the 270,000 residents of Luxemburg who
speak German ; and not much is heard about the German
minorities farther afield—the 17,000 in Esthonia, the 60,000
in Latvia, the 750,000 in Rumania, the 513,000 in Yugoslavia,
or the 577,000 in Hungary. There are almost a million
German settlers in Soviet Russia ! The simple truth is that

if German blood or language is to be regarded as justification
for a union with Germany, the Germans will control most
of central Europe.   There are 15,000,000 Germans outside
Hitler's boundaries, so great has been the ethnic penetration
of the Germans of the past.   These are ' the lost Germans '
whom Hitler has ever in mind and whose cause he has promised
never to forget.   Whether they all want to go back to his
rule is another question, but he is convinced that all of them
will want to do so when they learn of the blessings of National
Socialism.

' For every four Germans at home, one lives in exile under
a foreign flag,' say the Nazis, ' and they must all come back
to the German *Heimat*.'   On the very first page of *Mein
Kampf* Hitler said explicitly, in dealing with Austria and
Germany, that ' common blood must belong to a common
race '.   Later, in dealing with colonies, he stated that overseas
expansion should not be considered ' until the confines of
the Reich include every single German '.   It is clear that his
views on this matter have not changed.   Apart from his
speeches there is the obvious evidence of his propaganda
machinery in every country where German minorities are
to be found.   The machine functions in Switzerland, and
nobody interested in international affairs needs to be reminded
of its work in Austria and Czechoslovakia.   Palatable or not,
the plain fact is that Pan-Germanism is an active and immediate
political force in Europe.   Hitler's racial philosophy means
a fight for 15,000,000 Germans spread over more than a
dozen countries.   The only question that remains is : How
far will Hitler persist in this campaign ?   So far he shows
no sign of abating his propaganda, however much he may
officially deny it ; and we are confronted by the question :
Will he continue the campaign even if it means war ?   Or
is he sufficiently deluded by his own power to imagine that
he can secure territorial adjustments by a mere show of force
without having to use the reality ?   Every month that passes
sees a new emphasis on the racial basis of National Socialism ;
and every speech on race is an endorsement of Pan-Germanism.
It is the most dangerous form of Imperialism.

There is, however, one check.   The various tribes of lost

Germans are not equal recipients of propaganda. The Nazis, for instance, say nothing of their kinsmen handed over to Belgium and Denmark, and ignore the two-thirds of a million Germans in Hungary, although they are subjected to a most rigorous policy of Magyarization. The Germans in Yugoslavia suffer many wrongs, those in north Italy are denied all racial rights : but their time has not yet come. Germany works up campaigns only for the Sudeten Germans in Czechoslovakia, who receive (relatively at least) the best treatment of all the lost peoples. For the same reason much is made of the sufferings of the Germans in Danzig or Memel, while the Germans of the Corridor have hardly been mentioned since the signing of the Non-Agression Pact with Poland. The feeling of racial wrong, that is, varies not with the actual condition of the exiles, but according to the needs of Germany's general foreign policy. Their actual sufferings do not matter; the cynical truth being that each group of 'lost Germans' is used as a pawn on the wider chessboard of diplomatic *Realpolitik*.

Chapter Four

THE SOUTHERN DANGER ZONES

I.—Austria

The problem of Austria is a very complicated one for the
Nazis. Hitler himself has always had the outlook of a
southern German. To him, Germans and Austrians belong
to the same race. He obviously wishes to move the centre
of gravity of German life to the south. Disliking Berlin,
he spends as much time as possible in Bavaria, even directing
most affairs of State from there. He prefers Southerners
to Prussians, and, according to some of his intimates, would
like to see Vienna the capital of his neo-German Empire.

He has always looked with a kindly eye on the efforts
of the Austrian Nazis, even when obvious reasons of political
prudence have compelled him to disavow them outwardly.
In his formal processions he invariably assigns the place of
honour in the vanguard of the march to the Austrian Legion,
the Nazis exiled from Austria.

The movement for an *Anschluss*—a political union between
Germany and Austria—was dear to his heart from the outset.
When he became Chancellor, the Austrian Nazis thought
that the time had come for direct action, especially because
Goebbels so obviously favoured the step.

Austria, condemned to economic death by the partitions
inflicted on her by the Treaty, had been suffering for years.
Most of her industries had gone to Czechoslovakia ; her
markets should have been in Germany ; and the six impover-
ished mountain cantons left to her could not support the
city of Vienna. In the years immediately after the war,
most Austrians probably reacted to these conditions by
looking with favour on an *Anschluss* with Germany—certainly

an economic one, and possibly a political one. But common Germanism received a hard blow when Hitler rose to power. Vienna has always been notorious for its large Jewish population, and the easy-going Austrians in general were disgusted by the forceful methods of Nazidom. The cause of dictatorship, whether of the Italian or the German variety, was greatly set back by the *Heimwehr's* disgustingly brutal suppression of the Austrian Social Democrats. The Viennese looked at the holes made in their buildings by Major Fey's howitzers and cursed the very idea of Fascism.

Then came the thunderbolt of the murder of Dollfuss. While one can feel no sympathy for his Italianizing policy, or his dictatorial methods, or his ruthless treatment of political opponents, one must feel indignant at the method of his death. Nazi responsibility is beyond doubt. Whether the details of the final coup were arranged in Munich or not is a relatively unimportant question ; the main point is that, over a long period, Hitler had sanctioned a constant campaign against the Austrian Government, and his minions had relied on systematic terrorism, a policy to which the Nazi Press had offered every incitement. The assassination of Dollfuss was but the culmination of a long series of outrages on the part of the Austrian Nazis. They were aided by Germany at every turn, and when conditions became too hot for them in their own land they were given refuge— and sometimes signal honours—across the border in Germany.

Hitler's disavowal of such methods immediately after the assassination does not alter the situation. Theo Habicht had directed Nazi propaganda in Austria, blazing away from Munich. When Dollfuss banned the Nazi Party in Austria (June 1933) Habicht blustered and bullied, and did everything possible to rouse the Austrians to revolt. The Austrian Brown Book denounced Habicht and Frauenfeld as responsible for the campaign that led to the murder of Dollfuss ; but Hitler appointed these two men to the German Reichstag and eulogized the Austrian Legion.

Since then Dr. Schuschnigg has maintained the ban on the Nazi Party in Austria. Quite recently he stated that the country's foes were Communism, Nazidom, and Indifference ;

and his turn from Italy in no wise implied a move towards
Germany. The Austrian Government has so far succeeded
in keeping a precarious isolation ; but one feels, when in the
country, that it is caught between the pincers-grip of the
dictatorships on either side.

Schuschnigg achieved a great success by the Austrian-
German Agreement of July 11th, 1936, by which Germany
recognized the full sovereignty of Austria and agreed to treat
Austrian Nazidom as a domestic matter for that country.
For her part, Austria recognized herself ' to be a German
State '. What this meant is by no means clear ; and it is
certain that the agreement, even when supplemented by the
withdrawal of the prohibitive tax on German tourists, achieved
no vital changes in the situation. Relations between the
two countries remain in a state of flux, and incidents are
for ever arising as a result of Schuschnigg's penalization of
the Nazis. Those who looked on the agreement as a prelude
to an *Anschluss* have been proven wrong.

Austria is hopelessly divided, and that disposes of the
simplist solution of those foreigners who insist that a fairly
conducted plebiscite would clear up the situation. I spent
part of last autumn in a typical Tyrolean village up in a
valley above Innsbruck. The Nazis were strong there
and missed no opportunity of besporting the white stockings
which at that time were their emblem. The Government
had forbidden all the more obvious symbols. The people
in this valley—overlooked by the Italian gun-emplacements
on the Brenner—for the most part allowed their resentment
of Italy's seizure of ' the lost Tyrol ' to turn them towards
Germany. But the middle-aged men and women, while
pro-German, were by no means certain about their policy.
Fervent Catholics, they could not forget the refusal of the
murderers to allow Dollfuss the last sacrament as he lay bleed-
ing to death on a Chancellory sofa ; and they could not
overlook the gallant rally of Cardinal Faulhaber for their
faith in Munich. ' Better a lost province than lost souls,'
one old peasant said as he crossed himself before the crucifix
in his fields, ' and Schuschnigg at least leaves us our faith.'

It was near here that the hot-headed youngsters had taken

up arms the day after Dollfuss's murder, and some of them still resented Hitler's disavowal of their methods and his round-up of the Austrian Legion before they could dash across the frontier. 'High politics it may have been,' the local Nazi leader said to me, 'but high-sounding words cannot excuse desertion.' He blamed Hitler's advisers for what had taken place, because he still believed that the beloved *Führer* would never have been party to such an act of treachery.

In the same village were many Government supporters. Such a one was the local postmaster, who prevented my letter to Nazi headquarters in Munich from reaching its destination. But there were no believers in Starhemberg— 'the fly-by-night' they called him—and no members of the *Heimwehr*. It was odd, too, how little evidence there was of loyalty to Dollfuss. Some Austrian villages have their *Dollfussplatz*, but this town—typical of the Tyrol—had no relic of him, except an aged and discoloured poster bearing his portrait—and the portrait was cut in two !

One old man summed up Austrian opinion. 'My brothers are five miles away, down the other side of the Brenner. . . . Mussolini says that such as he can now use their own language again, but my brother's name has been Italianized, his children go to Italian schools, and the old repression goes on. We will have none of Italy. . . . Nor can we submit to the tricks of the Jews in Vienna. . . . Germans we are and always will be, but there is no short cut to Berlin for us. We suffer, but —thanks to the Virgin Mary—we survive. Hitler might make us prosperous again, but we should have to pay too high a price for a few extra shillings a week. You see our shops ; they are pitiably empty. But our souls are still our own, and we are all men of this village first—Homeland-Fronters or Nazis second. . . . We are buffers between Hitler and Mussolini, and all that we can do is to remain so. But does your England realize that, in acting thus and in keeping Germany and Italy apart, we are maintaining the peace of Europe ? You talk to me of the sins of the old Imperial Foreign Office in the *Ballhausplatz*. Mother of God, we are still paying for the errors of the past, if those errors you lay at our door. . . . Only one thing goes on—our Mother

Tyrol. We struggle on, only because of our mountains and
our valleys, and our Mother Church, and the thought of all
that we remember of Burg Insl, where Andreas Hofer fought
with scythes for our independence a hundred and more
years ago. That monument to Hofer yonder and this Virgin
above us (we were sitting under a polychrome decoration
of the Austrian Virgin on the wall) sustain us, even when
we are being treated as the shuttlecock of Europe, and even
when we are suffering from the new blockade the tariffs
all around us are imposing. We have only our memories
and our faith . . . so what can Hitler offer us ? '

The poignant sadness of riven Austria is summed up in
the quiet hopelessness of that beautiful Tyrol village. Young
and old are thwarted, they know not how ; and meanwhile
they accept Schuschnigg's moderating government. One
man struck a new note—he saw hope for *Austria Infelix*
only by a union with Czechoslovakia, but his was a lone
voice (although I heard a similar contention at other times in
parts of northern Austria).

On the whole, I should say that Austria wants Germanism,
but not Hitlerism, and is now much less content to accept
economic aid from Italy than she was a couple of years ago.
The *Anschluss* is no longer a spontaneous movement within
Austria, although there is intense underhand propaganda
from Germany the whole time, and at any moment an
explosion caused from without would stir up all the latent
bitterness that could lead to the crudest form of civil war.
One feels that the surface crust keeping down the volcanic
eruption is a very thin one.

Even if German agitation arouses the youngsters again,
it will be long before the Austrian Nazi Party regains the
popularity it had before the morning of Dollfuss's murder.
The bullets of the assassin Planetta and the manner of the
Chancellor's passing have effectively prevented that. Moreover, the doubt then implanted still persists. ' Our *Führer*
has sent orders to keep quiet and give no provocation,' said
my village Nazi chief, but his words lacked conviction.
He could not understand ; he doubted—in his eyes a movement that depended on perpetual aggressiveness was being

defeated once it sanctioned quietness. 'Doubtless the *Führer* knows best,' he said with a shrug, as he turned to dress in the traditional costume of his village for a church procession at another village up the valley.

That is Austria to-day. Gone is the certainty of a couple of years ago, when Nazis asserted that half of Vienna and at least two-thirds of the country folk would vote for them if there were a free election ; gone is the fighting faith in an *Anschluss*. 'We are Germans,' they say, and they will go no further. The material is still there—pliable if handled properly, but lacking the touch of the master hand. 'Holy Mother of Austria, keep us free ! ' ; this is their cry. They are in a wilderness and do not know if Munich is their city of promise or not. They wander and suffer, and see no end.

Meanwhile the well-oiled machinery of Nazi propaganda continues to pour out its material. The absorption of Austria is a subject very dear to Goebbels's heart. 'The little Doctor' has set his mind on Austria as the highway to central Europe, and the game of undermining a government is one he loves. The crude frontal attacks of Habicht are now no more ; the wily diplomatic tortuousness of ex-Ambassador Reith is also discountenanced for the moment : but Goebbels, from his radio base in Munich, continues to make use of the siren-call of German economic prosperity ('*Join us and double your wages!*') and to titillate the feeling of Germanic superiority by pointing to new Germany's successes in the diplomatic field. '*Österreich erwache !* ' cry the campaigners ; and the Austrians are torn in their perplexity.

Their dilemma is insoluble. Across the Brenner is assimilation to Fascism ; across the Inn is assimilation to Hitlerism ; and the Austrian wants neither of these. But he does so want to sell his crops and his high-grade cattle and the products of his hand-industries ; and he does so want to be proud of his race !

II.—*Czechoslovakia*

' Three and a Half Million Lost Germans '

A Czech diplomat once said to me : ' You cannot begin to understand German problems unless you see them from the south. Then they look entirely different.' His point was that the Austrian and Czech borderlands form the central axis of European affairs and that any trouble there would upset the equilibrium of the entire Continent. I am convinced that in these frontier-lands we have the real danger zone in Europe. While we may have heard more of other regions in this regard, the recent stress on ' the lost Germans ' has brought us closer to realities.

The conflict is one of fundamentals. Hitler sees Czecho-slovakia as an unwieldy agglomeration which has wrenched three and a half million ' lost Germans ' from the Germanic body and has failed to assimilate them in a Slav State ; while the Czechs, confident of their new-born nationality, are prepared to go to any lengths to keep their present frontiers, which, they say, are not only founded on history and geography, but are vital to Czech existence.

The Germans had reason for resentment, and much of Henlein's subsequent ' misery propaganda ' is based on fact. There is far more unemployment in the German districts than in the Czech,[1] and the Germans are inadequately repre-sented in official posts (a fact which the Czechs admit, but which they justify on the ground that they cannot take the risk of placing politically suspect men in key positions). The Germans say that the Czechs are a governing clique even in the purely Germanic regions, and the Government contracts go almost entirely to Czech firms. Much bitterness

---

[1] This is mainly due, however, to the restriction of world markets for industrial products in recent years, and especially to the closing of the market in Germany itself. As industrialists the Sudeten Deutsche were bound to suffer ; as industrialists largely dependent on Germany, still more so.

has also been aroused by the closing of German schools without adequate reason.

The Czechs foolishly adopted a policy of unification instead of a loose federalism. By the Minority Treaties and by the Czech constitution, the Germans were promised equality of rights. They took this to mean equality in a triune state of Czechs, Slovaks, and Germans; whereas Masaryk formed a 'National State of the Czechs and the Slovaks', with the Germans—who were twice as numerous as the Slovaks—possessing only the rights of a minority. In no sense partners, the Germans felt themselves tricked from the beginning.

In their resentment they lodged nineteen petitions before the League of Nations in six years, but without much result. Bereft of this last hope and now caught in the throes of the world depression, they listened to the voices from across the mountains, and the younger men in particular turned to Hitlerism—to the man whom Hindenburg had termed one of themselves, 'the little Bohemian corporal'.

From the autumn of 1933 onwards, Konrad Henlein rallied them in the S.D.P. (*Sudeten Deutsche Partei*). This was, in effect, a Nazi organization and took the place of the dissolved National Socialist Party. Nevertheless, Henlein has stated repeatedly that he does not want secession from Czechoslovakia. He denies the allegation that his orders come from Berlin and, on the contrary, asserts that his party springs from the racial and historical background of Czechoslovakia alone. He has seen Hitler only for a couple of minutes on a formal occasion during the Olympic Games. In Berlin at the time, I heard rumours from all quarters that this was a direct rebuff for Henlein's policy of compromise and a direct incentive to the extremists within his party to demand an open union with Germany. Henlein, in short, lacks the fanaticism of the true Nazi zealot. He uses the time-worn Nazi methods, his Press is clamant for Hitlerism, and his policy certainly dovetails in with that of Munich: but he is too conciliatory, too content with moderate gains, for the Nazi fold. He wants no more, he says, than equality of treatment for Germans and Czechs within Czechoslovakia; and he claims that 70 per cent of the Germans within the country support him.[1] In the elections of 1935 he obtained 1,250,000 votes more than any other party.

The Czechs have no faith in his protestations and are convinced that he wants separation and will declare himself when the time is ripe. They call his men *Crypto-Nazis*. It seems true that extremist elements exist within the Sudeten Deutsche Party and that, while some of these would be content with regional autonomy, others want nothing less than amalgamation with Germany. They dream of a ' totalitarian national state ' which will wipe out the imposing mountain frontier bestowed by Nature and replace it by an artificial racial line where the last ounce of German blood runs out near Pilsen and Reichenberg.

President Benes has steadily refused to recognize such claims. Any interference from Germany would be a *casus belli*, any aid to Nazi agitation outside the German frontiers would be an unfriendly act. Should any fighting minority attempt subversive activities, his State Defence Law (May 1936) allows martial law in the disturbed regions. As a precaution, care is taken to see that the National Socialist Party is not revived under new names.

Yet Benes professes much sympathy for the more moderate claims. After all, more than a fifth of the Czechoslovakians are Germans ; there has been much intermarriage ; the Germans have contributed largely to the composite civilization of the country ; and the great bulk of the Germans are quiet-living, sturdy artisans attached to the genuine democracy of Czechoslovakia. For such sections Benes promises an increasing degree of decentralization and a fair participation in political life. But autonomy he will not consider. He views it as quite unnecessary and as the first stage towards

[1] It must be noted that the last election was fought on the single question : Whether the Germans should have group-rights within Czechoslovakia ? Naturally very few of them opposed such a platform ; but this is no more ground for saying that Henlein speaks on all matters for the mass of the Sudeten Germans than for arguing that Hitler has the complete allegiance of 98 per cent of the Germans, because they agree with him on foreign policy, as stated in the plebiscites.

separatism. He will not concede Henlein's claim for 'a definite recognition of a dividing line for our people'.

While Benes can probably cope with the German minority within his borders, he can hardly do so if the discontent is stimulated from the German side of the frontier. The Nazis play on the grievances of their kinsmen in Czechoslovakia and even conjure them into existence. Undue publicity makes the discontent vocal and powerful, and thus a local problem becomes a major disturbing factor in international affairs. Official Germany must be blamed for this. The endless bombardments in the controlled Press could come to an end if the Hitlerites so desired ; and the movement within Czechoslovakia would die of inanition if the campaigns for ' the recovery of the lost Germans ' were called off in Germany. It is not a natural spontaneous agitation in Bohemia, because, after all, the people are not ' lost Germans ' in any real sense of the word. They are Bohemians and have had no political associations with Germany for centuries past. They have always had distinct traditions and a culture of their own ; and their only tie with Germany was the fact that their King was one of the seven Electors who chose the Holy Roman Emperor. To compare them with frontiersmen wrenched away by treaties after the last war (with Danzig or Memel or even Alsace) is absurd. If they are irredentists to-day (and one must reiterate that Henlein denies this), the movement lacks historical justification. Moreover, Benes has allayed much of the discontent by abandoning the earlier centralizing policy of Masaryk and by astutely turning to the *Activists*—those Sudeten Germans who advocate parliamentary co-operation with Prague. The *Activists* have always protested against any undue recognition of Henlein's claims, for they believed that he had merely capitalized the distress amongst his compatriots and the feeling of racial pride in the new strength of the Reich.

It is indeed doubtful if the great mass of Sudeten Germans would favour a secessionist movement against the Prague Government. Whatever happened, they would always be a minority—even in Germany—and no change of status could take place until after their Bohemian land had been turned into a battlefield. They may not love the Czechs, they may not relish rule from Prague ; but no alternative prospect is equally advantageous to them.

II.—' *The Bolshevik dagger at our throat* '

Some such realization may account for the increasing tension between Germany and Czechoslovakia in the last two years —the tension that started when Krebs and Jung, two of the Nazi extremists in Bohemia, were elected to the German Reichstag (March 1936). As the year went on, the tone of the Press in Germany became ever more bitter against Czechoslovakia. The reason for this became obvious at the Nuremberg Rally, because the thesis then presented was that the Czechs had betrayed the cause of civilization by becoming pawns in the hands of the ' Jewish-Bolshevists ' (although the pact between Czechs and Russians had escaped comment for many months after its conclusion). The legend of Russian aerodromes in Czechoslovakia came into being— Dresden and Munich could be bombed in a few minutes, Bavaria could be wrested from the Reich, industrial Silesia could be devastated, and Russian hordes could march unmolested towards western Europe—so ran the plaint. There was much talk of new strategic railways, of Russian experts at the aerodromes, and of new frontier fortifications. (For some strange reason the 1,250,000 Nazi leaders concentrated in Nuremberg at that moment, and huddled together on places like the Zeppelin-field—' five minutes from the Russian airports '—felt no sense of fear, although, had the Russian policy been as Machiavellian as they represented, here was a perfect opportunity for a swift annihilating blow !)

That the Nuremberg speeches were not merely for local consumption became obvious when Wächtler, the regional leader of the Bavarian Ostmark, revived the attack six weeks later. He specifically accused the Czechs of allowing the Russians to form an axial corridor running through the heart of Europe for 600 miles. The Red air force already had thirty-six aerodromes just over the German frontier, and now the Czechs were feverishly building strategic railways. The official news agencies reported this speech in all the main newspapers and endorsed Wächtler's claim that the peace of Europe was gravely imperilled. ' When a neighbour clumsily experiments with cholera germs, the anxiety to protect oneself against infection is not unjustifiable,' he said. A history professor (the allusion was to Dr. Krofta, the Czech Foreign Secretary) was rushing the world to war because of his candlelight intrusions into the grim realities of foreign affairs, and Germany could no longer view such happenings as of purely local significance.

The note thus sounded, the entire German Press became hysterical. Again and again they referred to themselves as the saviours of civilization, desirous of closing the breach in the dikes clumsily opened by the Czechs ; again and again they invoked the hoary analogy of themselves as the re-incarnation of the Teutonic Knights holding back the Asiatic hordes of destroyers, now brought up to the hitherto impregnable Moravian bastion through Czech perfidy. The Ostmark is imperilled, raved Wächtler, and if it falls, so will the whole of Europe !

In reply, the Czech Government repeatedly denied that they had made themselves ' a sally-port for Bolshevism', and invited German officials to investigate conditions on the spot. Overwhelmed by this blast of lying propaganda, they felt justified in their recent policies, and the only result of the Press campaigns, apart from inducing a feeling of insecurity all over Europe, was to throw the Czechs more than ever into the arms of France, Russia, and their partners of the Little Entente.

Part of the trouble arose out of misapprehension concerning the pact with Russia. This was described in Germany as an aggressive military pact aimed at the encirclement of Germany and the ultimate Bolshevization of Europe. This is ridiculous. The treaty can apply only in the case of defence. It is directed only against an aggressor—indeed, such aggression as can be determined by the League of Nations. It merely binds the signatories to come to each other's aid if attacked by an aggressor. The Czechs entered into the scheme only because negotiations for a general Eastern Pact had failed, and they have repeatedly stated that they would welcome the adhesion of Germany to such a system of pacts within the League.

Nevertheless, the Czechs have staked their national existence on the reality of Russian support in time of stress. A difficulty arose because at no point were the frontiers of the two countries contiguous. Russian aid (other than aerial) could come only through Poland or Rumania. The Czechs therefore rely on the Rumanian promise (given in exchange for an armaments credit) to complete the Czernowitz railway, which would allow troops and food to be rushed up from the Ukraine round the Carpathians.

Last year's Defence Law also allowed the strengthening of the frontier fortifications, especially in the Oder valley (guarding the coalfields) and at the dangerous Eisenstein gap. The Bohemian basin affords a natural protection against any thrust from the north-west, because of its mountains. Bismarck once said that ' the master of Bohemia is the master of Europe '. That is why Czechoslovakia can never cede this region, for an enemy holding the Moravian gateway could range at will over the whole of the Danubian lands. The latest Czech step to hold the passes is the formation of a militarized frontier force (November 1936), one of the aims of which is said to be the stiffening of the morale of the minority populations along the borderlands.

Czechoslovakia is enormously wealthy and strong. Despite the present industrial crisis, the country has consolidated itself; and it must be remembered that three-fourths of the industrial wealth of the Austro-Hungarian Empire was produced in the land of the Sudeten Deutsche. She is strong enough financially to subsidize less fortunate allies, like Rumania, and her armaments have been rapidly developed. The three States of the Little Entente have sixty peace-time divisions between them, and the Czech frontier fortifications are amongst the most complete in Europe. Her Slavonic populations are bitterly anti-Nazi and believe that their very existence depends on checking Germany's Imperialistic policy.

Imaginative strategists, who look on nations as pawns on a European chessboard, talk about a German invasion breaking down Czech resistance before France and Russia could come to their aid and then forcing the whole of central Europe to surrender. Such fantasies are absurd in the Europe of to-day ; they may have had some application to a crumbling Austro-Hungarian Empire, but they completely fail to take into account the consolidation of power and morale in Czechoslovakia in the last fifteen years. Czechoslovakia is far more likely to hold the ridges from Eger to the Oder. Land attacks on the Moravian gateway would involve losses that would make Verdun seem insignificant, and the resistance would put the entire German strategy out of joint.

The Czechs are fully aware of the importance of the 300 miles of the ' transversal Eurasian axis ' (the old Hamburg-Basra line) they have to control ; and they know that the only weakness which could ruin them would be the loss of Upper Bohemia to some foreign power. They survive as long as they retain the Bohemian bastion ; and as certainly they fall if they lose that natural guardian. That is why they can never consider the cession of any part of Bohemia to Germany, and that is why Hitler's persistence in a campaign to recover ' the lost Germans ' must inevitably lead to war ; and the Czechs have a saying : ' When Bohemia is aflame there can be no peace for the rest of Europe.' They must keep the mountain crescent of the Sudetes and the Carpathians ; they must guard the approaches along the Danube and through the Moravian gateway (between the two sets of mountains), and they must fortify the only other approach —down the Uzŏk Pass from the north-east. Thus only can they protect the middle Danubian lands ('the main military cross-roads of central Europe', Colonel Moravec has called them) ; and thus only can the new State retain its identity. It cannot be repeated too often that this is entirely incompatible with any expansionist policy within Germany. If Germany persists in wanting to absorb the Sudeten Deutsche, it means war.

Chapter Five

THE BALTIC PRESSURE-POINTS

I.—Danzig and the Polish Corridor

Hitler has always protested against the cleavage of East
Prussia from the rest of Germany. He made great attacks
on the Corridor in his campaigns before he became Chancellor
and openly stated that the arrangements about the Corridor
offended Germans more than any other part of the Peace
Treaties. On the eve of the elections of March 5th, 1933,
he made his melodramatic flight to Königsberg, and it was
expected that he would adopt an intransigent attitude when
in office.

Actually the position in the Corridor has been quiet,
except for economic disputes. In January 1934, Hitler
signed the Non-Aggression Pact with Poland and thus
postponed for ten years all hope of regaining the Corridor
or Upper Silesia for the Reich. Next month both Governments promised to control public opinion in their respective
countries, and, in March, the tariff war that had dragged on
for nearly a decade was ended. Hitler was obviously trying
to effect a breach in the ring of enemy powers encircling
Germany ; and he was most careful in his Reichstag speech
after the reoccupation of the Rhineland to reassure Poland
once again that he had no designs on the Corridor.

The eastern extremists within the Party thought that,
by this series of concessions, he had tied his hands without
any effective return ; and, by way of reaction, redoubled their
efforts to win control of Danzig. The Treaty of Versailles
had established Danzig as a free city protected by the League
of Nations. The town was to have a High Commissioner
appointed by the League. It was to be a unit in the Polish

Customs administration. There was to be a *Volkstag* (Diet) elected by universal suffrage, and the seventy-two members of the *Volkstag* were to elect a Senate. To alter the constitution there had to be a two-thirds majority in the *Volkstag*.

The first elections after the Nazi revolution in Germany gave the Danzig Nazis a clear majority over all the other parties together, and this position has pertained ever since. The last elections of 1935 gave them forty-three members out of a total of seventy-two. But they needed five more votes to secure a majority large enough to change the constitution, and all of their efforts have been directed towards this end. In November 1934, Dr. Greiser became vice-president of the Senate, and, since he was the general director of the administration, this meant a great increase in Nazi power.

The High Commissioner, Sean Lester, attempted to maintain a neutral attitude, but was hindered at every step by the Nazis and resigned in 1936.

The campaign for the ' co-ordination ' of the Government was then intensified. Attacks were made on all other parties. The Communist Party had been banned in May 1934, and drastic police action had been taken against all organizations of the Left. In October 1936, the Social Democratic Party was proscribed, and later the *Volkstag* took away the parliamentary immunity of deputies who were ' hostile to the State '. The onslaught was next enwidened to take in the Centre and the Nationalist Party, the result being that, by March 1937, the Nazis needed only two more votes to secure a two-thirds majority. By the beginning of May, owing to pressure on certain individual deputies, they had gained their point and could embark on the task of forming a new constitution which would make Danzig, like Germany, an *Ein-partei-staat*. The process of ' co-ordination ' was complete.

But the matter is not as simple as that. Danzig is definitely an international question. The League of Nations comes directly into the picture, and Poland has special treaty rights. Danzig is important to Poland economically and strategically, and the building of the new Polish port of Gdynia has not thrust the older Hanseatic city entirely into the background. The Danzigers are already deprived of the political and legal rights guaranteed to them in the League constitution, and to all intents and purposes Danzig is now ' co-ordinated ' on the familiar Nazi model.   But the Poles are not disposed to stand by and see the Nazis take over the city entirely. For one thing, they do not wish to see the Polish minority there treated as the non-Nazi Germans are being treated ; and, after all, the Nazis represent only 58 per cent of the population.

Herr Greiser, whose blunt and childish actions at the League Council made such a bad impression, did nothing to ease a complicated situation.   He often said that ' in Danzig, as in the Reich, there would be no distinction between the demands of the Nazi Party and the actions of the State ' and persisted in a direct policy of intimidation.

The possibility of a *putsch* appears slight, because Hitler is not likely to imperil Polish friendship for the sake of getting back 700 square miles of territory, as long as Poland can keep the *hinterland* that brings the port of Danzig most of its trade.   He knows that the Poles are not really very much concerned with minority rights in Danzig, and feels that a large scope exists in the new possibility of formulating a constitution that will go as far as possible in the direction of Hitlerism without alienating Poland.   About the League's part he does not worry.   Nor does he seem inclined to make ultimate incorporation of Danzig in the Reich an immediate issue.   In the near future he will probably be satisfied with a virtual Nazi dictatorship in Danzig, although in Germany last year I found an astonishingly widespread impression that Hitler could successfully carry off a coup in Danzig without any real fear of a war arising from it. The ultimate factor seems to be the limitations imposed by the need of keeping Poland's friendship.   As long as Hitler has any prospects in this direction, Danzig must wait.

II.—*Memel and Lithuania*

The Germans feel particularly bitter about Memel. It is the oldest German town in East Prussia, being founded in 1252 by the Knights of the Brotherhood of the Sword. It has never been Russian or Lithuanian at any time in its history. Germany always looked upon that part of her frontier as unalterable ; the frontier of East Prussia in the south has remained the same since 1422. She has always regarded that frontier as the dividing line between east and west, between Europe and Asia.

The Treaty of Versailles compelled her to renounce the Memel territory to the Allied Powers, and it was held for four years by a conference of ambassadors. The Lithuanians settled the uncertainty of ownership by a *coup d'état* in January 1923, when armed bands from Lithuania (in civilian clothes) drove out the French army of occupation and seized the land. Finally the Council of the League of Nations recognized Lithuanian sovereignty,[1] on condition that the terms of the Memel Convention were respected. Under this Convention, Memel was to be a separate unit under Lithuanian sovereignty with a large degree of local autonomy. Electors were to choose a Chamber of Representatives, and there was to be a Directorate possessing the confidence of this Chamber.

Germany protested from the outset against this arrangement. She claimed that one of her oldest possessions had been wrenched from her simply because Lithuania wanted a ' window ' on the Baltic ; and she argued that it was insensate to make this tiny province—1,100 square miles, with a population of only 150,000—a new European powder magazine.

Germany holds that the population of Memel is predominantly German, although races are so confused there that it is impossible to arrive at any finality. Side by side are Germans, Lithuanians, Memel-landers, and—the final complication—Lithuanians with German names and Germans

---

[1] Despite the fact that an investigating Commission sent by the Conference of Ambassadors found overwhelming proof of German preponderance in Memel, March 1923. Their report was distinctly anti-Lithuanian.

with Lithuanian names. Nazis claim that 68,000 of the people of Memel speak German, and that most of those whose mother tongue is Lithuanian understand German and have no desire to go to Lithuania. The towns, in particular, are mainly German. Moreover, nine out of every ten people in Memel are Protestants, whereas Lithuania is a Catholic country.

The Nazis also hold that the original Convention has been grossly abused by the Lithuanian Government; and here they are on firmer ground. They say that all personal and place names have been converted into Lithuanian forms; they claim that while the German parties secured a tremendous majority at all the elections for the Diet, yet the successive Directorates were such that only two had the confidence of the elected body. The Lithuanian governor also acted in a most dictatorial fashion, depriving the Memel-landers of their own schools, refusing to recognize the German language, dismissing local officials and replacing them by Lithuanians, and illegally dissolving the Diet. Towards the end of 1934, 126 Memel Germans were tried for treason in a most scandalous fashion, and most of them were sentenced to imprisonment. Such a protest was raised against four death sentences that they were commuted to life imprisonment.

The conflict became especially bitter over the 1935 elections, when the Lithuanians resorted to mass naturalization of thousands of their own subjects in order to vote in Memel, and at the same time disfranchised large numbers of German voters. A recourse to martial law also prevented freedom of speech and Press, and the Lithuanian Government intensified all those election tricks which had been condemned by Geneva in previous years. Their conduct throughout has been questionable, although they were only copying the methods the Nazis themselves had used at home. Despite all the unfairness, the German parties secured four-fifths of the votes. Lithuania obtained only five seats out of twenty-nine.

All through 1935 the Memel question was very acute. It died down somewhat last year owing to Nazi diversions elsewhere, but the radio propaganda from Königsberg and the surreptitious formation of Nazi cells continued. This

year the crisis has become worse, because Memel forms a
most important link in Germany's eastern strategy. Renewed
tension in Memel was an inevitable corollary of Hitler's
anti-Russian crusade.

If Memel is Lithuania's only seaport, it is Germany's most
practicable jumping-off place for an eastern expansion.
Lithuania has only 2,000,000 people and an army of three
divisions : it can offer little resistance to German troops
crossing the Niemen from Tilsit. And, as Alfred Rosenberg
never tires of saying (he was born in these Riga lands),
Lithuania leads to Latvia and Esthonia—weak powers both,
but lands that bring German forces to Russia's frontiers
and that would enable her to bottle up the Russian fleet in
the Gulf of Finland. With the small Baltic States, Germany
could hold a dagger at the throat of Soviet Russia. From
the Esthonian border to Leningrad is less than a hundred and
fifty miles. If Germany seriously fears Russia, she must
consider these possibilities, and a progress through the States
of the Baltic seaboard would have the further advantage
of not bringing her into conflict with Poland. The path
here is much easier than that through Czechoslovakia ; and,
assuming that Poland remains neutral under her non-
aggression pact with Germany, there is no other way to get
to grips with Russia.

The danger to Lithuania is so obvious that the Government
has shown signs that it is ready to patch up its old quarrel
with Poland (over the Poles' seizure of ' the Lithuanian
capital ' of Vilna) if the Poles will admit that any forward
policy on the part of Germany would be sufficient reason
for Poland to reconsider her whole policy. Hitler has never
concealed his opinion of Lithuania. He has ruled Lithuania
out of all of his peace proposals (except in March 1936, after
the reoccupation of the Rhineland, when he spoke of a non-
aggresion pact with Lithuania if certain reforms were instituted
in Memel—an offer which has never been revived and which
nobody took seriously at the time). He speaks of the
Memel-landers as ' blood relations who, contrary to laws
and treaty provisions, were attacked and torn from the
Reich in the midst of peace, and subjected to worse treatment

than criminals in normal States', and he has consistently criticized the Lithuanian Government.

Hitler also maintains that Lithuania is merely a Soviet outpost, and he repeats the old story that the Soviets have aerodromes here just as they have in Czechoslovakia. He looks with favour on the Fascist formations there, the 'Iron Wolves' of Woldemaras, the former dictator whose *putsch* three years ago failed so disastrously ; and he sees the 'Fiery Cross' of Latvia and the 'Liberty Fighters' of Esthonia as kindred spirits to the Nazis. The future of the Baltic, in his eyes, depends on the degree to which Soviet influence is ousted from Lithuania and to which the Fascist bodies triumph. Rosenberg has always been most romantic about reviving the spirit of the old Teutonic Knights, and much has been heard about a joint Baltic brotherhood, although there is probably very little practical move in this direction.

The final complicating feature in the situation is that the German elements in Memel are not united in their desire to come back to Germany. Some of them oppose Hitlerism ; many more realize that their town would be a third-rate little port in Germany, deprived of the rich agricultural *hinterland* on which its present prosperity is built up. If Lithuania cannot live without Memel, Memel would find it difficult to live without its Lithuanian trade.

But Hitlerism scorns such drab economics. To Hitler, Memel is the port that was the outpost of Germany for seven centuries. Every time Germans sing their National Anthem —*Deutschland über alles*—they are reminded of it. 'From the Maas to Memel. . . . *Deutschland über alles.*' Facts and statistics count for nothing. They feel that to lose Memel is like having a foot cut off—and to hand it over to the backward Lithuanians is to have the operation bungled by a quack doctor. Their sense of loss is aggravated by the insult. The Memel issue thus assumes more significance than its actual importance warrants. It is a symbol of national degradation, and the new Germany will be incomplete until it is incorporated again in the Reich ; and this feeling is quite independent of any scheme of eastern Imperialism. A German coup in Memel seems indicated by the logic of past events.

III.—*The Enigma of Poland and the Baltic States*

The Germans attribute great importance to the role played by Poland in eastern Europe. Poland is the 'bastion of peace' that keeps Russia and Germany from getting at each other. If Germany embarks on a policy of eastern Imperialism, Poland stands in the way, because, with the growing impossibility of the route through Czechoslovakia, the emphasis is coming to be on the north. Germany may respect her pact with Poland and go through the seaboard States, but, even if this involved no difficulties in the Corridor, the Poles know that ultimately they would be left isolated. A policy of neutrality while Hitler turned the Baltic States into 'war granaries' must be untenable in the long run, and the Poles are sufficiently realists to perceive this.

One of Hitler's earliest aims was to drive a wedge between the French and the Poles, and he relied on winning over 'the Colonel's group' which really ruled Poland for many years. They wanted to extend their peculiar form of feudalism—based on a landed aristocracy—to the smaller States on the Baltic; but Pilsudski's death weakened them and made possible the rival dictatorship of Marshal Rydz-Smigly, who wanted a policy determined by purely military considerations. This meant a turn of Poland towards France, culminating in the recent French credits for Polish rearmament.

As a corollary to this development, relations with Germany became strained, especially after the Nazi manœuvres in Danzig and the economic trouble in the Corridor.

On the other hand, there seems to be a general feeling in Poland that Germany will respect the non-aggression pact, which runs until 1944. The Poles feel that Germany can expand in a southern direction, in which case they can remain neutral. In central Europe there is thus a general idea that Poland cannot be depended upon to adopt any fixed policy. For the moment Colonel Beck is spending the money he obtained from France, is stressing the importance of good relationships with Germany, and is having trouble on every frontier; his only bright spot being the better understanding he has achieved with Rumania. All that one can say is that, in case of any major upheaval in eastern Europe, Poland's attitude is highly problematical. The Germans certainly think that they can secure Poland's neutrality if trouble is avoided in the Danzig sector. But speculation in futures in eastern Europe is a singularly fruitless occupation. Beyond that one cannot go, except to add that the feudal Fascists— the Radziwills, the Potickis, and their like—have certainly not disappeared from the Polish scene for ever. Poland has wavered in her policy for years. At the moment the army is pro-French, but there are many signs that the Poles are becoming more afraid of Sovietism than of Hitlerism, and they are not happy about the implications that stronger ties with France may have, in view of the existence of the Franco-Soviet Pact. Germany quite rightly places Poland in a different category from Czechoslovakia, in so far as fixity of policy is concerned ; and Captain-General Göring does more than hunt pigs when he goes shooting with the Radziwills in their principalities.

IV.—*Germany's Second Hope in the Baltic—Finland*

The Finns, because of their proximity to Russia and their fear of Communism, have strong Nazi tendencies. Baron Mannerheim, who freed his country from the Russians, leads a Fascist movement known as *Lappo*. Despite his failure to seize the government a few years ago, he is still the dominant influence with the officers and the landowners. His movement is in constant touch with Hitlerism, and he was, it will be remembered, the fourth member of the famous ' hunting-party ' at Rominten last year. Göring, Gömbös and Radziwill (the Polish reactionary) were the other three. He wants a Greater Fascist Finland, and he knows that Germany opposes the Kallio Coalition Government which took office in Finland last October, especially because its Foreign Minister, Holsti, wants a kind of anti-German Little Entente among the small States of the Baltic. Mannerheim's Fascists remain very strong, and, despite the temporary setback, Germany feels that she can rely on Finland to be in the anti-Communist camp, and from this it is a small step to Fascism. The German strategists speak of south Finland as being 'the key of the Baltic', and the Rosenberg group give it a fundamental place in their schemes. Berlin thus refuses to look upon the Holsti policy as the final expression of Finnish desires, especially since the Fascists have the elements that make revolutions—the soldiers, the landowners, and the students—on their side.

In the other Baltic States the Nazi outlook is much less favourable. Lithuania has a Fascist movement—the Iron Wolf of Waldemaras ; but this body failed to capture the government in the rebellion of 1934, and its leaders are at present discredited. Lithuania undoubtedly remains anti-Hitlerite. The clash between the two countries' policies makes this inevitable.

In Latvia an unimportant body called the 'Fascist Iron Cross'—the *Perkonkrust*—exists, but is violently opposed by the dictatorship of Karlis Ulmanis, which has been in power since 1934. Esthonia also possesses an authoritarian government, which is even more bitterly anti-Fascist because it owed its inception to a protest against the attempted *putsch* of the Fascist group called 'the League of Liberty Fighters'.

These three States see themselves as tiny units directly in the path of the German steam-roller. They know that they will be immediately occupied if Germany embarks on a scheme of expansion ; and they live in daily terror. They are turning to the idea of a 'Baltic barricade of peace', as proposed by Holsti and Finn ; but, even then, their concerted military strength would be negligible against the German hosts, even if each country presented a unified front instead of having Fascist bodies that look to Berlin for support. The outlook of the Baltic States is indeed a dark one.

Chapter Six

GERMANY AND WESTERN EUROPE

I.—The Obstacle of France

During his four years of power Hitler's policy has been diplomatically correct towards France, while strenuously attacking the French system of alliances, especially after the conclusion of the Franco-Soviet Pact. Hitler wishes to smash this system of encircling pacts ; and most people believe that he wants a free hand in recasting eastern Europe, while keeping France and Britain and Italy neutral in the west.

This at once raises the point : What is his real view about France ? He expressed his opinions at length on one occasion —from his luxurious prison cell in Landsberg. It is argued that he had not fully considered the problem at that time, and that a responsible statesman should not be saddled with the opinions he enunciated during his campaigning days. As against this, Hitler has reiterated the statements of *Mein Kampf* on a thousand platforms since that time, and he still compels every German family to buy the edition of *Mein Kampf*, in which the notorious passages against France remain.

In that book he said explicitly : ' France is and remains by far the most terrible enemy. This people, itself becoming more and more " negrified ", represents, because of its connexion with the aims of the Jewish world domination, a lurking danger to the continuance of the white race in Europe. For the contamination of the Rhine, in the heart of Europe, by negro-blood, is expressive not only of the perverse and sadistic thirst of revenge of this chauvinistic arch-enemy of our nation, but also of the icy-cold deliberation with which the Jew planned to start bastardizing the European continent from the centre.' On a previous page he said expressly : ' The inexorable and deadly enemy of the German people is and remains France ', no matter which party is in power there.

These statements (which are, incidentally, fair examples of Hitler's style) admit of no doubt. They can only mean that Hitler was violently anti-French. France must be destroyed—that is the gist of his attitude ; destroyed because of her military imperialism, destroyed because of her position on the Rhine, destroyed because of her domination by Jews and Communists. The hatred of a thousand years, backed as it is by unalterable facts of history and emotion, cannot be expunged by any goodwill speeches. The grim facts represented by the Maginot Line must be countered, and the only way of doing so is by brute force.

We must remember, too, that Hitler brought together his partisans on the allied issues—hatred of France and hatred of Jewry. For years before he wrote in *Mein Kampf* he had been talking of nothing else. He was stirred to the depths of his being by the occupation of the Ruhr and the resultant blows to German honour.

He had ranted about it at his trial, he had already accorded the murderer Schlageter a place of honour in his martyrology. France, in his eyes, was responsible for ' the dictate of Versailles ', and he felt much more strongly against her than against Britain. Later, when he became Chancellor, it was the French who wished to check German foreign policy : it was under Barthou that they tried to revive the throttling encirclement policy ; it was they who urged counter measures whenever Hitler broke a section of the Treaty ; and it was they who formed the Russian Pact which, more than any other single factor, occasions Hitler permanent disquietude. As the climax, Hitler felt that the French were far weaker than the Germans and that only their allies allowed them to make such a nuisance of themselves—this decadent country of corrupt politics and mutinous soldiers ; this land which refused to ' awaken ' and which held a gateway permanently open to Bolshevism.

Under these conditions it is difficult to say that Hitler

desires permanent peace with France. He very possibly
wants peace in the west until he has cleaned up the east in
accordance with his own ideas ; but his hatred does not
change because strategic reasons compel it to be dormant
for a time. Moreover, he knows quite well that France's
commitments are so involved that any trouble in which
Germany is involved in eastern Europe will, of necessity,
drag in the French. The destiny of France is linked with
the hemming in of Hitlerism ; and the future of Germany
is circumscribed until the French lose their present position
in European diplomacy. It is not so much a question of
hatred between individual Frenchmen and Germans (herein
the present position differs from that of a few generations
ago) ; the plain fact is that Germany cannot áchieve its openly
avowed aims without either breaking France or weakening
her to a degree she would not permit. Hitler looks east,
looks south, looks overseas : in each case, it is the French
who stand in the way ; and in each case if they were removed
the German aims might be realized. ' The French poison
our every breath,' said one of Hitler's lieutenants—and
Germans in their present frame of mind feel that they cannot
live without fresh air.

II.—*The Rome–Ber^lin Axis*

Italy and Germany have been flung together by a general
antagonism to their foreign policies. Mussolini has steadily
supported Hitlér in his treaty-breaking, and each government
gives a highly tendentious account of happenings in the
other's country over the officially controlled wireless. There
was a regular exchange of distinguished visitors last autumn,
culminating in Count Ciano's visit to Berlin at the invitation
of the German Government. Although Germany recognized
the conquest of Abyssinia, very little came out of the visits.
The two governments were shown to have a certain identity
of views on such matters as Spain, Russia, and rearmament ;
but the threatened ' vertical axis ' (from Berlin to Rome)
remained very nebulous after the interviews. Nevertheless,

both countries recognized General Franco on the same day and issued various diplomatic documents about Spain that were practically identical.

The basic truth is that the Germans have little faith in Italy's fighting power, and they feel that events in Spain support their estimate. Moreover, the two countries are in harmony only because of their common enemies. Their policies conflict in so many essentials, and difficulties are avoided only by not being mentioned. Central Europe is a permanent barrier between them, so much so that it is difficult to envisage an Italo–German *bloc* based on a permanent identity of interests, however much their present isolation may force the two countries together. The Germans will not surrender their plans of a *Mitteleuropa* ; and they do not really respect the Italians. Indeed it is difficult for them to find a place in the Nazi racial theory for these Mediterraneans. Yet it would be erroneous to preclude any possibility of united action between the two on such general grounds. An immediate threat might draw them together, despite Mussolini's critical estimate of Hitler, and despite the German feeling about the Italians.

The Italians are not popular in Germany, but Germany is not in a position to pick and choose her friends, and she at least knows that Mussolini believes in the efficacy of swift blows and will not hesitate to use force in settling international disputes. The understanding between the two totalitarian States then, however uneasy it may be, dominates international affairs for the moment. Germany and Italy are partners in dividing Europe into two camps on doctrinal differences. They are hastening a conflict between rival political ideologies —meanwhile central Europe can wait, although German grumblings against Italy's new understanding with Jugoslavia show how real are the differences between the two dictators.

Chapter Seven

THE COLONIAL QUESTION

Germany has assigned a special place to colonies in her campaigns for *Gleichberechtigung*. The day of May 7th, 1919, when the Council of Three announced the decision to deprive Germany of her colonies on the grounds of 'colonial unworthiness', is still an occasion for mourning in Germany. When a country like Portugal retained her overseas possessions, Germany, despite the improvement in her colonial rule during the Dernburg period and despite the loyalty of her African *askaris* in the long fighting, was left without a 'place in the sun' and, in addition, with the stigma of unworthiness upon her. The Versailles Treaty has been practically torn to ribbons, but Sections 118–27, the colonial sections, are merely given added importance because of the destruction of the others.

Germany had built up a colonial empire of a million square miles (five times the area of the Reich itself) in a single generation. But, coming late in the colonial race, her possessions were, for the most part, undesirable. She had invested only £20,000,000 in them ; they had cost her more than she received and, when war broke out, they provided only one-half of 1 per cent of Germany's total trade. As outlets for population, they were even less important, because the number of Germans in them was less than 20,000. With one exception, the colonies fell at an early stage of the war. Only in East Africa was von Lettow-Vorbeck, as a result of his consummate military tactics, able to hold out with a handful of *askaris* and whites until the Armistice.

Secret agreements between the Allies had made arrangements for the disposal of the colonies before the war ended ; and it was this hypocrisy, together with the talk about mandates being a sacred duty of civilization, that most annoyed the Germans. It was obvious from the first that there would be little practical difference between mandates and annexations.

Within Germany, Dr. Schnee (himself a former governor of East Africa) and Dr. Schacht organized nation-wide colonial propaganda long before the Hitlerites thought of it. In the early days of the movement at least, Hitler had no interest in colonies, and it is doubtful if, even to-day, he is ' a colony man '. In *Mein Kampf* he definitely relegated the colonial question to an obscure position. Pan-Germanism must come first. He said : ' Not till the confines of the Reich include every single German and are certain of being able to nourish him can there be a moral right for Germany to acquire territory abroad.' Again : ' The German people have no right to dabble in a colonial policy as long as they are unable to gather their sons into a common State.' Although it has been claimed recently that these passages have been misinterpreted, they seem quite clear.

Nevertheless, he allowed Ritter von Epp, himself an old colonial soldier, to organize a colonial department within the Party and, from time to time, turned on a torrent of propaganda. In Hitler's first two years of power the campaign was waged unofficially. The great strength of the private societies which worked in this direction is one of the surprising features of Nazi Germany, and Hitler may have come to realize that he had overlooked a powerful instrument of propaganda.

Throughout 1934 he was divided on the matter. The private associations were making the Germans ' colony-minded ', and Göring, himself the son of a colonial governor, had placed himself whole-heartedly behind von Epp's agitation. He roared about ' our stolen colonies ' and formally handed over to his new political police the ' Tradition ' of the East African Protectorate police. ' The German people needed colonial territory if it were not to suffocate at home,' he cried.[1] It was he who was largely responsible for the nation-wide celebrations that year of the fiftieth anniversary of

[1] This speech in May 1934 was the first occasion on which a Nazi minister openly spoke of a restoration of colonies.

German colonization and for the issue of a special set of stamps commemorating colonial leaders.

But there was no uniformity of opinion within the Party, and many Nazi advisers followed Dr. Darré in arguing that Germany should think only of the Reich in Europe. A member of Darré's staff criticized the colonial campaign as an unwanted reversion to an outmoded psychology, and quoted with approval Hitler's own dictum that 'we are finally done with the pre-war colonial and trade policy and are now proceeding towards the territorial policy of the future'. Hitler Youth, it was said, should not be led astray from their main duty by stories of colonial romanticism. In particular the localists attacked a famous novel, *Volk ohne Raum*, which Hans Grimm had written in 1925 and which had become a permanent best-seller under the new régime. Described as the Bible of the colonists, it was attacked as false teaching by those whose vision was limited to Europe. It certainly provided the expansionists with an appropriate slogan.

Having to decide one way or the other, Hitler practically came round to the colonials at the Nuremberg Rally of 1934, although still in a very half-hearted way. At that gathering Hess, speaking as his deputy, stated that colonies were not a luxury for Germany but an economic necessity, and that the return of the colonies would be the necessary corollary of the return of the Saar. Here were two new notes—the diplomatic and the economic. The diplomatic argument appealed to Hitler, who became convinced, by 1935, that the idea of *Gleichberechtigung* should be extended so as to include 'colonial equality' as well as diplomatic and military equality with other nations. Throughout 1935 he worked up this argument and made the colonial question one of 'national honour'. He even made Germany's return to Geneva contingent upon a satisfactory solution of the colonial question, purposely linking up the two matters in order that foreigners should see that Germany viewed the return of her colonies as a vital question of diplomatic prestige.

It was left for von Epp to bring in still another aspect.

'The colonial demand is comprised for us to-day in two words—bread and honour,' he said. Thus the Nazis joined forces, on one question at least, with Dr. Schacht, because Schacht had been arguing for years that colonies could solve most of Germany's difficulties. Schacht holds that colonies could provide the raw materials, the markets, and the outlet for excess population, all of which Germany needs so badly. He raised this claim as early as 1929, at the 'Young Plan Conference' in Paris, but was laughed at when he argued that colonies were absolutely indispensable for the economic existence of Germany. He insists, however, that colonial markets should be under German administration and the German currency system. Exactly why colonies would 'redeem' Germany's economic plight, instead of further weakening her, is not clear : Schacht limits himself to mere assertions that they would have this result, despite past experience that such colonies as Germany possessed would prove endless sinks for new expenditure rather than immediate sources of profit. Schacht's arguments might apply to a Belgian Congo or a Java, but it is unlikely, to say the least, that such colonies would be handed over to satisfy Germany's demands.

Schacht's propaganda was intensified through 1936, and most Germans came to believe that colonies would lead them out of their economic troubles. *Lebensraum*—room to live—would solve everything. After the formulation of the Four Year Plan, the belief became almost fanatical, and Germans to-day think that the plan could easily be carried through if they had the raw materials and markets of the colonies.

At least ten colonial bodies kept the agitation at fever-heat, and during the year the colonial department of the Party (under von Epp) interfered more directly in the campaign, thus displacing the German Colonial Society which Dr. Schnee led. In the spring all existing colonial societies were amalgamated into one huge body, the Reich Colonial League. The official Press made virulent attacks on 'the colonial-guilt lie', and the propaganda culminated in Göring's famous speech in the *Sportspalast* on October

28th—a speech which, for unpremeditated frankness, rivalled that of Hitler when he said, at Munich, nine months earlier, that Germany must act as France and England had done. 'They did not argue. They took what they wanted. So shall we.'[1] Now Göring echoed this brutal directness by saying : 'We possess no colonies. They were stolen from us after an unfortunate war. We are told to buy raw materials with gold. We would be ready to do so if all our gold had not been stolen from us, too.' Lest this be not sufficiently clear, Dr. Goebbels explained it two days later and excitedly declared : 'We will, of course, take up the fight against the world for our colonies.' The British Ambassador was ordered to point out that Britain could not accept the implications of these last two speeches.

Although Hitler is still said to view the colonial agitation primarily as a question of prestige, or even as an instrument which can induce Britain and France to make concessions in Europe, leading Nazis continued an uncompromising campaign. Bitterness was added to their argument by the fact that Japan and Italy had left the ranks of ' the have-nots ' and acquired territorial possessions to exploit. Herr von Ribbentrop joined Schacht in making much of this point and added the new note that the *Führer* saw, in the facilities provided by colonies, the most important means by which the standard of life within Germany could be raised.

Out of this medley of arguments, Germany has brought her colonial campaign almost to the point at which she can present concrete demands. Her kite-flying experiments came to a temporary end when the strength of British and French opinion on the question was demonstrated and when the falsity of her argument that the British Dominions would not be prepared to support Britain (at least in so far as war was concerned) was revealed. Nevertheless, the campaign at least had the result of making the German viewpoint known to the world, and there is no doubt that it will be raised again when the time is ripe, although Hitler, despite his so-called conversion to ' colonial realities ', still appears to view purely European matters as the most important.

[1] This speech was drastically censored in the German Press.

The second weapon employed by the Nazis was propaganda within the colonies. By the nature of things, this was not so obvious in the lands under mandate to Japan and Australia and New Zealand. Its main scope was in Africa, especially in South-West and East Africa.

Starting in 1932 in South-West Africa, the Nazi movement reached such proportions that the Union Government forbade it in 1934. Although only 31,000 Europeans live in the territory, a Commission of Inquiry[1] reported early in 1936 that they 'are inordinately preoccupied with politics'. It also found that the agitation was directly inspired by the Party's Foreign Department in Berlin, and that agents had been sent out ' for the Nazification of all German institutions in the country'. The German flag was even substituted for the Union flag on public buildings ; schoolchildren were taught the Nazi interpretation of history ; branches of the Hitler Youth were formed ; and the *Deutscher Bund*, the political party through which the naturalized Germans express themselves, became a completely Nazi body. The Commission said explicitly : ' There is no room for individual thought or action in the Bund. It has become a voting machine pledged to political and, at that, foreign dictation ; the individual is dragooned into conformity by threats of reprisals and persecutions.'

The Germans in South-West Africa thus became ' co-ordinated' under the rule of a foreign power. Although Germany had assented in 1923 to the naturalization *en masse* of the Germans there, she now interfered so much with their lives that they had become *verpflichtet* (under an obligation) to Berlin again, as the Commission reported. Since then the local Government has maintained a rigid opposition

[1] The Commission was appointed as a result of a resolution of the Legislative Assembly of South-West Africa, requesting, by a two-thirds majority, the incorporation of the mandated territory as a fifth province of the Union. The most striking evidence was that seized in police raids on the Nazi headquarters at Windhoek. The Commission reported in March 1936 (Paper No. 26), but its members could reach no unanimity about the question of incorporating the mandate in the Union. They agreed, however, that the smooth functioning of the mandate was impossible if such intervention by a foreign government like Germany were to continue.

to any extension of Nazi influence. The Youth Movement has been declared illegal, and its leader expelled, and the Union Government has stated that it has as little intention of abandoning the mandate as it has of abandoning its own territory, although it would be content to continue the separate administration of South-West Africa as at present (December 1936). More difficulties have been experienced because the *Deutscher Bund* viewed the failure of the Union Party to secure incorporation as a victory of their own, and they have become increasingly assertive. Inquiries I made in South Africa in March 1936 demonstrated convincingly that the noisiness of the Germans in South-West Africa increased in proportion to the assertiveness of Göring and von Epp at home. Von Epp, in particular, has always shown a special interest in this province, because of its strategic importance, its diamonds, and its pastoral possibilities. Moreover, it is one of the few ex-German colonies where white families can live. Even in 1914 over 1,600 German children lived there permanently.

While the tensity of feeling over South-West Africa raises it to a position of priority amongst the German colonies, it was not the only scene of colonial activities. In Tanganyika, which abuts on Kenya, Germans received appointments from the Nazi Party, and at one time even carried their ideas of a shadow State so far that they attempted private courts to try cases between themselves. Although the German population is for the most part orderly, there has been a steady economic penetration of Germany in the last few years, and there appears to be a quiet belief that the mandate will some day revert to Germany. The natives, however, are not anxious to go back, and it must be remembered that Tanganyika has over five million natives to fewer than 8,500 Europeans. Moreover, it does not provide any of the raw materials Goebbels describes as essential, except cotton, and then only 55,000 bales a year.

The other lost colonies are not very important. Germany had less than two thousand people in Togoland and the Cameroons before 1914. France received most of these colonies and has succeeded in displacing all but a handful of German settlers, but in the fifth of the Cameroons that fell to England, the Germans regained their original supremacy. To-day they call the products of the British mandate ' German bananas '.

In the Pacific, Japan has the northern islands and it is unlikely that Germany will ever do anything about them. She is more concerned with those parts of New Guinea and Samoa which are under Australian and New Zealand mandates respectively. New Guinea is a vast tropical colony, not yet fully explored and with its resources practically undeveloped. The discovery of enormously rich placer gold deposits has changed its outlook, although German propaganda has paid more importance to the copra, which would allow the Pacific colonies to help Germany's shortage in essential fats.

When the question of actual restoration is mooted, one difficulty is met at the outset. It is not known whether she wants back the actual colonies she previously held, or whether she wants a general reshuffling. It would appear from recent articles in the inspired German Press that she is fully aware of the deficiencies of her former colonies and that, if Schacht's ideas are to be carried out, Germany must receive an entirely different kind of empire. There have been many disturbing references of late to colonies in the hands of ' weak Powers ' like Portugal.

If the demand is limited to the former colonies, it will centre on South-West Africa and Tanganyika. Feeling in the Union makes it extremely unlikely that she will ever get back the former without war (especially because Great Britain dare not risk an open conflict with the Union on such a matter in the present state of imperial relationships). Her prospects are much brighter in Tanganyika, and the defiant cry of the planters (even as supplemented by the threats of the Kenya Protection League), that they would fight to the death, can be put down to the sectional interests of a group which, after all, includes only a few thousand men. Togoland and the Cameroons are not important enough to bother about. The Pacific colonies held under Dominion mandate do not raise the same complicated problems as South-West

Africa. Samoa is remote from New Zealand, and Australia probably does not feel sufficiently strongly about New Guinea to fight for it, although it is always easy to raise an alarmist cry in Australia about the colony being a base for enemy aeroplanes.

Taking the colonial plea on its wider aspects, it seems rather beside the point to argue about Germany's ' colonial unworthiness ', especially from wartime Blue Books that give only part of the truth, and that little most tendentiously. Propaganda has made us believe that every German colonial administrator was a von Trocha, that all natives were treated as were the Hereros, and that the cleansing revolution which Dernburg instituted in 1907 simply did not exist. For one von Trocha there were many Dr. Solfs, Dr. Schnees, von Rechenbergs. Germany had little time after Dernburg to put her reforms into operation, but, even so, her colonial policy had become most scientific. It is extraordinary how, of all the war-atrocity stories, that about German colonization has lasted the longest ; and it is little wonder that Germany —the Germany which administered New Guinea, Samoa, and East Africa as she did—should resent the stigma of permanent unworthiness to rule subject peoples when, say, the eternal scandal of the Portuguese colonies is allowed to continue without offending the nose of civilization. Moreover, whether the original verdict was right or wrong is beside the point ; no great resurgent nation will for ever submit to carry such a verdict. True or not, it is a slur on her racial pride and, as such, will have to be removed. As a student of colonial policies I can find no adequate reason why it should ever have been imposed ; as a realist in international affairs I can see nothing to justify it from the political angle in the world to-day.

On the other hand, one cannot doubt that the German arguments in favour of a new colonial empire are palpably weak, unless one limits them to national prestige. How can the colonies be described as an outlet for surplus population when they included less than twenty thousand German inhabitants in 1913, and when Hitler is making every effort to increase the birth-rate to-day ? How can they bring her raw materials or markets when only one two-hundredth of Germany's trade was with them, and when they do not produce such articles as the flax, hemp, and jute she needs ? How can they relieve her economic plight when they must involve enormous initial expenditure ? The main products from the ex-German colonies are gold from New Guinea, diamonds from South-West Africa, sisal from Tanganyika, and cocoa and bananas from the Cameroons ; and it is difficult to see how any of these are products without which Germany cannot live. In cold fact, the institution of tourists' marks did more for German economy than would any conceivable colonial empire she could build up. Schacht's argument that colonies are essential to the economic recovery of Germany is completely untenable. He is not arguing from facts, and he must know full well that Germany's *devisen* problem would be solved long before she could secure any return from colonies, even were she granted them to-morrow.

The colonial question, then, becomes, in reality, one of national prestige and diplomacy. If Germany demands colonies to ' complete her nationhood ', it is useless to argue about legal and technical points, or about the manner in which ' the haves ' obtained their existing empires. The point is—are the great Powers convinced that Germany (alone amongst them)[1] should be denied colonies for ever, and, if so, are they prepared to fight a new world war on such an issue ?

I am not yet convinced, however, despite the popularity of the colonial campaign in Germany (it extends even to cigarette cards), that Hitler looks upon colonies other than as a bargaining weapon in diplomacy. Despite all the clamour, he has made no formal demands for restoration of colonies, although he has not been backward in formulating his other wishes in foreign affairs. On at least three occasions in the last eighteen months, the colonial agitation has been cut off as suddenly as it began, a clear indication that it is viewed as subordinate to wider diplomatic questions. It would almost appear as if the realists in Germany to-day had little wish to be burdened with actual colonies, while using

[1] Except Czechoslovakia and Poland.

them as a convenient propagandist instrument. There is certainly no doubt that Germany has a very strong colonial argument both inside and outside the Reich; and the test of the statesmanship of 'the haves' will be the way in which they face this claim when it is presented, assuming, of course, that it is presented in a fitting manner. Any application of 'the policy of surprises' to the colonial field can mean nothing but an immediate war.

There are apparently three arguments used against giving Germany back some of her colonies—that she is unfit to rule colonies; that she agreed to their loss in the Treaties; and that the natives may not want it. The first two of these were doubtful at any time and have been outmoded by the rise of the Third Reich. The third is also unproven. Nobody appeared to think it worth while, in 1919, really to inquire what the natives thought, and it seems a little disproportionate to allow the unascertained wishes of small native groups to weigh against what may possibly be the preservation of world peace, especially when we think of recent fighting in Morocco, Abyssinia, and even North-Western India. The proposal, recently mooted in England, for a plebiscite amongst the natives led to charges of hypocrisy in Germany; an accusation of appalling ignorance would have been more tenable, for the idea of asking the unsubdued headhunters, say, of New Guinea, whether they preferred British or German rule could have only emanated from an insane asylum or from some philanthropic society that thinks facts completely unimportant.[1]

It is also objected that we cannot renounce mandates, but what of Iraq and Syria? It is argued that we 'could not think of' handing over people from British rule; but what was moral in 1919, when entire provinces of Europeans were cut away from their fatherlands to allow enemies to put guns in favourable positions, has become immoral in 1937. We argue that most of the German colonies were worthless; the German naturally retorts: 'Why, then, keep them?' We say that Germany might militarize the natives;

---

[1] Natives have a tendency to say what will please the questioner, and it would be ridiculous to question them on events of a quarter of a century ago.

Germany points to the Black Army of France, and the native forces we have in India. We say that Germany might treat the natives as she treats the Jews ; there is no answer to this. It is the one grave flaw in the German position ; but as against it is the fact—admitted in German writings on colonies, nowadays—that it pays for colonization to be scientific, and that winning over native populations is good business, to put it on its lowest plane. Finally, there is the political argument that it is of no use to give Germany colonies because the granting of this demand will not satisfy her. This argument is beside the point ; the only relevant facts here are that Germany has a good colonial claim, that (rightly or not) the German public believe that they are being scandalously treated by a group of sated and hypocritical powers which hold all the colonies to-day, and that the colonial bitterness engenders a frame of mind in Germany that may well lead to a war which the Germans will fight as a holy crusade. The main opposition to the return of some of the German colonies comes from the diehard Conservatives, a few honest (but, I believe, misinformed) Liberal intellectuals, and the interested inhabitants of one Dominion. Their respective weapons are stubborn pride, unreasoning philanthropy, and fear ; and it is probable that, if the British public fully realized the issues at stake and the facts on both sides, they would feel that Germany had as good a case for colonies as she had to re-enter the Rhineland. The subject is far too important to be obscured by the mists of misrepresentation or inapplicable theories ; it is an issue directly affecting world peace, and only Hitler's preoccupation elsewhere and his intrinsic lack of interest in the colonial question (as such) have kept it damped down until the present time. Whether we like it or not, whether we think the German arguments sound or not, the question must be faced.

Meanwhile the campaign in Germany goes on. Even many of the circles of cardboard on which glasses of beer rest have colonial propaganda on them, and in the inns are copies of Hitler's remarks on colonies given at the *Partei-Tag* of 1936. ' Germany cannot reconcile herself to the loss of her colonies. The right of the German people to live is as great as that of any other nation.'   Under each is the huge lettering, *Vorkämpfer heraus*.   Some people have said that giving Germany back her colonies is like paying Danegeld, a curiously inept analogy which the Germans counter by saying that the British, who have always criticized the French for making the Treaty of Versailles ' the Bible of European affairs ', and who have acquiesced in breaches of it in all other directions, keep a closed mind about those sections of the Treaty which deal with colonies.   It is unfortunate that the Germans should have singled us out in this matter, but our responsibility at the Bar of history is great, alike on grounds of justice, political expediency, and the preservation of peace.   (The Germans have not even ruled out the possibility of submitting to safeguards regarding the natives as long as, in Schacht's words, nothing is done that is unworthy of Germany's place among the nations.)   Colonial redistribution is one of the world's greatest problems, and must it be said that we are considering sectional vested interests and arid legal technicalities (such as where sovereignty resides in a mandate) when the peace of all is at stake ?   It was Edmund Burke who said that ' nothing is just but in proportion and with reference '.

Chapter Eight

CONCLUSION

It is impossible to give any final evaluation of the National Socialist revolution in Germany, even of its first four years. There can be no longer any doubt as to the extent of that change. Because it was comparatively bloodless we, too, readily lose sight of its extremely revolutionary aspects. The Nazi leaders claim that their process is an evolution that will take centuries to complete, and they ask that no final judgement be given on the necessarily brusque events of the initial transitional period. This seems a fair request.

It is inconceivable that Nazidom shall remain in its present inchoate stage. Nobody now expects a realization of the Twenty-Five Points of the original Party programme. Indeed, most developments have been in a very different direction. Feder's programme is an historical curiosity. The only query is whether the mind that conceived *Mein Kampf* (and it has never been settled how much of that book was Hitler's and how much the work of Rudolf Hess) has changed in its approach to world problems.

At present Germany has a popular dictatorship, with opposition effectively stifled, with the one significant exception of the Church. But there is no permanence in the membership of the governing cabal. Already a noticeable move to reaction has set in, and already there is a turn towards the army. I am of opinion that, apart from Hitler's own tremendous popularity, this is the most significant feature of present-day Germany. Month by month last year one saw the growing power of the army ; and it is not far-fetched to imagine a Germany in which the army, retaining the *Führer* as a willing figurehead, will take control of the land.

The cumbrousness of the present Party machine must necessitate a considerable pruning, and undoubtedly many excrescences of the Party will go, especially in the local districts, where most of the opposition is still to be found on the part of the people. The old Civil Services are still practically intact, and the Junkers have not been seriously harmed under the Third Reich. If the future sees a further consolidation of the army, the Civil Services, and the landed magnates, it would only witness a continuation of the tendencies of the last few years. 'The New Germany is becoming the Old Germany—the real Germany. Hitlerism will become a reversionary process, getting back to the stage before the degradation and the alien ideas of the Weimar republic '— this was the view expressed again and again in Germany last year.

The Nazis themselves say that many of the features of their rule which seem so undesirable to us are phases of transition and will moderate themselves with the passage of time. If there is a move towards the army, this process of moderation will be accelerated. It has always been difficult to explain why the mass of the people accept restrictions on their liberties (especially in such matters as religion) and why they acquiesce in a lowering of their standard of life. Up to the present, if we except the constant element of constraint, the explanation has been in the feeling of sacrifice for the more immediate objective—the restoration of Germany's national pride. But, now that equality has been achieved, the main justification of the restrictions (at least, in the people's eyes) has disappeared, and Hitler is finding it increasingly difficult to whip the dying horse of sacrifice for ' the peace-time war '. The comparative coolness with which his anti-Russian crusade and his intervention in Spain were met demonstrates that. Thinking people in Germany are well aware that many a purely Party cause masquerades under the guise of nationalism, and most of them know that the army would not stoop to such tricks.

Army rule would lower the emotional *tempo* of the New Germany and would substitute an ordered frame of mind (however limited in its concepts) for the erratic uncertainty of the present régime. It would also solve the problem of the subterranean opposition—for many of the movements which have been driven underground at the moment, but which still undoubtedly exist, object primarily to the Party aspects of Hitlerism rather than to its nationalism. The disinterested type of nationalism that the army would pursue fits in with so many aspects of German life to-day.

Even abroad, any such move might not be unwelcome. In the countries bordering Germany I heard repeatedly last year the view that anything was preferable to the terrible uncertainty of the present régime. Even granting the militaristic viewpoint of the army—even accepting its ulti-mately expansionist aims—neighbours would at least know what the aims were ; they would know how the military mind works ; and they would know that it would never act until it was ready. It is always the uncertain, the un-predictable, that causes the trouble in international affairs ; here has been Hitler's greatest menace in the past.

Many experts declare that Hitler is practically an army spokesman now. While this is to a large degree true, the difficulty at present is that Party pressure may force him into drastic action unwanted by the army (the Rhine occupation and the anti-Russian crusade are cases in point). But Hitler has always been an army man. He delights in military functions, and has always played with military bodies. His whole development has been in that direction ; and the long list of helpers cast aside—the list that included Drexler, Strasser, Röhm—is by no means filled. Various sections of the Party have been sloughed at opportune moments ; and it is abundantly obvious in the Germany of to-day that the process which cleared up the Brown Army must be applied to other extraneous elements of the Party which can have no place in the clear-cut evolution of Hitlerism. So far Hitler has built up a ' One Party State ' ; it seems as if that State is in process of becoming an ' Army State '.

But those who spoke of this development in Germany always added one qualification—' unless war enters as a complicating factor '. It is admitted that many tendencies of Hitlerism, unless diverted in the near future, may lead to war ; and it is admitted that some of the opportunists who are at present powerful in Germany would risk the final throw of war rather than lose their power.

Goebbels has repeatedly stated that the end—the continuance of power in the hands of the Nazi governing minority—justifies any means, and that he who shrinks from drastic measures is a traitor. The position may arise, then, in which some grave crisis—the failure of the Four Year Plan, for instance—may precipitate war ; and even ' their grey eminences ' of the Reichswehr may prefer this (with all the subsequent reshufflings) rather than face a total collapse of Germany. War would clarify the German situation, for better or for worse ; without war there can only be a continuance of the present confusion, unless there is a whole series of ' purges ', and endless repetition of ' Nights of the Long Knives ' in the direction I have referred to above.

One further line of development may be considered. Hitler may achieve his avowed goal ; he may consolidate the entire nation along the lines he wants. If this is so, the outlook for peace would still be clouded, because Hitler's consolidation is contingent upon ideas—such as economic *Autarky*, military aggressiveness, a dashing foreign policy, and a general Imperialistic ideology—which, of necessity, would lead to war. He cannot achieve some of these without war, and if he does not achieve them, the people will feel deluded, and in that case Hitler's consolidation will not be successful. That is his basic dilemma. If he persists in the policies he has enunciated, he plunges Europe into war ; if he abandons them, he can no longer maintain his position within Germany.

Logically, then, the success or the failure of Hitlerism brings war in its train. A German diplomat insisted, however, that one further variant existed—that Hitler might become so strong that every other country would surrender everything that he wanted. As this implies the complete disappearance of six nations and the mutilation of several others, it may well be dismissed as a practical possibility. Yet a striking number of people in Germany believe in it. They think that a sufficiently strong Germany can obtain satisfaction of her demands by asking peremptorily and by letting it be known that she has the necessary force and will not hesitate to use it. The only comment needed on this is that war lies in that direction, too.

From whichever angle we approach the question, then, we come to the inevitability of war, unless Hitler modifies his teachings and methods or unless there is a peaceful transition to some other régime. I firmly believe that, unless some unexpected international incident crops up, German evolution will take the form of a rapid transformation of the present régime, as I have indicated above.

Hitler himself has never stated that he will not go to war. He has always professed a love of peace ; but in the same speeches he has said that German honour will not be satisfied until the granting of certain demands, which, by their very nature, could not be given up by other nations until after a defeat in the field. The whole teaching of Hitlerism is to justify war as an instrument of policy in certain contingencies, and there is hardly a boy in Germany who does not view the preparation for ultimate war as the most important aspect of his life.

The position reduces itself to this. Hitlerism cannot achieve its aims without war ; its ideology is that of war. Hitler started with an ideological preparation years before he came to power ; he added to that a military preparation ; and now the structure is crowned by an economic mobilization of all the country's resources. The sum of these is staggering. Hitler has worked up Germany to such a state that the people are ready to accept war at any moment. His instruments of propaganda would interpret it as a struggle for survival forced on her by malicious enemies—an attitude of mind which months of continuous propaganda and a Party Congress almost led me to believe myself. Finally he is in a position to exploit all the capacities of sacrifice and heroism that are so fine in the German people.

That is what makes the German position so tragic. The nation has been duped in the sense that it has been launched along a road that can only lead to disaster. The nation may be reborn, it may be ' a new Germany ', but, unless it learns the habit of political and economic collaboration in international matters, it is a nation confronted by ultimate ruin and disillusionment. That is the infinite tragedy of it all, for the Germans of the last two decades have had more than their share of suffering, and the middle-aged and the old so sincerely want peace in the land for the rest of their time.

CPSIA information can be obtained
at www.ICGtesting.com
Printed in the USA
BVHW041216150620
581541BV00015B/919